Work-Based Learning

Level 2
NVQ/SVQ

TEAM LEADING

Bethan Bithell

Nigel Parton

Bernadette Watkins

ALWAYS LEARNING

PEARSON

Published by Pearson Education Limited, Edinburgh Gate, Harlow, Essex, CM20 2JE.

www.pearsonschoolsandfecolleges.co.uk

Heinemann is a registered trademark of Pearson Education Limited

Text © Pearson Education Limited 2012
Edited by Julia Bruce
Designed by Tek-Art
Typeset by Phoenix Photosetting, Chatham, Kent
Index by Indexing Specialists (UK) Ltd
Original illustrations © Pearson Education Ltd
Cover design by Pearson Education Ltd
Cover photo/illustration © **Superstock:** Beyond

The rights of Bethan Griffiths, Nigel Parton and Bernadette Watkins to be identified as authors of this work has been asserted by them in accordance with the Copyright, Designs and Patents Act 1988.

First published 2012

15 14 13 12
10 9 8 7 6 5 4 3 2 1

British Library Cataloguing in Publication Data
A catalogue record for this book is available from the British Library

ISBN 978 0 435 07785 3

Printed in Spain by Grafos S.A.

Acknowledgements
The authors and publisher would like to thank the following individuals and organisations for permission to reproduce photographs:

Picture Credits
Alamy Images: ableimages 201, Bernd Tschakert 139, Fancy 131, Francesco Gavazzeni 204, Juice Images 86, MBI 41, Moodboard 36; **Corbis:** Chicasso / Blend Images 103; **Getty Images:** Jon Feingersh / Stone 228, moodboard / the Agency Collection 60, Reza Estakhrian / Stone 215, Tom Pidgeon 172, VCL / Alistair Berg / Taxi 2; **Press Association Images:** Ng Han Guan / AP 120; **Shutterstock.com:** Aspen Photo 146, auremar 20, baranq 95, Blend Images 226, DelicatePhoto 233, Dragos Iliescu 28, Goodluz 72, mangostock 170, Michal Kowalski 62, Patricia Hofmeester 210, Ragne Kabanova 244, Ron Hilton 30, Sylvie Bouchard 157, Vartanov Anatoly 165, Yuri Arcurs 143; **www.imagesource.com:** Rob Lewine 76

Web units
Alamy Images: Brian Southam D12, Image Scotland F17-21, Juice Images E10-13; **Corbis:** Kerim Okten / epa B11, Phil Boorman / cultura D12-10; **Getty Images:** Cynthia Lum / WireImage F17, Monty Rakusen / Cultura F17-10; **Shutterstock.com:** holbox D12-23, Tamara Kulikova E10, Yuri Arcurs D12-14; **SuperStock:** fstop B11-16

All other images © Pearson Education

We are grateful to the following for permission to reproduce copyright material:

Figures
Figure in B5 and E10 from "How to Choose a Leadership Pattern", *Harvard Business Review*, Vol 36, pp.95–101 (Robert Tannenbaum and Warren H. Schmidt, 1958), copyright © 1958 by the President and Fellows of Harvard College. All Rights Reserved; Figure in D1 John Adair's model on working with others, source: http://www.johnadair.co.uk/, copyright © John Adair; Figure in D1 from *The Mathematical Theory of Communication*, University of Illinois Press (Shannon, C.E., & Weaver, W.) copyright © 1949, 1998 by the Board of Trustees of the University of Illinois. Used with permission of the author and the University of Illinois Press; Figure in D5 and D10 from *Motivation and Personality, 3rd edition* (Maslow, A.H., and eds Frager, R.D., Fadiman, J.) copyright © 1987. Printed and electronically reproduced by permission of Pearson Education, Inc., Upper Saddle River, New Jersey; Figure in D10 adapted from 'Conflict and Negotiation Process in Organizations' in *Handbook of Industrial and Organizational Psychology, 2nd edition*, Vol 3, Consulting Psychologists Press, Palo Alto, CA (Thomas, K. Eds Dunnette, M.D., and Hough, L.H., 1992) p.660, copyright © 1992 by L. M. Hough. Adapted by permission; Figure in E15 from "How Competitive Forces Shape Strategy", *Harvard Business Review* (Porter, M.E., 1979), copyright © 1979 by the President and Fellows of Harvard College. All Rights Reserved; Figure in F17 from 'Ansoff Matrix' by Igor Ansoff, http://www.ansoffmatrix.com. Reproduced with kind permission of the Ansoff Trust.

Screenshots
Screenshot in D5 from MS Project screenshot. Used with permission from Microsoft, Microsoft product screenshot reprinted with permission from Microsoft Corporation.

Tables
Table in B5 from "Developmental sequence in small groups", *Psychological Bulletin*, Vol 63 (6), 384–399 (Bruce Tuckman, 1965), Group Facilitation, Spring 2001. Source: American Psychological Association.

Text
Extract in B5 and D1 from "Team Roles" by Meredith Belbin, www.belbin.com, Reproduced with kind permission of Belbin Associates; Extract in F17 from the Arts Council England Charter, www.artscouncil.org.uk/publication_archive/customer-service-charter.

Every effort has been made to contact copyright holders of material reproduced in this book. Any omissions will be rectified in subsequent printings if notice is given to the publishers.

Websites
Pearson Education Limited is not responsible for the content of any external internet sites. It is essential for tutors to preview each website before using it in class so as to ensure that the URL is still accurate, relevant and appropriate. We suggest that tutors bookmark useful websites and consider enabling students to access them through the school/college intranet.

Contents

 www.contentextra.com/management

Username: Team

Password: Leader

The accompanying website includes the following additional units for this qualification:

B11: Manage or support equality of opportunity, diversity and inclusion in own area of responsibility

D12: Participate in meetings

E10: Make effective decisions

F17: Manage customer service in own area of responsibility

NVQ Unit numbers

The unit numbers used in this book are those used by the Council for Administration (CfA), the Sector Skills Body for Management. However, awarding organisations use different unit numbering within their specifications. The table below maps the unit numbers of the most popular awarding organisations to the CfA numbering.

	Edexcel	EDI	ILM	OCR
A1: Manage personal development	1	CU855	F/600/9469	A01
D1: Develop working relationships with colleagues	2	CU856	H/600/9660	D01
E11: Communicate information and knowledge	3	CU857	H/600/9724	E11
D5: Plan, allocate and monitor work of a team	4	CU858	Y/600/9669	D05
B5: Set objectives and provide support for team members	5	CU761	M/600/9600	B05
B11: Manage or support equality of opportunity, diversity and inclusion in own area of responsibility	6	CU859	M/600/9628	B11
C1: Support team members in identifying, developing and implementing new ideas	7	CU860	L/600/9636	C01
D10: Manage conflict in a team	8	CU861	R/600/9685	D10
D12: Participate in meetings	10	CU863	H/600/9688	D12
E10: Make effective decisions	11	CU864	F/600/9715	E10
E12: Manage knowledge in own area of responsibility	12	CU865	T/600/9730	E12
E15: Procure supplies	13	CU866	L/600/9734	E15
F17: Manage customer service in own area of responsibility	14	CU867	D/600/9804	F17

How to use this book

This book has been written to help you achieve your NVQ (or SVQ, if you are based in Scotland) Level 2 qualification. It covers the mandatory units and a range of optional units from the 2010 standards, giving you a broad choice of content to match your needs.

Throughout you will find the following learning features.

Key Terms

Essential terminology and phrases are explained in clear and accessible language. Where these appear in the book, the first instance of the word appears in **bold** so you know there is a definition nearby.

Activity 10 minutes

Use these tasks to apply your knowledge, understanding and skills. These activities will help you to develop your understanding of the underpinning theory and key techniques you will need in your day-to-day working life. Each activity includes a suggested time for completion, which will help you to keep track of your learning.

Functional Skills

You may be taking Functional Skills alongside your NVQ – if so, these are opportunities for you to apply your English or mathematics skills in a team leading role.

Portfolio Task 20 minutes

These tasks cover grading criteria from the NVQ standards and can be used to generate evidence for your portfolio. You should discuss the activities with your assessor to agree what types of evidence can be gathered.

Checklist

These features help you to identify important information or steps in a task that need to be completed.

Team talk

See how the unit applies to the world of work, and get best-practice hints and tips for making the most of your time in the workplace.

Links to Technical Certificate

If you are taking your NVQ as part of an Apprenticeship, you will need to complete a Technical Certificate qualification. Key topics from the Technical Certificate are covered in more detail within units of the NVQ, as identified through this feature. There is a range of different qualifications that can be used as the Technical Certificate (see www.contentextra.com/management for a document mapping the topics against the most popular qualifications), so check with your assessor which qualification you will be completing.

The website can be accessed using the following details:
Username: Team
Password: Leader

Unit A1 Manage personal development

This unit focuses on planning, measuring and assessing the progress you make in work as you develop your skills. Through this unit you will develop your understanding of the skills you need for your job role and reflect on your own knowledge and skills. You will identify objectives through development reviews with your manager and will monitor your progress towards achieving these objectives.

Planning your development within your work role is important as it helps you make sure that you are working towards your organisation's performance requirements.

Through appropriate discussion at your workplace, you will agree personal objectives with your line manager that will improve your performance and help you to keep your skills and knowledge up to date. You can measure the progress you make to see whether you are meeting your objectives.

You will produce your own development plan, which will identify the activities and processes needed to advance your career prospects within your organisation and to enhance your performance within your work role.

What you will learn:

- Be able to identify and agree performance requirements of own work role
- Be able to measure and progress against objectives
- Be able to identify gaps in skills and knowledge in own performance
- Be able to carry out and assess activities within own development plan

Links to the Technical Certificate

If you are completing your NVQ as part of an Apprenticeship Framework, you will find the following topics are also covered in your Technical Certificate:

- The attributes, work objectives, authority and responsibilities of a team leader
- Assessing own development needs
- Preparing and reviewing a Personal Development Plan
- Identifying ways to improve own performance

Key Terms

Goals – things that you are trying to achieve.

Job description – detailed statement of the tasks involved with a particular work role.

Objectives – tasks you have set to help you to achieve your goal.

Performance development review (PDR) – identifies objectives and targets and areas for improvement. Performance development reviews are also referred to as staff appraisals.

Person specification – a document to identify the essential and desirable skills and knowledge to complete the job role.

Procedure – step-by-step set of instructions to ensure a standardised approach to workplace activities.

Be able to identify and agree performance requirements of own work role

How to identify and agree performance requirements of your own work role

In your workplace, your individual performance is very important to help your team to achieve its targets. Further, your individual performance and the performance of your team will help your organisation to meet its overall **goals** and **objectives**.

Through discussion with your line manager, you will have the opportunity to identify and agree your work role performance requirements. Your line manager or human resource department will provide you with documents that will give you an accurate overview of what is expected of you and what tasks you are expected to undertake in your work.

Your job description

Your day-to-day tasks will be listed in your **job description** and its contents will tell you what your employer expects of you at work. This information can help to identify your performance requirements.

Your line manager may use your job description to agree what is expected from you in terms of your performance. This is likely to happen in one-to-one meetings between you and your line manager, at supervision meetings, or perhaps more commonly at staff appraisals. These appraisals are sometimes known as **performance development reviews (PDRs)**.

PLTS

Through reflecting on your job role you will be assessing yourself (RL1).

Functional Skills

If you read and understand your job description to identify your job role as part of the assessment for this learning outcome, you will be practising your Functional English skills Level 1 in Reading.

Portfolio Task 1   20 minutes

Links to LO1, Assessment criterion 1.1

To succeed in your job role, you must understand the key tasks that you are responsible for. Make a list of your key tasks and to whom you are accountable.

If you haven't already got a copy of your job description, please speak to your line manager and ask for one.

Are there any differences between the content of your job description and your responses to the above task? If so, you may wish to discuss these with your manager or assessor.

You should also reflect on the terms and conditions contained within your contract of employment to identify requirements of your job role. These terms and conditions can have an impact on the way you carry out your role and will include details of your holiday entitlement, what to do if you are unable to attend work due to illness and the number of hours you are expected to work each week, under normal circumstances.

Person specification

Being aware of the skills and knowledge you currently possess, and those you need to successfully fulfil the requirements of your job role, can enable you to identify any knowledge gaps that you may have.

You may be in possession of a person specification, perhaps issued to you by your human resources manager when you initially applied for your current position. This document will list the essential or desirable skills, attributes and knowledge necessary to successfully fulfil your job role and will help you to identify any knowledge gaps.

The format of your person specification may look similar to Table A1.1:

PERSON SPECIFICATION		
Job Title: Team Leader **Department:** Finance **Location:** Southport		
Requirements	**Essential**	**Desirable**
Personal attributes	Good communication skills Well organised Good timekeeping Meeting deadlines	Work as part of a team Work on own initiative Speak Welsh
Knowledge/ qualification	GCSE English Grade C or above GCSE Maths Grade C or above RSA Word and text processing Knowledge of: – employment law – SAGE accounts	Team Leading Level 2 NVQ Conflict Resolution training
Experience	Controlling payroll Maintaining financial documentation, e.g. ledgers, profit and loss	Some team leading experience is desirable

Table A1.1: An example person specification.

Once employed by your organisation, you may have realised that you do not fulfil all of the criteria featured in the desirable section. There may be gaps in your development you have identified. You can use this as a basis for discussing training needs with your managers.

Checklist

In order to carry out a thorough assessment of your current work role performance remember to:

- refer to your job description and person specification
- access and keep up-to-date with workplace policies
- keep up-to-date with amendments to **procedures** that have a direct impact upon your job role.

Activity 10 minutes

Identify the positive aspects of each skill listed below:

- personal and interpersonal skills
- numerical skills
- communication skills
- technical skills
- information processing skills
- information technology skills
- leadership skills.

Quality standards

Workplace procedures can help to ensure that everyone works to the same standards of quality. Procedures can be described as a set of step-by-step instructions for everyone to follow. This means that everyone should be working towards the same standards when they carry out the same tasks.

Here are some examples of working towards high quality standards.

- Exercising effective leadership – As team leader, you should monitor processes and examine ways to improve them. It is important to communicate the need for continuous improvement and offer praise to team members when appropriate.

- Communicating objectives effectively – Your SMART objectives (see page 9) should always be developed with quality in mind. It is very important to communicate your organisation's objectives and your departmental or team's objectives to everyone on a regular basis. Objectives previously devised may have to be reviewed and perhaps rewritten, as internal and external influences affect the way things get done.

- Encouraging a **holistic** approach – It is important that you are enthusiastic about developing yourself – perhaps through training activities – in order to work to the standards expected of you. Similarly, your team members may benefit from training to meet quality standards. Aim to develop your own communicative skills and encourage regular feedback from your team members. It is also important to involve your team in the decision-making process and the introduction of new procedures, so that they feel that their opinions are valued. This will enhance morale and motivation, in turn helping to achieve the expected standards of quality.

- Resources allocation – To ensure quality standards are met and objectives are realised, it is important that resources are monitored and controlled. Usually resources can be identified as:
  - time
  - money (finances)
  - equipment/materials
  - people (i.e. human resources).

- Processes – Quality of output depends on you and your team having knowledge of your job content, work systems and process. Knowledge of your organisation's policies and the procedures you work with can help you to minimise the risk of mistakes being made by you and your team.

It is important that the whereabouts of your policies and procedures is communicated effectively to the team, to minimise the risk of errors. Just telling your team members where to find these is not enough.

> **Key Term**
>
> **Holistic** – everyone working together, for example to achieve objectives.

The content needs to be shared, discussed and periodically reviewed to ensure quality standards are met. Similarly, performance to date should be discussed and reviewed regularly.

You should evaluate your approach to dealing with these aspects of your work to identify whether you would benefit from further development of some of your skills.

Your development needs should ideally consider an approach to ensuring that your customers or service users receive a high standard of quality at all times. It is important, therefore, if your customers' expectations are to be satisfied and sustained, that you make yourself aware of the quality standards your organisation works towards.

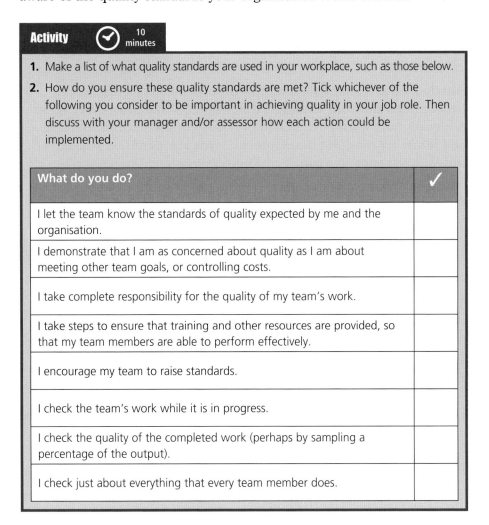

Activity ⏱ 10 minutes

1. Make a list of what quality standards are used in your workplace, such as those below.

2. How do you ensure these quality standards are met? Tick whichever of the following you consider to be important in achieving quality in your job role. Then discuss with your manager and/or assessor how each action could be implemented.

What do you do?	✓
I let the team know the standards of quality expected by me and the organisation.	
I demonstrate that I am as concerned about quality as I am about meeting other team goals, or controlling costs.	
I take complete responsibility for the quality of my team's work.	
I take steps to ensure that training and other resources are provided, so that my team members are able to perform effectively.	
I encourage my team to raise standards.	
I check the team's work while it is in progress.	
I check the quality of the completed work (perhaps by sampling a percentage of the output).	
I check just about everything that every team member does.	

If you are to develop yourself to become an effective leader, it is important to identify and understand the policies and procedures that have an impact on your job role.

Be able to measure and progress against objectives

Your organisation will have set itself objectives and goals that it wants to achieve in order to be successful. To help the organisation achieve these objectives, teams and departments will have their own objectives to work towards. Because of this, each individual in the team plays their part in ensuring that the team is successful.

Ways that measure progress against work objectives

Examine the following techniques that can help to identify and measure progress.

Performance development reviews (PDRs)

Also known as a staff appraisal, this process involves a discussion between you and your manager, which should take place every six or twelve months. Your current and previous performance is reviewed and future training and development needs are identified and agreed between you and your manager. These development needs can be translated into personal objectives to enhance your performance and, ultimately, that of your organisation.

The PDR enables you and your manager to reflect on your recent performance and to identify a pathway for future development. It is a two-way process that will give you the opportunity to request future training activities that you think will develop yourself further.

The PDRs that you take part in with your line manager and the supervision meetings that you attend, will help you identify and agree personal objectives. It is important that both you and your line manager agree personal performance objectives, which reflect the content of your job description, as these will enable the progress you make to be monitored and measured.

Ideally, you should feel that the process motivates you to continue with your cycle of **continuous professional development (CPD)**.

Monthly supervision meetings

These meetings will feature a discussion between you and your manager to examine the personal objectives that have been set and agreed for you. The process will look at what progress you have made over the previous month and set targets for the following month (your overall personal objectives will be broken down into smaller step-by-step targets, to ensure that you are progressing well in your work role). This will also help identify whether any additional guidance is needed to enable you to meet those targets.

Key Term

Continuous professional development (CPD) – training and fact-finding that helps you to keep up to date with changes taking place in your industry.

Continuous professional development (CPD)

CPD is a vital part of any job role and enables employees to keep up to date with the latest ideas and changes taking place in their industry.

Devising SMART objectives

When your personal workplace objectives are agreed it is likely that your manager will refer to the acronym **SMART**. This is a series of steps that ensure objectives are realistic and achievable. If not, you could become demotivated. This is because a badly designed business objective may not measure the progress you are making. So, make sure you can measure the outcome of your objective, for example, you have reduced the number of accidents by 10 per cent in a given time period.

Objectives should be SMART, which means that they are:

S   Specific
M   Measurable
A   Achievable
R   Realistic
T   Time-bound

For example, 'Conduct four staff supervisions by March 31st 2012.' This is a SMART objective because it relates to a specific target (conducting staff supervisions), it is measurable (there are four staff appraisals), it is both achievable and realistic and is time-bound as it needs to be completed by a specific date.

By devising SMART objectives, the activities agreed for your development will not only be realistic and achievable, but the progress you make towards achieving your personal objectives will also be measurable. This will enable you and your manager to establish how successful your progress along your development pathway is.

Key Term

SMART – Objectives should be specific, measurable, achievable, realistic and time-bound.

Portfolio Task 2 15 minutes

Links to LO2: Assessment criteria 2.1

Devise three SMART objectives to assist you with the planning of your development pathway.

Explain to your assessor why it is important to set objectives.

PLTS

By thinking about your development pathway, it will encourage you to generate new ideas and explore new possibilities (CT1, IE1).

Be able to identify gaps in skills and knowledge in own performance

Your job description informs you of the tasks you are expected to undertake on a day-to-day basis. However, your organisation will focus on providing a quality product or service to ensure that it successfully meets its customers' expectations. This means that your role, and the role of everyone else who works in your organisation, is equally important and needs to be continuously developed to meet the challenges of your industry. The mix of skills and knowledge that the employees possess in your organisation will, collectively, contribute to successful outcomes and the achievement of business objectives.

Knowledge and skills required for own work role

To enhance the quality of the product or service that your organisation provides, you and your team will need to identify any gaps in your knowledge and update your skills.

The role of the team leader

Imagine that you take part in a leadership survey. One of the questions asks you what personal skills an effective team leader should possess. How do you think you would respond?

By being aware of your own performance as you work towards your personal objectives, you may be able to identify gaps in the skills and knowledge you currently possess. You may find that some aspects of what you do would benefit from improvement.

You and your team may also work towards **key performance indicators (KPIs)**, which establish targets that have to be achieved within a given time frame. It is important to be able to achieve these targets.

To be able to identify whether or not your skills and attributes would benefit from improvement, you may initially reflect upon what your workplace is likely to expect from a good team leader. For example, your workplace may expect you to:

- have good interpersonal skills (verbal skills *and* non-verbal skills – these skills may include use of tone when speaking, words used, eye contact and use of facial expressions)
- be an effective communicator, show respect, be polite and offer feedback
- be a problem solver and monitor the work of your team
- be effective at dealing with relationship difficulties (such as conflict situations)
- be a good listener, act decisively and avoid favouritism within the team
- manage time effectively (for example, keeping a diary)
- set objectives, goals and targets and plan the work of the team

Key Term

Key performance indicators (KPIs) – targets for performance that can be measured, for example sales volume expected each month.

- be comfortable using information technology (where appropriate)
- be able to process information effectively and prioritise tasks accordingly
- be a good decision maker and involve others in that process
- have sufficient technical skills (such as using equipment)
- monitor resources effectively (for example, stock control and reducing waste)
- have good knowledge of the product or service you provide
- be aware of who your organisation's stakeholders are
- act within the limits of the authority given to you
- identify the development needs of yourself and your team members
- empathise with and support your team members
- be able to lead your team effectively.

This is a long list, but it is useful to reflect on these points in order to identify what skills, if any, you think you may need to develop further.

Portfolio Task 3 15 minutes

Links to LO3: Assessment criterion 3.1

In order to be effective as a team leader, it is necessary to have the right skills and knowledge to enable you to carry out your job role to the best of your ability.

Make a list of the knowledge and skills that you think are necessary to be an effective team leader.

PLTS

This task will encourage you to analyse, evaluate and judge appropriate skills and knowledge needed to be an effective team leader (IE4).

Using a SWOT analysis

The knowledge and skills you possess will also help you to plan the work of your team members to meet the requirements of your organisation. The success of your planning process, and the way you communicate your plans to your team, largely depends upon the development of your skills and attributes.

A useful tool to examine the skills and knowledge you possess, as well as areas for development, is a **SWOT** analysis. SWOT stands for:

S   Strengths
W   Weaknesses
O   Opportunities
T   Threats

Key Term

SWOT – a technique for identifying areas for improvement. SWOT stands for Strengths, Weaknesses, Opportunities, Threats.

In order to complete a SWOT analysis, consider what your strengths and weaknesses are, what opportunities are available to you and the threats you need to be aware of. Your strengths and weaknesses may be training you have or have not received, your confidence and your skills.

Opportunities can be training that is available internally or externally and threats can also be internal or external. Have a look at the table below for some examples:

Strengths	Weaknesses
Good communication skills	Managing conflict
Knowledge of job role	Meeting deadlines
Good team player	Using databases
Confident when dealing with customers	
Using SAGE accounts	

Opportunities	Threats
Conflict resolution training – external	Lack of time to complete training
Time management training – internal	No support from manager
Shadowing staff member to obtain training on databases	

PLTS

This activity will encourage you to think creatively by generating and exploring new ideas in the opportunities section of the SWOT analysis and encourage you to ask questions about what threats are preventing you from realising your goals. This activity will also make you evaluate your strengths and limitations (CT1, 3; RL1, 2, 3, 5).

Portfolio Task 4 20 minutes

Links to LO3: Assessment criterion 3.2

Carry out a SWOT analysis on yourself, identifying your personal strengths and weaknesses and opportunities for future development. You can also identify threats that may present themselves as obstacles. Ask your line manager and colleagues for their opinions.

Table A1.2: An example of a SWOT analysis.

With your SWOT analysis completed, you can plan actions that will assist your continuous professional development (CPD). You may have already identified a gap between the skills you need to perform well and those you currently possess. This analysis will present opportunities to consider for future personal development.

Once you have identified what your responses are, an action plan can be drawn up for you and your manager to plan your development activities. These can be discussed in your monthly supervision meetings and your responses can be built into your PDR for consideration.

Action planning

Action planning is a process where you and your manager can identify actions needed to achieve the objectives that have been agreed. Initially, you may use a three step approach:

1. Where am I now?
2. Where do I want to be?
3. How will I get there?

By drawing up an action plan, both you and your manager (or your human resource manager) can identify what actions should take place to ensure progress. This can be measured by introducing a 'By when' column into your plan so you know when your actions are completed.

A suggested action plan template is shown below.

Title:						
Name:						
Date:						
Action/Task	**By whom**	**By when**	**Resources needed**	**Completed/ date**	**Review date**	**Manager signature**
Attend time management training	Me	End of July	Time and materials	30th July		

Table A1.3: Template for an action plan.

Self-appraisals

Your SWOT analysis will have enabled you to examine any threats that present themselves as obstacles and to identify opportunities for improvement. It is important to be aware of these obstacles and make efforts to minimise or eradicate them so that they don't affect your progress. Having conducted a SWOT analysis, an action plan should be produced with timelines for your improvement activity.

It is often useful to examine an area which you (or others) have identified as a weakness and develop a **self-assessment** process. Examine the template below:

Key Term

Self-assessment – evaluating the success of your own performance.

Leading a team meeting – Self-assessment					
Date of meeting:					
Topic discussed					
Self-assessment item	**What went well?**	**What didn't go well?**	**What needs improving?**	**What should I do to improve it?**	**By when?**
Encouraging all to participate					
Speaking clearly					
Time management of my meeting					
How I clarified the points made by others					

Table A1.4: Template for a self-assessment.

Conducting a SWOT analysis for yourself is a useful self-appraisal but there are other things you can do, such as obtaining feedback about your performance and behaviour from others in your workplace.

Consider obtaining feedback from:

- your line manager (and/or other managers)
- colleagues working at the same level as you
- members of the team you lead
- customers you deal with (if appropriate).

In terms of analysing your behaviour generally, you may also wish to obtain feedback from members of your family and friends whose opinions you value.

Think about how you will capture this feedback. Will you do it verbally and make notes, or will you do it more formally by using a feedback questionnaire? Your questionnaire would need to explain who you are, what you want the respondent to do and why you want them to do it. (For example, you want to improve your workplace performance.)

You wouldn't need to ask many questions, but for your identified areas of performance or behaviours you could ask:

- What do I do well?
- What do I not do well?
- How could I improve what I do?

Always finish your questionnaire with a 'Thank you' and explain where the form should be returned to and by when.

Dealing with negative feedback

It's not always easy to accept criticism or negative feedback but everyone has to at sometime! What is important is how we accept it and deal with it. Remember, what appears to be negative feedback may encourage us to reflect on our current behaviours and perhaps change the way we do things. This could result in positive outcomes.

Here are some ways to handle feedback that appears to be negative.

- Ask yourself, what is the purpose of this feedback? Is it justified?
- When you respond to criticism be assertive but not aggressive.
- Stay as calm as you possibly can.
- Think positively because the feedback may be valid!
- Ensure you listen carefully to what is being said (if you are anxious, you may not listen properly).
- Try to empathise (for example, 'Yes, I can see how this will have upset you').
- If you are angry, ask to meet again later (sometimes a break away from your conversation will calm you down).

Remember

When assessing your own listening skills, ask yourself whether you let the other person speak without interruption. You cannot listen properly if you are talking!

Consider the model below:

Figure A1.1 The importance of feedback.

Activity 🕐 20 minutes

Spend some time investigating the communication process further, by researching the work of Wilbur Schramm (1955). A particular focus should be on exploring the areas of encoder and decoder.

Although simplistic, this model suggests that feedback is important and enables the sender to obtain clarification that the message has been received and understood by the recipient. It also enables the recipient to clarify any points that are uncertain with the sender.

Communication is about getting the right message, to the right person at the right time.

After conducting your SWOT analysis and obtaining feedback from others, it may be useful to reflect deeper on the aspects of your job that you wish to develop. A self-assessment document such as the one below may help you to do this. (Please note: these are examples only – the areas you have identified for development may be different.)

General Self-Appraisal Form

Date of self-assessment:..

My views on my performance and behaviours to date:

1. The quality of my work

2. My ability to lead my team effectively

3. My ability to plan work with my team to meet targets

4. My technical skills

5. My ability to communicate effectively

6. My ability to empathise with my team members

How valuable has any training I have received over the last 6 months been? What training would I like over the next 6 months?

Figure A1.2 A self-appraisal form

Stress management

Sometimes you might find yourself in a stressful situation in your personal life, which can affect your mood. These feelings can be transferred into the workplace, sometimes creating tension and even leading to conflict with others. Similarly, stressful events at work may result in strained relationships with family or friends outside of work. Stress management therefore is very important and when examining the concept of personal development, it is useful to be aware of the effects of stress, for example:

- mood swings
- unusual/out-of-character behaviours
- eating and drinking disorders
- smoking (perhaps more than usual)
- being very emotional.

Such behaviours can be counter-productive to what you are trying to achieve as a team leader. Prolonged exposure to stressful situations may even lead to serious illness such as heart disease. It is extremely beneficial to control stress levels wherever possible. Some of the effects of a stressful environment on your team may include:

- colleagues leaving their jobs
- increased levels of absenteeism (requiring 'cover' from others who in turn, may become stressed also)
- a less efficient team not meeting its targets
- lowered levels of output, resulting in disappointed customers.

The good news is that stress can be managed. This can be done through relaxation strategies (watching a film or pursuing a hobby), healthy diets, taking exercise (even brisk walking) and talking through problems with others. Planning time sensibly and setting realistic targets (refer back to SMART) will also help. In extreme cases, it is worth talking to your doctor, a manager, an occupational health therapist, or friends and family members.

Identify opportunities and resources available for personal development

For your organisation to meet its overall business objectives and safeguard everyone's job, team objectives must be met. This in turn means that the personal objectives of every employee must be met and is why personal development activity is so important.

Development opportunities can be in the form of on-the-job training, off-the-job training and distance learning, which will now be discussed in detail.

Activity 10 minutes

List what you consider to be causes of stress and the likely impact upon your team.

Remember

Causes of stress may include work being too challenging or not challenging enough!

Some stress can actually be good for you (such as the stress you feel before giving a presentation, which produces adrenaline and makes you perform better).

On-the-job training

1. Mentoring – You may be allocated a mentor who will be somebody who understands the procedures and needs of the organisation. This person will act as a buddy to guide you as you develop and grow into your job role. During regular face-to-face meetings, your mentor will give you regular feedback on the progress of your development.

2. Coaching – A suitably qualified member of staff will help you to develop your skills and knowledge by showing you the best way to do things and sharing their knowledge and skills with you.

3. Shadowing – You will be given the opportunity to work alongside an experienced member of staff to gain first-hand experience of how they carry out their tasks. This enables you to observe, question and learn from experience.

4. In-house training – You may attend various training sessions in your workplace to increase your personal development.

Off-the-job training

1. College courses – At college you have the benefit of mixing with individuals from other organisations who bring their own workplace experiences into your discussions and activities. It is an opportunity to learn from other students as well as from your tutors.

2. Private training providers – This provides many of the same benefits as attending training in a college, as you may mix with people from other organisations.

Distance learning

There are clear advantages and disadvantages to developing your knowledge and skills through distance learning. These are listed in Table A1.5.

Advantages	Disadvantages
– Can study at own pace – Don't need to travel – Can choose when to study – Can chat online with other candidates – Have one-to-one chats with tutor online	– Cost of purchasing hardware and software – Lack of social interaction – Technical problems can disrupt your study – No face-to-face interaction with peers and tutors, e.g. activities – May be time-consuming waiting for feedback on work

Table A1.5: Advantages and disadvantages of distance learning.

PLTS

This activity will give you the opportunity to carry out research and plan suitable training. Also, it will help you to generate new ideas and explore new possibilities on the type of training you would like to attend (IE 2; CT 1).

Key Terms

External training – training available outside your organisation, e.g. college courses.

Internal training – training available within your organisation.

Remember

It's always useful to be open to new ideas and observe the way that other people do things. Never stop learning from others!

Portfolio Task 5 45 minutes

Links to LO4: Assessment criterion 4.1

To assist you with your development plan, identify what general training is readily available to you, both **internally** and **externally**. For example, your organisation may run regular in-house health and safety training days for its managers or, perhaps there is a waiting list to attend an external widely recognised management course. Once you have found out what is available, list your findings in a table.

As you continue to develop yourself, you should constantly review your personal objectives. Your career path can be planned by thinking about what you want to achieve within given timescales. Consider planning your goals as follows:

- Within 1 year – aim to achieve your short-term goals.
- Within 3 years – aim to achieve your medium-term goals.
- Within 5 years – aim to achieve your long-term goals.

Planning in this way may appear straightforward but it is important to find ways to remain committed to your plan and to motivate yourself. Think about how you can reward yourself when you achieve a milestone in your development journey.

The benefits of meeting your challenges are increased self-esteem through what has been achieved and increased levels of self-confidence as you go about your day-to-day tasks.

For advice on career development, you can speak to your local careers advice service, visit a library or examine newspapers, trade journals or the internet. Be aware that in terms of your personal development opportunities, it is often useful to speak to your human resources manager, and your line manager. Your staff appraisal, or PDR, is a useful vehicle for this type of discussion.

How do you learn

You may find it useful to examine how you learn so that you know how best to improve your skills. Management theorists have carried out research into the steps you will take when learning. One of these theorists introduced a learning cycle.

Kolb's experiential learning cycle

David Kolb created a learning cycle in 1979 to identify the way people learn. He looked at four points:

- Learning and what was felt during a period of learning. An example of this could be using a particular computer program for the first time, and assessing it.

- Thinking about how useful the period of learning was.
- Looking at ideas and theories related to the learning experience. In terms of using a new computer program, this stage would be to understand how it functions.
- Testing the learning. In our example, this would mean using the new program to try out what has been learned.

It can be helpful to identify your own learning style as some people learn more by visual means whereas other people learn more from doing something (a hands-on approach).

Theorists Honey and Mumford described the following types of learners:

1. Activists (do something) – People who actively enjoy the challenges that new learning experiences offer.
2. Reflectors (think about it) – People who like to stand back and review a learning experience in a thoughtful way.
3. Theorists (make sense of it) – People who like to think the learning experience through in logical steps.
4. Pragmatists (test it out) – People who like to try out new ideas and enjoy problem solving and decision making as part of a learning experience.

These four learning attributes can also be seen as a learning cycle.

Activity ⏱ 30 minutes

Spend some time researching David Kolb's learning cycle. From your research, create your own diagram of the cycle. Discuss with your manager how you could use this cycle in practice.

Figure A1.3 Honey and Mumford's learning cycle.

Activity ⏱ 45 minutes

Spend some time researching into the work of Honey and Mumford (1986) and identify your own preferred learning style. Discuss your findings with your manager and assessor.

Manage personal development Unit A1

Checklist

Skills requirements

When evaluating what skills and knowledge gaps you may have, remember to look at:

- communication skills
- listening skills
- time management skills
- stress management
- leadership skills.

This unit has prepared you for taking part in your PDR (staff appraisal) with your manager. Through this process and by following the steps that have been discussed, you will have identified aspects of your work role that need developing.

Now ask yourself the following:

1. What are my main responsibilities at work?
2. What have I done well over the last 6 months?
3. What knowledge and skills have I learnt over the last 6 months?
4. How have my new skills and knowledge helped in my job?
5. What have I not done well in the last 6-12 months?
6. What further training and development would improve what I do?

When you reflect upon the opportunities you have identified, it will be necessary to plan your training needs so that you can update or improve your skills and knowledge accordingly. You and your manager may wish to develop a plan similar to the one shown below:

Identified opportunities for development	Skills/knowledge gap	SMART objective	Resources and/or support from others	Training opportunity
Reviewing the performance of your own team members	How to conduct a PDR	To complete PDR training by June 30th	Staff Time Training material Training budget	Internal one-day training course

Table A1.6: A possible training plan template.

Your line manager and Human Resources department will need to agree with you when and where your training activity will take place.

A plan similar to the one on page 20 is useful to clarify in your own mind, and that of your manager, what requirements have been discussed and agreed. However, your organisation may prefer to use a document similar to the one below.

Name of post holder: Date of today's review: Date of last review:		Name of manager:		
What skills/knowledge do I need/want to develop?	What actions must I take to achieve this?	What resources and/or support will I need?	Target date for completion	Target date for review with manager
Development objective 1: Managing conflict in the workplace	Attend an in-house training session	Time to attend and training materials	30th July	30th August
Development objective 2:				
Development objective 3:				
Post holder's signature:		**Manager's signature:**		

Figure A1.4: Personal development plan template.

Remember that the aim of your development activity is to enhance, update or improve your current performance. Once you have successfully completed your training and development activities, you should revisit your SWOT analysis and the corresponding action plan. For example, you may want to examine whether the identified weaknesses have now been fully addressed and possibly become strengths. You may have also minimised the threats that presented themselves as obstacles to your development, and you may even have realised some of the opportunities that you identified.

Portfolio Task 6 60 minutes

Links to LO3, LO4: Assessment criteria 3.3, 4.1

Examine the contents of the Personal Development Plan document above and devise a similar document of your own. Spend some time completing your document to establish what skills you wish to develop. Once you have completed this task, make sure you discuss your findings with your line manager.

HH LEARNING CENTRE
HARROW COLLEGE

Be able to carry out and assess activities within own development plan

Plan activities in own development plan that address identified needs

To help you to plan your development activities, it may be useful for you to prioritise each stage along the following lines:

- costing – the cost of the training programme, travelling and materials

- timescale – the length of training programme and your availability to fit the training schedule alongside your workplace and family commitments

- availability of training and development – taking steps to identify which colleges provide suitable training to meet your budget and what opportunities are available in-house for mentoring, coaching and shadowing

- assessment – how much work is involved with the revision and preparation required for assignments and examinations? Can you realistically meet the targets and workload for these requirements?

- support – will you get the support you need from your managers, family members and friends to make sure you complete your studies on time?

- suitability – it is always a good idea to discuss with your line manager the suitability and identification of the people you will shadow, be coached or mentored by.

This process should be followed for each of your other identified priorities. (for example, time management).

Managing your time

As with many aspects of work life, time is a very important resource. Your personal development will require strong time management skills. You will be expected to complete your training and development activities on time and within given deadlines.

Managing your time effectively can reduce levels of stress levels in work. Consider the suggestions below for effective time management.

- Use timed agendas in your team meetings.
- Use planning aids (for example 'To do' lists) and prioritise activities into urgent, important and non-urgent categories.
- Fill in time-sheets to see how long tasks take to do and monitor this.
- Be prepared to delegate tasks to others in your team (as appropriate).
- Ensure tools, equipment and materials are always easily accessible to avoid wasting time searching for things.

- Don't encourage unnecessary interruptions from others (for example, drop-in visitors).
- Everyone is tempted to have a chat in the corridor or staff room, so examine how you can save time here!
- When using the telephone or emailing, aim to be concise.
- Use tools such as Gantt charts and action plans to assist you with your time management.

A Gantt chart is a time management technique devised by Henry Gantt in 1917. The chart offers a visual representation of what has been scheduled to ensure tasks are carried out in a timely manner.

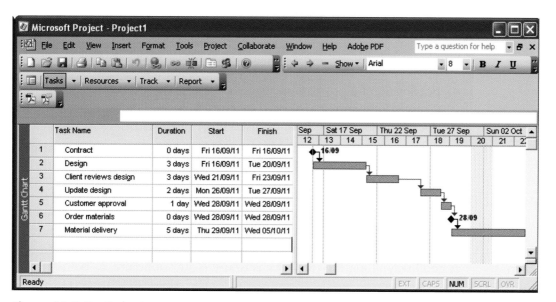

Figure A1.5 Gantt chart.

The chart above shows the order in which tasks must be done and the length of time each should take.

Managing your time effectively will help you achieve the goals you have for your personal development activities in a timely manner and assist you on a day-to-day basis in your workplace, as you and your team achieve your targets. This can result in enhanced job satisfaction for everyone.

Of course, managing your time effectively can also reduce the possibility of you (and your team) becoming stressed at work.

Think carefully about how you manage your own time. Do you still have enough time to do the following:

1. Meet with and spend quality time with all of your family members?
2. Pursue your main hobbies and interests?
3. Meet your home-life deadlines?
4. Meet your college or studying deadlines?

Collecting feedback from colleagues on development activities

The value of feedback

In the 1960s Douglas McGregor, a management theorist, carried out some research into the characteristics of a successful team. It is worth examining this research to establish whether it has any resemblance to the way you work with your team members.

McGregor suggested it is important that team members listen to each other, respect each other's views and that decisions made are reached by consensus. He further suggested there should be a workplace culture that allows team members to freely express their views. He was of the opinion that this should happen in an atmosphere that is comfortable and relaxed.

With regard to the concept of feedback from others, McGregor suggested that:

- Feedback, of a positive or negative nature, should be given or received regularly and should be constructive. Then feedback should not create an atmosphere of discomfort or mistrust.
- If there is disagreement, then this should be openly discussed between all parties concerned to minimise the risk of disruption to the team's work.

Wherever possible, the feedback you receive should be evaluated and analysed in a quiet and relaxed atmosphere. Do this by yourself: you can share your views with others later and approach the feedback you have received as a positive overview of areas in which you could improve. A good way of getting feedback is to use a questionnaire, as below:

Feedback Evaluation Questionnaire on my Performance

Recently I attended an Assertiveness Course at Healbridge College. In order to evaluate the effectiveness of this course, I would be very grateful if you could spend 5 minutes answering the following questions:

1. I am more assertive when allocating work

   Yes   No

2. If yes, please explain how:

3. If no, how can I be more assertive?

Thank you for taking time to complete this form.

Please return it to .... by ....

Figure A1.6 An example evaluation questionnaire.

Portfolio Task 7 90 minutes

Links to LO4: Assessment criterion 4.2

Getting feedback from colleagues and your manager following a development activity is important for your development as a team leader. Therefore, prepare a brief questionnaire to find out their opinions and/or views on whether the activity has made you more effective.

Once you have received your questionnaires back, prepare a brief document summarising what has been said.

Assess the success of development plan activities

After attending training, it will be necessary to assess how successful your development activities have been.

Portfolio Task 8 10 minutes

Links to LO4: Assessment criterion 4.3

Use the template below to enable you to assess whether your team leading skills have improved.

Team Leading Skills – Self-Assessment

Using the following scale to evaluate your team leading skills.

Scale: 1. Excellent   2. Very good   3. Good   4. Fair   5. Poor   6. Very Poor

Please circle the appropriate score.

Skills/Ability	Score
Communication skills	1 2 3 4 5 6
Decision-making skills	1 2 3 4 5 6
Patient with others	1 2 3 4 5 6
Supportive	1 2 3 4 5 6
Able to work with colleagues	1 2 3 4 5 6
Honest and trustworthy	1 2 3 4 5 6
Treating colleagues and staff fairly	1 2 3 4 5 6
Respecting others' views	1 2 3 4 5 6
Assertiveness	1 2 3 4 5 6

Knowledge area	
Technical knowledge	1 2 3 4 5 6
Staff members skills	1 2 3 4 5 6
Policies and procedures	1 2 3 4 5 6
Commercial awareness	1 2 3 4 5 6

PLTS

Through working on this task, you will engage with issues that affect you. This task will allow you to discuss any issues of concern you have identified with your manager and review progress (EP 1, 2, 3; RL 1, 4, 5).

Functional Skills

This activity will help you develop your Functional Skills in English: Reading and Writing. Your questionnaire will need to be presented in a logical sequence with an appropriate language and structure. Your document will need to highlight the key points noted in the questionnaire and your work will include generally accurate punctuation, spelling and your meaning must be clear.

PLTS

This activity will enable you to review progress on your team leading skills (RL 3).

To manage your personal development, you will need to work through the following stages:

- Personal development plan
- Training plan
- Self assessment and feedback
- Performance development review

Performance development review (PDR)

In addition to reviewing your SWOT and action plans and obtaining feedback from colleagues, you and your manager can assess the success of your development activities by reviewing what has taken place together. This can happen by examining the personal development plan previously agreed and reviewing your achievements to date.

During your PDR interview, your line manager will review your past performance and development activity and is likely to use a document such as the one below, which you and your manager can complete together. This will evaluate your personal training and development activity to date and identify any further development that may be required.

Performance Development Review					
Dates of training	What I did	Reasons why	What I have learnt	How I will use these new skills/ knowledge	What further development is needed in this area?

Table A1.7 An example form to be used in your performance development review.

Portfolio Task 9 45 minutes

Links to LO4: Assessment criterion 4.3

Use the table below to assist you in evaluating your current position, identifying where you would like to be in the future and the opportunities available to you. Discuss this action plan with your line manager during your next PDR and/or supervision meeting. You can use this as a piece of evidence for your portfolio.

Personal Action Plan	
Staff name:	
Period from:	**To:**

Where am I now?

Where do I want to be?

How will I get there?

Date for review:

Staff signature:	Date:
Manager signature:	Date:

Portfolio Task 10 30 minutes

Links to LO4: Assessment criterion 4.3

Write a short reflective account on the success, or otherwise, of recent training. Was the training useful, if not why not? Give reasons for your views.

Manage personal development **Unit A1**

Team talk

Catrin's story

My name is Catrin. I'm 32 years old and employed as a team leader in a national cleaning company. The company has a contract with local hospitals and with smaller construction firms. I currently lead the team I was a part of. I have been a team leader for two months now and I'm finding it hard to manage my team. As we were previously work colleagues, they will not take me seriously and ignore my orders. Also, I have a new starter who is not working to the quality standards of the organisation. I'm worried that my manager is going to pick up on this very soon.

When I was appointed to the team leader role two months ago, I was given no training and I have no experience in dealing with under-performing staff.

Top tips

Catrin could speak to her colleagues and managers to find out what her strengths and weaknesses are. She should ask for training in managing a team.

It may also be beneficial for Catrin to set out a plan of where she would like to be in five years' time.

Ask the expert	
Q	I have a one-to-one meeting with my manager next week. What do I need to do before the meeting in order to raise my concerns with my manager?
A	You will need to evaluate your own performance and identify the knowledge and skills gaps you think you have. This can be done by: ■ completing a SWOT analysis to identify your strengths, weaknesses, opportunities and threats ■ conducting a self-appraisal ■ researching internal and external training and making a list of the training you think will help you to be a more effective team leader.

What your assessor is looking for

In order to demonstrate your competency within this unit, you will need to provide sufficient evidence to your assessor. You will need to provide a short written narrative or personal statement explaining how you meet the assessment criteria. In addition, your assessor may ask you questions to test your knowledge of the topics identified in this unit.

Below is a list of suggested documentation that will provide evidence to help you to prove your competency in this unit:

- performance development review documentation
- supervision documents
- notes taken during one-to-one supervision meetings
- own training plans
- own job description
- completed feedback questionnaires.

Task and page reference	Assessment criteria
1 (page 4)	1.1
2 (page 9)	2.1
3 (page 11)	3.1
4 (page 12)	3.2
5 (page 17)	4.1
6 (page 21)	3.3, 4.1
7 (page 25)	4.2
8 (page 25)	4.3
9 (page 27)	4.3
10 (page 27)	4.3

Unit D1 Develop working relationships with colleagues

In this unit you will look at how positive working relationships with your colleagues can help to make a team more successful. You will be learning about the work of various theorists, including Bruce W. Tuckman, John Adair, Dr R. Meredith Belbin and Robert E. Quinn.

You will be investigating the importance of professionalism and respect in creating productive working relationships and reflecting on leadership styles, team development and dealing with difficulties in the workplace. You will also learn about effective communication when dealing with internal and external customers and colleagues.

What you will learn:

- Understand the benefits of working with colleagues
- Be able to establish working relationships with colleagues
- Be able to act in a professional and respectful manner when working with colleagues
- Be able to communicate with colleagues
- Be able to identify potential work-related difficulties and explore solutions

Links to the Technical Certificate

If you are completing your NVQ as part of an Apprenticeship Framework, you will find the following topics are also covered in your Technical Certificate:

- The role of a team leader when developing and maintaining working relationships
- Conducting a skills audit and planning the work of a team
- Understanding team development
- Leadership styles
- Dealing with conflict in a team

Key Terms

Group – people coming together with a common interest, e.g. group of football supporters.

Team – people working towards the same objective or common goal, e.g. football team.

Remember

For any team to be successful, a mix of appropriate skills and attributes among the team members is required.

Understand the benefits of working with colleagues

If you are working for an organisation, you will find yourself working with others and it is important at the outset to understand the implications of this. **Groups** and **teams**, for example, are not the same. A group of people may get together to go and watch a football match; they share a common purpose – watching football – but that is all. A team of people work together with the aim of achieving the same goal or objective. So the football side that spectators go to watch *are* a team. Specific skills or knowledge are not necessary to be part of a group but they are important elements of a successful team.

In other words, a *group* of people who simply share the same interest do not need to work towards a specific objective, whereas a *team* of people will have a holistic approach towards achieving a specific objective and must work closely together to achieve it.

Stages of team development

When examining what defines a team, it is useful to explore the work of Bruce Tuckman (1965), who developed a theory of 'Stages of Team Development'. Tuckman suggested that a group of people works through the following processes to eventually become an effective team.

- Forming – When the group comes together there can be power struggles and conflict because they are unsure of each other.
- Storming – The leader's authority is challenged at this stage of development and members can be disruptive.
- Norming – At this stage there is more stability in the team as people begin to accept each other and become more willing to listen to their leader: they willingly accept more responsibility.
- Performing – Team members become more creative and happily put ideas forward which enhances team performance.
- Mourning – If the team is disbanded or perhaps a team leader is moved or leaves, the team can go through a process of mourning.

In your workplace, you will work alongside colleagues at different levels. Some colleagues will be easier to work with than others as we all have different personalities. You should however make efforts to build effective working relationships with everyone.

The benefits of productive relationships include:

- a friendlier working atmosphere
- the increased likelihood of targets being met
- a more enjoyable work experience
- a better service for customers
- a higher level of morale.

What is a productive relationship?

Think about the relationships you have with your friends and family members. To be able to sustain a long-term relationship you often have to consider other people's feelings and make efforts to compromise, but also, in a **tactful** way, let them know how you feel. The same can be said for the workplace, where efforts have to be made to:

- communicate effectively
- minimise conflict
- show respect to others
- value the opinions of others
- be willing to reach a compromise.

There may be occasions where you witness personality clashes in the workplace just as you do with friends and family. If this happens, knowing how you should deal with the conflict is important.

In your workplace, you will interact with colleagues at the same level as yourself, with colleagues who manage you and perhaps with colleagues that you supervise in your own team. Without productive working relationships and effective liaison between people working at these different levels, it can be difficult for individuals, teams or departments, or even the organisation as a whole, to meet its objectives and goals.

Similarly, without a **culture** of respect, honesty and openness, it may be difficult to maintain a motivated workforce which enjoys the challenge and satisfaction of achieving goals and objectives. The customers or service users that use your product or service will also benefit from productive working relationships as their requests will be met with a speedy and efficient response. This may result in positive feedback for your team.

To help create productive relationships in your team, think about the following examples of good practice:

- Providing the correct training to do the job.
- Demonstrating effective time management.
- Ensuring everyone knows the procedures to be followed for a standardised approach.
- Creating good working conditions.
- Promoting **diversity** and **equality**.
- Conducting regular staff appraisals.
- Managing and minimising **conflict**.

Being aware of your own behaviours and the behaviours of your colleagues can help you to build an effective and efficient team. It is possible that you sometimes behave negatively towards others without even realising it! Perhaps you shout or snap at members of your team when you are feeling stressed and this may result in them feeling demotivated or undervalued, which can affect the performance of your team.

Key Terms

Conflict – disagreement between individuals or groups.

Culture – the behaviour and beliefs of the organisation that affect the attitudes, decision making and management style of the staff; the way things are done.

Diversity – having a variety of people from different backgrounds.

Equality – equal opportunity and treatment for all.

Tact – making sure you don't offend or upset someone by what you say or do.

Remember

The way you view yourself, is not always how others view you!

Qualities and attributes required to build an effective team

Consider how the qualities and attributes that you possess can help to build a team that works efficiently and effectively. Some of these are:

- effective communication (including listening and questioning skills and correct use of body language)
- enthusiasm, commitment and motivation
- technical/professional competence
- the ability to offer and receive constructive feedback
- a balance between competition and cooperation
- keeping promises
- praise and recognition (without rewarding poor performance)
- ensuring rules and regulations are accepted and followed
- not giving unreasonable demands or abusing the power you hold
- being well organised and planning effectively
- having patience and understanding
- possessing the ability to make well-informed decisions and judgements
- a supportive nature
- observing and managing team behaviour
- creating and working within a pleasant culture/team spirit
- holistic approach towards achieving goals
- being aware of **authority** and **standards**
- displaying effective leadership, direction, **delegation** and negotiation.

Key Terms

Authority – the right to control or command others.

Standards – rules or judgements about levels of behaviour and quality of work.

Delegation – giving direction and focus to others by allocating suitable tasks to them.

Activity 10 minutes

Consider how important the attributes or skills of a leader are for each of the following categories. Record your thoughts along with a reason for each of your opinions.

- Being an effective communicator
- Supporting the team
- Sharing ideas
- Showing respect
- Involving the team in decision making
- Being approachable
- Being polite
- Valuing your team members' contributions
- Knowing your team members' strengths and weaknesses
- Treating all team members fairly
- Praising your staff when appropriate
- Effective delegation

Components that make up an effective team

If you conducted a survey to find out what team members would like from their organisation, the responses you get might include:

- strong leadership and a sense of direction
- recognition and reward
- motivation and a high level of morale
- mutual respect, trust and support
- regular reviews and training updates
- reliable, loyal and dependable team members
- a shared sense of purpose
- making best use of resources and skills
- being able to learn from mistakes
- enjoyable work
- delegation that will stretch them
- effective communication
- an atmosphere/culture that enables conflict to be resolved
- a team that is well informed about its responsibilities
- sound procedures to follow
- a culture of quality
- openness and honesty.

The team leader should remember they are in the centre of a network of people.

Planning work effectively

When you allocate work you must do so fairly but you must also make the best use of your team's strengths. This will mean knowing your team's strengths and weaknesses and who you should allocate tasks to. You will need to control the resources that each team member needs to carry out their role effectively.

Your line manager is likely to have discussed your departmental budget with you and it is important that you don't overspend on resources. As team leader you will not have overall control of your budget, but you can help your manager to monitor it. You can discuss this process in your meetings.

Use the strengths of each person in the team to make the team effective.

Holding regular one-to-one reviews with your team members can help to address any concerns that may have an impact on your planning process. Your discussions with team members will give you the opportunity to monitor and measure performance and then compare the results against targets. Often key performance indicators (KPIs) will be set and these are likely to be quantifiable. An example of a quantifiable KPI is to make or sell a given number of products in one week or month.

SMART objectives should be set for yourself and your team and whether these objectives will be met largely depends upon:

- sufficient resources being available
- tasks being organised well
- the quality of the work being monitored (for example, is it being rushed?)
- the progress of the work in hand being monitored
- work rotas being produced and distributed.

Planning aids may assist you and your team to achieve your objectives and these can include:

- Gantt charts (refer to Unit A1)
- schedules (what is to be achieved and by when)
- 'to do' lists (what must be achieved daily/weekly)
- visual boards/wall boards (for example, to plan staff holidays/sales targets etc.).

Checklist

SMART stands for:

- Specific
- Measurable
- Achievable
- Realistic
- Time-bound

Remember

Ideally contingency plans should be in place to address a situation should something go wrong with your planning process. In other words have a back up plan in place to deal with uncertainties. For example, if there is a power cut in a hospital, then a generator will automatically switch on.

Unit D1 Develop working relationships with colleagues

Regardless of how well work is planned, things may go wrong. Should this happen it can have a negative effect on working relationships and may lead to a conflict situation in the team. You must be prepared to deal with this to avoid the situation getting worse. (See D10 Manage Conflict in a Team.)

Portfolio Task 1 10 minutes

Links to LO1: Assessment criterion 1.1

Identify the advantages of having productive working relationships with your colleagues.

Write down your views and discuss them with your assessor.

PLTS

Through discussing with your assessor the advantages of having productive working relationships you will be generating new ideas and exploring possibilities (CT1).

Sharing views and opinions

Briefings and **brainstorming** activities can encourage your team to share their views and opinions. This will enable you to question and clarify points raised to confirm that you recognise and understand their needs and concerns.

Be mindful that some people are naturally shy and less likely to speak out in front of other people. These people may have excellent views or genuine concerns to share. Know your team members' characteristics and if you think they are shy, you could let them discuss things with you on a one-to-one basis (for example, in your monthly supervisions).

Key Term

Brainstorming – a technique used to resolve a problem, share ideas and encourage creative thinking whereby all participants come up with ideas spontaneously in a group-discussion environment.

Be able to establish working relationships with colleagues

Organisations can be structured in different ways. This is often due to how they have grown and developed. Many business organisations began with one person (or a small group of people) who had a good business idea and identified a need for a product or service in the market place. Then, as an organisation receives more orders or contracts from customers, its structure will grow because more staff members are employed.

Identify colleagues within own and other organisations

Once organisations have grown to more than a handful of people they need to develop a management hierarchy and may even be structured into departments.

Spend some time researching the different types of structures referred to here. Then, by speaking to your manager, decide which type of structure your organisation has.
Discuss your findings with your assessor.

PLTS

Completing this activity will give you the opportunity to demonstrate your ability to generate new ideas and research alternative types of organisational structures. Through discussions with your manager, you will evaluate your findings and judge the value of the information you have found which will support your conclusions (CT 1, 3, 5; IE 1, 2, 3, 4, 6).

Small and medium-sized enterprises (**SMEs**) or larger organisations will often have:

- Chief Executive/Managing Director/General Managers
- Senior Management Team/Board of Directors
- Middle Managers
- Supervisors/First Line Managers
- Team Leaders
- Operatives.

An organisation that has all the employees listed above has a 'hierarchical' structure. Other types of structures are:

- geographical – often used by large retailers who have many branches in many different regions of the UK (for example, Tesco or B&Q)
- matrix – often used for one-off projects such as motorway bridge or a car manufacturer producing a limited edition
- product-based – likely to be used by an organisation that makes a variety of related products. For example, a pharmaceutical organisation may produce different types of specialist medicines, vaccines and sterile supplies.

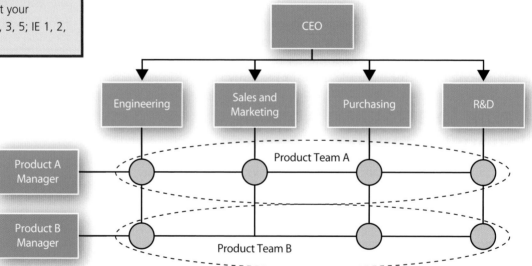

Figure D1.1 Example of a matrix structure.

Often, colleagues who work in other departments or functions in an organisation are called **internal customers**. These colleagues or internal customers should be treated with the same respect as external customers who buy your product or use your service.

Activity 20 minutes

Having identified your organisation's structure, now draw it or obtain a copy of your organisational chart from your manager. Use your drawing or chart to identify:

- the different **functions** (or departments) in your organisation and write a brief description of what each does
- how many colleagues in each department are at each level and list them
- the number of managers
- the number of **auxiliary staff** (caretakers/cleaners)
- the number of team leaders
- the number of staff in your own team.

Key Terms

Auxiliary staff – workers that provide additional support.

Function – an internal activity part of the organisation, e.g. Finance, Human Resources.

Internal customer – colleagues in other departments within the same organisation.

Small and medium-sized enterprise (SME) – an organisation with fewer than 500 workers.

External colleagues

From time to time, you may have to liaise with outside organisations, for example, to organise a delivery of materials. How you relate to people working in these organisations is very important. Effective working relationships will help you to get better results, for example, suppliers' extra effort to deliver on time.

Confidentiality

Confidentiality is vital to ensure a strong working relationship with your team and for the reputation of your organisation. It is very important when dealing with both internal and external colleagues. For instance, it could be quite damaging to the organisation and its reputation if sensitive information reaches competing organisations.

When dealing with colleagues, be aware of the Data Protection Act 1998 (often referred to as DPA 1998). This act makes it illegal to pass on information about someone to another person or organisation unless you have received permission from them to do so.

If a colleague confides in you and you later repeat that confidential information to someone else, they may pass on the information to another person. It is only a matter of time until others in your team or organisation hear it too.

The consequences of breaking confidences in this way can be very serious and damaging to working relationships. The colleague who confided in you will never trust you again and you may lose respect from the rest of your team members should they find out.

Approaching the right people

Identifying colleagues at other levels in your organisation and knowing who to contact in external organisations can speed the process of obtaining answers to queries and questions. For example, if you have a query about stock, you should know who to make direct contact with at your **suppliers**.

Activity 10 minutes

Think about who you deal with on a regular basis in other organisations. Who are these organisations and why do you contact them? Why should you make efforts to get on well with your contacts?

Key Terms

Confidentiality – respecting someone's request to keep information private.

Supplier – an organisation that provides resources, e.g. stationery supplier.

Activity 10 minutes

Find out about the eight principles of the DPA 1998.

Consulting the right people at the right time can help you to resolve problems quickly, enabling you to prioritise the work of your team. Resolving queries quickly can reduce your own stress levels.

Agreeing roles and responsibilities

You and members of your team are likely to have been issued with job descriptions. These documents outline the tasks you are expected to undertake in work. They will help you to set objectives and targets for your team. Meeting these aims and targets is vital if your organisation is to achieve its overall business objectives.

Through staff appraisals and monthly supervisions, you will be able to clarify and agree the roles and responsibilities of each team member. It is important to agree these rather than dictate them, so that your team members feel involved in the decision-making process. This can in turn lead to improved team performance.

Knowing the strengths and weaknesses of each of your team members can help you allocate specific tasks to someone who has the right skills and attributes. It would be pointless to delegate a task to a team member who didn't possess the right skills and attributes and the team member would probably feel demotivated as a result.

Checklist

Roles and responsibilities of your team members can be agreed during:

- appraisals
- supervisions
- team meetings
- one-to-one discussions.

PLTS

Discussing your findings with your colleagues will help you to generate ideas, ask questions and question your own and other people's assumptions (CT 1, 2, 4).
This activity will give you the opportunity to explore issues from different perspectives (IE3).

Activity 45 minutes

Examine Belbin's work and try to identify which role you fall into. Belbin devised a questionnaire to help match individuals to roles. You could complete this yourself and ask your team members to complete it. The results could help you with the planning and allocation of work in your team. Discuss your responses with your assessor.

Portfolio Task 2 60 minutes

Links to LO2: Assessment criteria 2.1, 2.2

1. Identify six internal colleagues working in your organisation and list their roles and responsibilities. Also, identify three external organisations/contacts you regularly work with and their role in enabling your team to meet its objectives. List your findings in tables.

2. If you can, discuss what you have recorded in part 1 with your colleagues. Do they agree with you?

Belbin's work roles

Dr R. Meredith Belbin suggested that teams benefit by including individuals who complement each other with their skills, personalities and attributes. He identified nine key roles:

- Co-ordinator – a good communicator who is confident and in control.
- Shaper – an extrovert person who welcomes new ideas and challenges.
- Plant – a creative person who often proposes new ways of doing things.

- Monitor/Evaluator – often introvert by nature, this person is analytical and views things objectively.
- Implementer – this person is a good organiser and likes to see a job through to successful completion.
- Resource investigator – this person is enthusiastic and reacts well to challenges.
- Team worker – a person who is good with people, is stable and supports others.
- Completer-finisher – this person is very conscientious and often a perfectionist.
- Specialist – this person is very dedicated and provides knowledge and skills that are in rare supply.

Belbin suggested that a balance of roles is necessary for a team to be effective. When you carry out research into team roles in the Activity, take steps to identify the negative aspects of each role in view of their contribution to the success of a team.

An effective team is made up of many different personality types and skills.

For example, it would be counter-productive to place four completer-finishers in a team of five people working on the same task. There needs to be a sensible balance of shared attributes and skills if a team is to be successful.

John Adair's model on working with others

John Adair's model is helpful when analysing your own approach to working with others.

The model suggests that in a workplace, the needs of an individual, the needs of a team and what must be done to get a task completed, should be analysed separately. In other words a team leader should think about:

- what must be done to get a task completed
- how to encourage the team to work **holistically**
- what each individual will need to perform well as part of the team.

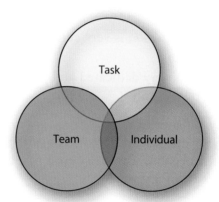

Figure D1.2 Adair's model on working with others.
Source: http://www.johnadair.co.uk, ©John Adair.

Interpersonal skills

Being aware of your own interpersonal skills – your verbal and non-verbal skills – can help you to build effective relationships with colleagues at all levels. When dealing with your manager for example, you may adopt a more formal approach than you would with your own team members. Being approachable to others in your organisation will enable you to access information and suggestions for best practice that you can share with your team.

Obtaining and sharing information with others, both inside and outside your organisation, is known as **networking**.

In 2002 the theorist Dr John Quinn developed an idea that networking within your organisation can be a powerful tool. Because you know and trust your colleagues, you are likely to accept the knowledge that they share with you through discussion. You can use this information to help with your decision making. They too will use the information you give to help them with their own decision making.

Networking and effective working relationships can help to achieve successful outcomes because:

- customer service will be enhanced and their expectations are more likely to be met
- a positive message about the work of the organisation will reach **stakeholders**
- there will be mutual support in the team for a standardised approach to quality.

Development of team members' skills

When gaps in the workforce are identified, it is likely that the organisation will either recruit new members of staff who hold those required qualifications and skills or select existing employees to undergo additional training and development in order to fill those gaps.

If existing employees are developed further, they may recognise this as an opportunity to improve their own performance or perhaps view it as career enhancement.

Skills audit

The purpose of a skills audit is to identify the skills that employees have and any need for new skills in the team. The result is then benchmarked against the skills the organisation needs for future success.

The audit will establish what employees are currently capable of doing and what qualifications they currently hold. This identifies any gaps between skills and knowledge the organisation holds at the time of the audit and what skills and knowledge it needs to be successful in the future. The process is useful when, for example, the organisation wishes to expand its operations.

> **Checklist**
>
> A skills audit will help you to identify:
> - who is the best person for the job
> - what skills and knowledge is needed to improve the team
> - which team members are being under-used and could be given more challenging roles.

> **Remember**
>
> Ultimately, a satisfied workforce results in a satisfied end users of the product or service you provide.

Be able to act in a professional and respectful manner when working with colleagues

Working with colleagues brings with it responsibilities that everyone in the team must take on board. Behaving in a professional manner will encourage mutual respect between team members and will encourage team bonding.

Displaying professional behaviour

There are many factors that can influence professional behaviour and policies and procedures are there to help ensure everyone works to the same standards and within a safe environment. One of the policies that your organisation is likely to have is a health and safety policy. This will outline how the organisation expects everybody to behave to ensure a healthy and safe working environment, which includes anyone who visits your workplace.

Health and safety in the workplace

The conditions your team members work in can have a direct impact on performance and productive working relationships.

Staff members in any workplace want to know that they are working in suitably ventilated, hygienic environments. Minimising the risk of danger and communicating to your team how this is being done can have a positive impact on the quality of work. Remember you should communicate to your team the importance of regular risk assessment activities.

The Health and Safety Executive (HSE) is a government body that exists to investigate any serious accidents or incidents related to health and safety in the workplace. It also has the power to close down organisations while investigations are carried out or, in some cases, close the organisation down completely. To minimise the risk of accidents, you should make sure that codes of practice, policies and procedures are followed by everyone in your team.

You can encourage a flexible approach to tasks by adjusting rotas and work roles from time to time. This will give everyone in your team the opportunity to experience each other's roles. By having a multi-skilled team everyone will be aware of the hazards and risks associated with each other's role and this will help to minimise the possibility of accidents.

Remember

Your organisation has health and safety obligations placed upon it, and its employees have rights (for example the right to work in a safe and healthy environment). There are also obligations placed upon the employee (for example they are responsible for the health and safety of everyone they work with).

Activity 30 minutes

Spend some time researching the following and then discuss your findings with your assessor. (A brief overview of the purpose and content of each will be sufficient.)

- HASAW 1974 responsibilities for employers
- HASAW 1974 responsibilities for employees
- The Factories Act 1961
- The Offices, Shops and Railway Premises Act 1963
- The Health and Safety (Display Screen Equipment) Regulations 1992
- COSHH 2002
- The EU Working Time Directive 2003

Leadership styles to encourage professional behaviour

The style of leadership you adopt can have an effect on the performance of your team and your workplace relationships and help you to promote professional behaviour. Your team members will observe your own workplace behaviour and will respond to supportive leadership.

Management theorist Kurt Lewin promoted the view that there are three main leadership styles:

- Autocratic – this type of leader is dominant. The leader makes decisions on their own without speaking to the group and sets deadlines and tasks for the team without consulting members.
- Democratic – this type of leader makes decisions by consulting with the team, but still maintains control of the group. The style allows the team members to decide how the tasks will be undertaken and who will perform the tasks.

- Laissez-faire – this type of leader allows the team to make their own decisions about their roles and managing their own tasks. There is very little leadership.

From Lewin's work you may be able to identify which style you adopt as team leader. Often, however, circumstances that arise will force you to change your style. For example, you may usually be a democratic leader but if a crisis requiring urgent attention occurs, it is likely that you may switch to an autocratic style. Similarly, if someone has been selected to work on a special project because of their strengths and expertise, you may take a step back and use a laissez-faire approach.

You should aim to use a leadership style that will help you to develop a team of high performance. This is likely to be the democratic style as it generally gets the best results. Because team members feel involved in the decision making process, they feel motivated and commit themselves to meeting targets.

Leading by example

Leading by example is a phrase you may be familiar with. Being professional as you go about your daily tasks will not only enhance your own self-esteem; it can also make your job more enjoyable. This can be because your professional behaviour will minimise the risk of errors and will increase the respect you get from colleagues in your organisation. This in turn will increase your levels of motivation and morale, rubbing off on members of the team you lead.

Some managers like to operate an **open door policy**. This technique removes barriers between the team leader/manager and team members. On occasion, team leaders/managers will operate this policy on certain days or times during the week so that they have sufficient time and privacy to carry out their own tasks and meet their deadlines. Other managers, however, encourage team members to call in at any time during the working week.

Consider the following aspects of professional behaviour.

- following procedures
- understanding your organisational policies
- ensuring internal/external customers get the best possible service
- being punctual and having a positive attitude
- avoiding conflict
- having an appropriate dress code
- being considerate towards others
- communicating the right messages on time
- having good time management
- giving and accepting constructive feedback.

Key Term

Open door policy – when managers literally leave their office door open so that any member of their team can approach them with queries or concerns without feeling intimidated by having to knock on the door and wait for a response.

Activity 30 minutes

When you lead by example, your team members are likely to mirror your actions. Reflect upon your own behaviour and identify what aspects of your workplace behaviour you would like to change or improve. Discuss your responses with your assessor.

Remember

The trust you build with your team will help you to earn respect.
If a team member wants the rest of the team to show them respect, they must earn it!

Checklist

When trying to gain trust always remember to:

- show commitment
- fulfil promises
- be fair and consistent
- give support to the team
- listen to the views of the team.

Checklist

When communicating with colleagues remember to:

- make sure the message is clear
- make sure the message says what it needs to say
- give the message to the necessary people
- check the message will be understood
- make a record of the message as necessary.

Earning respect

Respect must be earned. As team leader, your team members should trust you to make the right decisions that will benefit both them and the organisation. Deliver this and it will earn you their respect.

Suggested ways to gain trust and earn respect are to:

- show your own commitment to the work of the team
- never make promises unless you know you can keep them
- be consistent and fair in the way you deal with your team members
- be open with your team, telling them exactly what is expected of them
- let the team know that any difficulties have your full support and commitment
- always listen to the views of your team members and let it be known that you value their opinions and input
- offer sincere and public praise when it is due.

All the above behaviours can help you to develop a team that has the potential to perform at a high level.

Responsible behaviour in the workplace

Consider the real-life example of a local government manager who was horrified and surprised when a female member of his team took out a grievance accusing him of bullying her. As a very popular and mild-mannered manager, he was shocked to learn that his light-hearted banter in the office was thought of as offensive by the female team member and some of her colleagues.

This example illustrates that what we think is innocent and acceptable behaviour can sometimes upset others! It pays to examine how we act and to think about how others in the workplace view us.

Sometimes the way we communicate with others in the workplace can help and sometimes it can damage our working relationships. Getting the right message to the right people at the right time is very important. Regardless of the method of communication being used, it is important to consider:

- the speed with which you communicate (does something need resolving immediately?)
- the clarity of the message (is it a clear message being sent to others?)
- the detail of the message (does it say what it needs to say?)
- the distribution of the message (is it reaching everyone it should?)
- the intelligibility (is the information in the message reaching the right people who need it and will they understand it?)
- auditability (can records of the communication be kept?).

Expectation of behaviour

When managing your team, you should make it clear that rules must be followed. There is therefore an expectation of behaviour. This is called role behaviour. Rules for behaviour are generated by cultural values, workplace ideas and standards. Rules can take three forms:

1. permitted – what may be done
2. proscriptive – what should not be done
3. prescriptive – what should be done

Remember that policies within an organisation are what managers say can or cannot be done (for example, anti-bullying policy).

Activity 20 minutes

Write your responses to the following statements and share your views with your assessor.

1. A manager should operate an 'open door' policy.
2. A manager should leave his or her staff alone unless they are making a mess of things.
3. A manager should avoid getting drawn into discussions about personal problems of others.

Portfolio Task 3 5 minutes

Links to LO3: Assessment criterion 3.1

List four factors that demonstrate professionalism and discuss these with your assessor. Which do you think is the most important?

Be able to communicate with colleagues

Communicating clearly

As you go about your daily activities in your organisation, it is important to consider:

- who you are communicating with
- what you are trying to achieve.

Remember, the **tone** and language you use is likely to vary, depending on who you are communicating with and the situation you are in.

Effective communication

Good communication is fundamental to good team working. It is vital that certain basic aspects of working within an organisation are communicated efficiently, effectively and in a timely fashion. For instance:

Key Term

Tone – the sound of the voice in reference to quality and pitch, e.g. loud and aggressive when angry.

- the codes of practice of the organisation
- instructions for using equipment correctly and safely
- health and safety procedures (it is likely that your organisation will need to update you and your team regularly on health and safety matters
- what to do in an emergency situation
- the organisation's dress code (if appropriate)
- the organisation's policies, procedures and code of conduct.

It is always a good idea to get your team members to acknowledge that they have read and understood instructions, policies, procedures and the code of conduct.

Activity   30 minutes

With your assessor, discuss and write down how you think your language and tone might differ when you communicate with the following people. Give examples where possible.

- A close colleague.
- Your team leader/co-ordinator.
- Someone from another team, but on your level.
- A middle/senior manager.
- A customer.
- A supplier.
- Your G.P.
- A close member of your family.

Now think about:

- how you would start a conversation with each of the above
- how you would respond to each of the above if they were to interrupt you while you were working on a complicated task.

Getting the message across

Often the way we communicate with others can either support or damage working relationships. Getting the right message to the right people at the right time is very important.

Messages should be brief, clear, to the point and legible. It is sometimes necessary to adjust the content of the message, or adapt it in some way, so that it meets the needs of the recipient and is fully understood.

Activity   10 minutes

Emphasise, Acknowledge, Reflect and Summarise (EARS) is a model you can use when communicating with your team. Using the internet, research the EARS model then record your findings to establish how you can apply the model when communicating with your own team.

The concept of **noise** in the context of communication relates to anything that distorts the message in any way and can include physical noise, illegible handwriting, use of jargon/acronyms not understood by others or perhaps chewing gum when talking on the telephone.

If you were to analyse it, you might find that you communicate using different methods, techniques or language when dealing with colleagues at different levels in your organisation. It is useful to reflect on this, to make sure you communicate in the best possible way with everyone you work with. You may communicate formally with senior managers or customers, but more informally with team members of suppliers you deal with.

Portfolio Task 4 — 20 minutes

Links to LO4: Assessment criterion 4.1

You give information to your team on a day-to-day basis. Explain to your assessor the types of information you give and the techniques you use to share this information. Provide evidence of how you communicate with your team. This evidence could be in the form of minutes of meetings, emails, action plans and informal reports.

Keeping everybody informed

In the workplace, it is important to keep everyone informed of:

- delays
- changes
- new staff/staff leaving
- major decisions
- new ideas.

Failure to keep everyone informed can result in rumours, which can be damaging to morale and motivation. Effective communication breeds trust and loyalty from team members and can help to build positive working relationships. The flow of information is very important but there is no point in sending a message unless it is accurate, timely and clear.

Shannon and Weaver's communication model

Examine the following model by Shannon and Weaver. This illustrates that messages must be clearly structured to aid understanding.

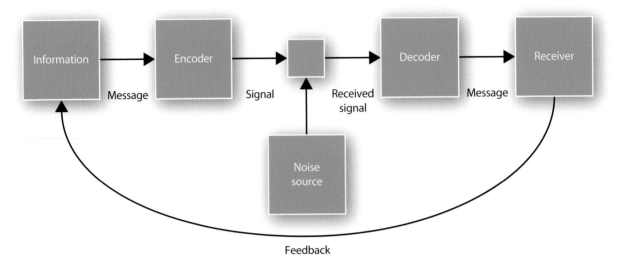

Figure D1.3 Shannon and Weaver's communication model.

Verbal and non-verbal communication

In organisations effective communication can be verbal or non-verbal. Some examples are shown in the table below.

Verbal	Non-verbal
Team meetings	Reports
One-to-one discussions (supervisions)	Memo
Interviews	Fax
Briefings	Email
Telephone	Letters
Voicemail	Surveys/questionnaires
Video conferencing	Texting
	Social networking (businesses)
	Internet
	Intranet and extranet

Table D1.1 Types of verbal and non-verbal communication methods.

Receiving and clarifying own understanding of information

When you receive a message from internal or external customers and colleagues, you should make sure you fully understand what is being said to you. This means you should clarify with the sender of the message what is being said and you can do this by questioning them or asking them to repeat the message. This will help to minimise any errors as you go about your daily tasks.

You can:

- record the message received (tape, files, minutes, notes etc.)
- go back to the sender of the information and ask for clarification
- speak to others to obtain their views and understanding of the information.

With reference to Shannon and Weaver's model of communication, it may be helpful to examine the decoder section and aim to minimise barriers associated with this.

Listening skills

Listening is a skill. **Body language** plays a part too, when responding to colleagues. Your verbal response and your body language may give different messages. For example, if you don't make eye contact or you have your back turned towards the person you are talking to, it could leave that person feeling undervalued and they may not approach you in the future. You may then miss out on excellent ideas or suggestions to improve the work of the team.

Barriers to effective listening include day dreaming, not really listening to what is being said, or perhaps pre-judging what you think is being said before you've listened to all of the facts. You should try not to interrupt the other person when they are talking because you cannot listen when you are talking yourself. To show that you are listening intently, you could use phrases such as 'Oh I see' or 'Aha' and appropriate body language can help too, such as gestures or a nod of the head at the right time.

> **Key Term**
>
> **Body language** – movement or positioning of the body that demonstrates the person's views and opinions on a topic, e.g. frowning when not understanding.

Portfolio Task 5 10 minutes

Links to LO4: Assessment criterion 4.2

Provide evidence to your assessor where your manager has asked you to complete a task that is new to you. Explain to your assessor how your manager communicated the requirements of the task to you and how you checked that you have understood the task correctly.

> **PLTS**
>
> By seeking new challenges and working towards goals you will show initiative and evidence of your commitment to your manager and your organisation (CT 1, 2).

Be able to identify potential work-related difficulties and explore solutions

Potential work-related difficulties, leading to conflict of interest, may include:

- not adhering to health and safety requirements (for example, not wearing protective clothing)
- bullying and harassment
- underperformance of team members
- personality clashes between team members or others
- inadequate training so people don't know how a task should be done
- poor communication
- conflict between team members
- discrimination or unfair treatment
- inadequate resources to do the job (for example, lack of equipment)
- rumour and gossip
- lots of changes taking place
- high levels of stress in the team
- unhappy customers
- problems with suppliers
- poor working conditions affecting team morale
- unrealistic targets or deadlines to meet.

Portfolio Task 6 20 minutes

Links to LO5: Assessment criterion 5.1

Prepare a list of difficulties you have experienced or witnessed at work and explain to your assessor what happened. Also, explain to your assessor your involvement in resolving these difficulties.

Identifying problems

You should monitor the progress you and your team members are making towards the achievement of each of your team and individual objectives. It can be helpful to insert **milestones** into your progress schedule. A useful tool for this is a **Gantt chart.** As each milestone is reached, there is opportunity for you to congratulate and praise your team for their hard work. This process will make the working relationship between you and your team members stronger and will increase levels of morale.

Key Terms

Gantt chart – a horizontal bar chart used to plan and monitor a project.

Milestones – marking out when stages of progress will have been made.

However, when milestones are not reached, it is important that you investigate the reasons why this happened. It could be due to lack of **resources**, faulty equipment or perhaps underperformance of the team. If this is the case, then corrective action should be taken by you to resolve the issue or problem.

Before taking corrective action you should think about the following:

- Was the task given to a team member(s) too difficult or unrealistic?
- Is a team member(s) not capable of doing the task? Do they need training?
- Was the team member(s) capable of doing the job, but simply chose not to perform well?
- Is there some other difficulty within the team such as bullying or **discrimination** that is affecting performance?

You may take corrective action by reviewing your targets to make sure they are SMART or you may hold face-to-face discussions with your team members to establish if there are difficulties preventing the team from performing effectively.

Having planned your team's work, it is the duty of the team to work holistically towards achieving your SMART objectives. Be aware however, that **sub-groups** can form in your team. This might happen for many reasons such as people siding with one party involved in a conflict situation or perhaps some people are eager to work alongside particular colleagues. Sub-groups can prevent a team from working holistically towards the achievement of its objectives and team leaders need to evaluate the negative effects this may have on team work.

To monitor performance against standards or **KPIs** you could:

- observe processes being undertaken by the team
- sample products or work in progress (WIP) periodically
- review procedures with the team periodically
- collate and analyse data on performance
- monitor error and reject rates
- encourage everyone to work towards quality systems in place such as **ISO9000**.

Resolving identified potential difficulties

Some causes of difficulties

Disagreements and conflict situations should be investigated as soon as you become aware of them. Reflect on your leadership style and how you deal with conflict, or how your managers have dealt with conflict situations that you have witnessed.

Key Terms

Discrimination – treating a person differently from others because of their background, sexuality, religious belief, origin, age, disability or marital status.

KPI – a key performance indicator or standard to work towards such as sales targets or reducing the number of complaints.

ISO9000 – an industry-wide recognised quality standard.

Resources – a source of help, materials and time to assist with completion of a job.

Sub-groups – smaller groups within the team created to work on individual projects or tasks. Sometimes the team unofficially splits itself into smaller groups because of conflict or disagreements between team members.

Remember

Depending on the outcome of your strategies for corrective action, you may have to seek support from your managers to make sure the problem gets resolved as quickly as possible.

Unit D1

Develop working relationships with colleagues

Conflict can arise as a result of:

- organisational factors – unfair treatment and practices, poor communication or workloads that are too challenging or not challenging enough
- personal factors – unfair treatment by an individual (for example, a line manager), inappropriate behaviour, bullying or poor attitudes in work.

See Unit D10 Manage conflict in a team for further information.

Generally difficulties arise inside the workplace due to disagreements, misunderstandings and underperformance. Outside of the organisation difficulties can arise because of supplier problems or complaining customers (for example, because of poor quality products).

There may also be occasions when you have witnessed or experienced personality clashes in your workplace. This is often because people have different thought processes, opinions and attitudes towards the way things should be done, which can lead to work-related difficulties.

To avoid conflict situations therefore, people's behaviour needs to be managed. In the best of situations, a team of people who have different opinions and attitudes can actually be productive if they are managed properly.

In any workplace, there can be:

- 'can't do' team members – These people may underperform because they haven't received the correct training and development or perhaps tasks have been delegated to them beyond their current capabilities. With correct guidance they could perform the task successfully and would be willing to do so.
- 'won't do' team members – these people, regardless of how much training support and guidance is given, will not make any effort to carry out their tasks, expecting others to carry them. Not only is this unfair to other team members, but it can also cause frustration and **demoralise** other team members, sometimes leading to confrontation and conflict in your team.

'Can't do' people can be **coached**, **mentored** or trained to improve their performance but 'won't do' people can present problems. During one-to-one discussions, offers of support and training may not have resolved the problem and unfortunately it may be necessary for your manager or human resources to instigate disciplinary procedures.

It is also likely that in your team, you will have:

- type A personalities – these people are prone to high levels of stress and can become very frustrated
- type B personalities – these people are more relaxed, take things in their stride and tend not to become stressed.

Key Terms

Demoralise – undermine an individual resulting in morale and team spirit being destroyed.

Coaching – giving of advice or instruction by an expert on a particular topic.

Mentoring – personal training, advising and counselling of an individual by a more experienced person.

Resolving difficulties

Once potential difficulties have been identified, whatever the cause, action must be taken to minimise or reduce the likelihood of them occurring in your workplace. Often, it is only when it is too late and a difficulty has escalated into a large problem that action is taken to rectify it. It is far better to plan ahead, be prepared for any eventuality and more importantly, plan how you can deal with it. There are many things you can do to manage the difficulties you experience, including:

- improving communication
- using team-building activities
- having customer service training
- holding in-house sessions on all policies and procedures
- having health and safety training
- reviewing PDR meetings and what should be included
- giving feedback more frequently.

Portfolio Task 7 20 minutes

Links to LO5: Assessment criterion 5.2

You have recently being experiencing problems with a member of staff. This member of staff has always met her deadlines and has always presented work that meets the organisational standards. However, recently she is late presenting work and the quality of the work is substandard. Explain to your assessor how you would deal with this situation. Write up your discussion for your portfolio.

PLTS

This activity will give you the opportunity to discuss issues of concern in relation to others, while developing options to resolve the concerns (RL 1, 5; EP 1, 2, 3).

As team leader in a conflict situation you should:

- intervene to stop the problem getting worse
- try to calm the situation and the people involved
- speak to the parties involved to negotiate a solution or an acceptable compromise
- ensure all team members are fully aware of the organisation's policies, procedures and code of practice – and understand them!
- refer colleagues to others, depending on the circumstances (for example, to your line manager/human resources/counselling service)
- avoid favouritism.

Functional Skills

This activity will allow you to present information in a clear way using appropriate language. You will be given the opportunity to practise your Functional Skills English Level 1 Speaking skills during your meeting with your assessor.

Team building

If you intend to introduce team-building activities to help your team members to bond, and to help resolve potential difficulties and conflict, you must understand that different team formats exist. This will depend upon the size and nature of your organisation.

Different types of teams include:

- project teams – team members are selected to work together on a specific project for a given period of time (for example, producing a limited edition product that offers extra functions)
- cross-functional teams – team members are selected and withdrawn from a number of different functions (or departments) to pool their expertise for major events, such as change management or development of a new product
- virtual teams – team members from different branches or even countries use techniques such as video conferencing to work together on specific projects and may never meet face to face
- self-managed teams – team members work alongside each other with no obvious leader. Members often take it in turns to lead the team and accept more responsibility and decision-making powers.

It may be easier to plan team-building events and rotas for a team that works together on a day-to-day basis. However, with other types of teams – for example, those put together for long-term special projects – the planning can be more difficult.

In your team you may supervise between two and twenty team members, with you as the team leader reporting to your line manager. Effective working relations between you and your team can be improved if you involve members of your team in decision making and the setting of your SMART objectives. This will encourages a holistic approach whereby everyone works efficiently towards the goals you want to achieve.

As team leader, you should think about the best way to support your team. You can do this informally by offering praise and constructive feedback via one-to-one discussions or team briefings or you may do this on a more formal basis through staff appraisals or monthly supervision meetings.

You can further support your team members by encouraging their personal development through training, coaching or mentoring activities.

It is also important to make sure that every member of your team is aware of the content of your organisation's policies and procedures. Team members need to know where to find these and that they are expected to read and understand them. This will encourage a standardised approach towards the quality of the work being done, which will in turn lead to better performance, reduced risk of conflict and enhanced customer satisfaction.

Remember

When difficulties occur – especially major ones – make sure you keep your manager informed and fully aware of the situation.

Remember

Be aware of your own limits and seek support from others when you need to.

Some team leaders like to reward their team members for performing well. Even small gestures, such as taking in cakes to share, can be a strong morale booster and make the team feel appreciated. A gesture such as this can help to build trust and mutual respect between the team leader and the team. Do not underestimate the power of the words 'thank you'. Given at the appropriate time and for the right reasons a simple but sincere thanks can be very rewarding for team members and will be appreciated.

Giving feedback

When you have a problem in your team, you may have to explain to a team member that their current behaviour is unacceptable. You could do this by offering **feedback** on their performance or behaviour. This should be done in private and as quickly as possible, so that the situation doesn't become more serious.

Think about the best way to give the feedback. It should be phrased in such a way that it is accepted as constructive and helpful advice, otherwise your colleague may feel demotivated by what you say, further affecting their performance or behaviour. Consider the use of the praise sandwich:

1. Say something positive about them/their performance.
2. Insert the feedback into the conversation.
3. Discuss another positive aspect of their work.

Key Terms

Feedback – views of others on the performance and/or behaviour.

360° appraisal – everybody giving feedback on the performance and behaviour of an individual.

Figure D1.4 Feedback sandwich.

The boxes in the figure read:
- I've noticed how clean and tidy your work area is at the end of your shift, which is great.
- You really need to stop being late in the mornings.
- Before you go, I'm very pleased that you always meet targets.

Checklist

Give feedback that is:
- constructive
- to the point
- helpful.

Activity — 20 minutes

Spend a few minutes reflecting on how you think you behave at work. Then write down your thoughts. Be honest with yourself and consider whether you are perhaps too aggressive or too passive when dealing with others.

If you use a technique like the praise sandwich, your colleague is more likely to accept the feedback you are giving. You will have surrounded the criticism with positive aspects of their performance or behaviour.

A **360° appraisal** system is when everyone gets the opportunity to appraise each other's performance. For example, your team members review your performance and you get the opportunity to review your line manager's performance and so on. Not all organisations use this system as many prefer to use the normal appraisal systems. However, it is a useful process for you to find out your team's opinions about your performance.

Checklist

Remember the praise sandwich is made up of:
- positive comments
- feedback
- positive comments.

Team talk

John's story

My name is John and I currently work for Mental Health Care, a private health care organisation in Wrexham, North Wales. I have recently been promoted to team leader within my department. I currently lead a team of ten health-care staff, who are all fully trained and experienced in their areas and two new staff who are learning on the job.

Recently, I have been experiencing some problems with one of the new members of staff. She is becoming aggressive to other team members and as a result she is creating negativity in the department. Team objectives are not being met and the staff sickness levels have increased. Performance and customer service is suffering and I feel everything is getting out of control. My line manager has expressed her concern and wants to know how we can resolve this situation.

Top tips

John needs a way to monitor team performance so that he can identify problems and deal with them before they become too serious. He could consider monthly one-to-one meetings with staff to discuss their objectives and any concerns. This would be done in confidence.

When situations arise, as in the example above, John should consider agreeing an action plan with the aggressive member of staff to address and monitor future behaviour. John should also offer to arrange as much support as possible such as counselling, additional training or a review of flexible working arrangements if there are problems at home.

Ask the expert	
Q	How should I deal with this situation to get everything back on track?
A	The first thing John needs to do is identify the cause of the problem. John should arrange a one-to-one meeting with his member of staff to ascertain the cause of her aggression. She may have personal issues that need addressing or be experiencing difficulty dealing with the work or workload. She may require counselling or training in aspects of her job or in dealing with people. The one-to-one meeting will: ■ identify the problem/cause of difficulty ■ allow John to challenge the inappropriate behaviour and outline the appropriate workplace policies and procedures, for example, bullying and harassment ■ prevent the situation from escalating or getting out of control ■ help to agree courses of action ■ identify whether it is necessary to refer the matter to somebody else within the organisation such as manager and/or counsellor.

What your assessor is looking for

In order to demonstrate your competency within this unit, you will need to provide sufficient evidence to your assessor. You will need to provide a short written narrative or personal statement, explaining how you meet the assessment criteria. In addition, your assessor may need to ask you questions to test your knowledge of the topics identified in this unit.

As part of your assessment process, your assessor may wish to conduct observations of work-related tasks that you are carrying out.

Your assessor may wish to observe you:

- during team meetings where there is a two-way communication between you and your team
- giving feedback during team meetings
- agreeing targets, roles and responsibilities.

A list of suggested documentation follows that will provide evidence to help you to prove your competency in this unit.

Functional Skills

If you take part or lead a team meeting, you will be given the opportunity to practise your Functional Skills English Level 1 in speaking and listening. You will make relevant contributions to discussions, respond to the opinions and views of others in the team and present information clearly using appropriate language.

The work products for this unit could include:

- examples of emails/memoranda sent to the team informing them of changes to policies or procedures
- minutes of team meetings where information is shared with the team
- staff rotas and/or work schedules
- action plans allocating roles and responsibilities to the team
- staff appraisal forms
- one-to-one supervision documentation managing a difficult situation
- notes to manager informing them of a difficult situation between team members.

Your assessor will guide you through the assessment process as detailed in the candidate logbook. The detailed assessment criteria are shown in the logbook and by working through these questions, combined with providing the relevant evidence, you will meet the learning outcomes required to complete this unit.

Task and page reference	Assessment criteria
1 (page 37)	1.1
2 (page 40)	2.1, 2.2
3 (page 47)	3.1
4 (page 49)	4.1
5 (page 51)	4.2
6 (page 52)	5.1
7 (page 55)	5.2

Unit E11 Communicate information and knowledge

At work, you will communicate with your team, other colleagues and your customers all the time. This unit explains the principles and benefits of communicating information and knowledge in an effective manner. By improving your own communication skills, you should help to improve those of your team, which could also help to improve the overall efficiency of the organisation.

It is important to plan communication. You should know what your intended **outcomes** are and the needs and requirements of your audience. Different methods of communication can be used in different circumstances and these methods will be explored in greater detail to help you learn how to communicate in the most appropriate and effective way.

The final section of the unit will explore how to modify communication techniques in response to feedback that you may receive. Receiving feedback allows you to develop your communication skills.

What you will learn

- Be able to identify the information required, and its reliability, for communication
- Be able to understand communication techniques and methods
- Be able to communicate information and knowledge using appropriate techniques and methods
- Be able to adapt communication techniques and methods according to target audience response

Links to the Technical Certificate

If you are completing your NVQ as part of an Apprenticeship Framework, you will find the following topic is also covered in your Technical Certificate:

- Developing working relationships with colleagues

Be able to identify the information required, and its reliability, for communication

Effective communication with other people in a team ensures that:

- everyone is clear about what is happening and what is going to happen
- the information being communicated is clear, concise and at the right level of detail for the recipient
- the team can work efficiently and meet its goals and objectives
- the team can sustain good working relationships with each other
- no one is left out or unsure about what is happening.

It is therefore vital that any information communicated is relevant and reliable.

> **Key Term**
>
> **Outcomes** – the end result of an activity which can also be measured or quantified.

Good communication in the workplace will lead to better productivity.

Explain the information and knowledge that needs communicating

Effective teams have effective communication channels in place. There are many forms of communication open to you and at any given time you need to use the most appropriate method to ensure that the information being communicated is timely, delivered to the right people and in the right level of detail.

In a business environment you will be communicating both formally and informally using different methods including verbal and written forms. You will also be communicating in more subtle ways, for example, via your **body language**.

Communication in organisations can be complex as there are some specific factors to consider including:

- the flow of information within the organisation
- the culture of the organisation
- the systems and processes that are in place
- the degree of complexity of the information
- any organisational politics that may be in place.

The principles of effective communication

Communication involves the transfer of information between people. The effectiveness of that communication – the level of understanding and interpretation of what is being communicated – will depend significantly on some or all of the following factors.

- Is the information being communicated easy to understand or complex?
- Are the parties involved in the communication known to each other?
- Is the communication formal or informal?
- Is the information that is being communicated specific or general?
- Are there any barriers in respect to the information that is being communicated?

The principles of effective communication are to:

- ensure that the information is clear, concise and at the right level of detail for the recipient
- ensure that all parties are clear about what is being communicated
- listen actively to what is being said
- ensure that communication is a two-way process.

As a result of applying these principles, you, your team and your organisation should reap the benefits and be able to work more productively. By building positive working relationships, the organisation should see:

- improved commitment and co-operation of individuals
- improved enjoyment of their roles by individuals
- increased output, productivity and efficiency
- improved supportive working within teams and across other team boundaries
- less resistance to change.

> **Key Term**
>
> **Body language** – the gestures, postures or facial expressions of a person.

Communicating information and knowledge

All organisations have a purpose. This is sometimes written in a mission statement and describes the organisation's aims. In order to achieve its mission, the organisation will also set a number of key objectives. These objectives will be SMART and will be assigned to individual teams or members of staff within the organisation. (See Unit A1 for a detailed definition of SMART.)

It is imperative that you and your team members know and understand the specific objectives that have been assigned to you, as this is how your performance will be measured. You need to put a process in place to communicate and manage these objectives on a regular basis. Team meetings provide a good forum for discussing and agreeing targets and current performance. In a team-meeting environment, you can share information and knowledge to increase the overall efficiency of the team and also discuss any ideas for improvement. Some team members may have specialist knowledge that they can share with the rest of the team.

Induction and training

All team members must have the relevant skills and knowledge to undertake their job. Once they are equipped with these elements, they will be competent in their role. As a team leader it is part of your job to ensure that all of your staff are competent at what they do. This will involve training your staff when they join the organisation. Initial basic training about the organisation and the job is sometimes called induction. Also, you will need to support your staff members on an ongoing basis by providing both formal training (this could be within your own organisation or external) and on-the-job training and support. Don't forget that systems, processes and customer expectations are evolving all the time, so a team member who is trained and competent today, may not be competent in six months' time, so this should be monitored.

Appropriate methods

Always discuss verbally any issues that are important, sensitive or potentially contentious. Other forms of communication are not appropriate when it is a matter of an important nature. How would you feel if you received an email or a letter informing you that there was a change to your organisational structure pending? You would probably prefer to be told about it in a team meeting by your manager.

Collaboration and collective decisions

Communication is also about agreeing things together. Collective decisions where the whole team is on board are more powerful and more likely to work than those decisions imposed by the team leader. You may need to admit defeat when you are out-voted by your team!

By **collaborating**, team members can share their values and the vision of the organisation, develop a team spirit and absorb the information that they need to work well with each other. Trust, mutual respect and honesty between all team members is vital. Always try to keep people informed on a regular basis, both in relation to general issues and their individual performance.

Performance standards

As an organisation, you will have certain standards that you need to work to. These are sometimes called **performance standards**. These may not always be written down and some will be specific and some will be general. For example, a general performance standard would be to treat all colleagues and customers equally and fairly. It is likely that this will not be written down anywhere but will be implicit in the day-to-day operations of the business. You may think that this is common sense (and it is), but what you need to consider is do all of your team members understand the importance of treating everyone equally, fairly, courteously and with dignity and respect, and do they know how to do it? This is why it is important for you to understand all of your organisation's performance standards as these will have a direct impact on how you operate your team.

Examples of specific performance standards could be to 'respond to customers' emails in two working days' and 'answer the phone within five rings'. Performance standards are also often associated with producing an item or service to an agreed quality. Your organisation may not have specific performance standards in place, but if they do, you need to familiarise yourself with them because it is likely that you and your team's performance will be judged on some of these elements. Once you know what the standards are that you need to work to, you can put in place processes to achieve them.

The following flow chart will help you to structure how you meet your organisation's performance standards.

Key Terms

Collaborating – working together.

Performance standards – standards of service or quality that the organisation will strive to achieve.

Remember

You could have specific day-to-day or week-to-week targets that you need to achieve, but you also need to achieve those targets to agreed performance and quality standards.

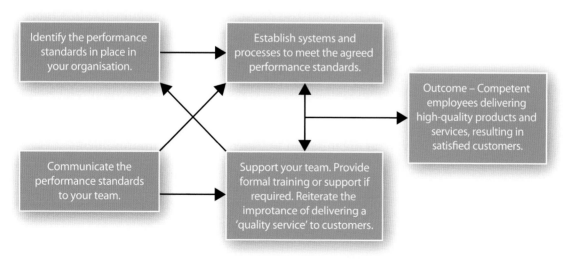

Figure E11.1 Performance standards flow chart.

PLTS

By understanding the specific purpose and mission of your organisation you will be able to plan how you can work with your team to communicate that vision. You will also need to plan how you can actively work with your team to allow them to participate and be creative in achieving the team's objectives that link to the vision (EP; CT; IE; SM).

Functional Skills

If you carry out research involving reading texts including work-related documents as well as internet research in order to complete your portfolio task, you may be able to count this as evidence towards Level 1 and 2 Functional English: Reading. Remember to keep records of all of the documents, handbooks, guidelines that you study, along with the websites you visited, as you will need to document the reading research that you carried out.

Portfolio Task 1 60 minutes

Links to LO1: Assessment criterion 1.1

Find out what the purpose of your organisation is. If your organisation has a mission statement, get a copy of this for your portfolio. Write up a short personal statement describing your organisation's purpose/mission and how this links to your job and your team's roles and responsibilities. Consider any specific objectives that your team has and describe how you achieve them.

Identifying the target audience requiring the information and knowledge

As a team leader it is likely that you will interact with individuals, groups of people and outside organisations on a regular basis. Your target audiences could include:

- your own team members
- other teams within your organisation
- other individuals within your organisation
- your manager and other managers within your organisation
- external customers and suppliers.

Communication and information can flow upwards, downwards or horizontally throughout an organisation as follows.

- Top-down communication – for example, from team leaders to other employees. Examples of this type of communication includes briefing sessions or newsletters.
- Two-way communication – the most common method of communication within organisations. On a day-to-day level, this will occur naturally as you interact with your colleagues and your manager. It should also occur when you communicate in a more formal environment, for example, in team meetings. Other examples of two-way communications include appraisal meetings, suggestion schemes or employer surveys.
- Horizontal communication – similar to two-way communication, but also allows for teams as well as individuals to work collectively across team boundaries. For example, teams may work together within an organisation to develop business improvements.

Planning communication

When you are communicating, you need to ensure that you meet the specific needs of the person or group you are addressing. You can achieve this by planning what you are going to say and by asking yourself what the audience requirements are. By working through this process you can identify the correct communication method and be sure to meet both the audience needs and your intended outcome. If you do not know what the audience's requirements are, you will not be able to provide them with the relevant information that they need.

To ensure that what you want to communicate meets both your intended outcomes and the audience needs, you need to communicate in the right format, at the right time and in the right level of detail. By doing this you will be meeting both your own needs and the needs of the person you are communicating with. The most effective method is to carefully plan what you are going to communicate. The checklist below will help you.

Checklist

Ask yourself these questions when you are planning your communication:

- WHO – is the communication with?
- WHY – am I communicating with this person? What are my outcomes?
- WHAT – am I communicating? Be very clear and specific.
- WHEN – is the best/right time to communicate with them?
- HOW – can I use the right level of detail in the most appropriate format?

Portfolio Task 2 60 minutes

Links to LO1: Assessment criterion 1.2

Identify your own target audiences. Write a short personal statement to describe the different people that you communicate with and try to classify them into two or three groups. Also collect any relevant evidence demonstrating your recent communication with them. This could be presentations, emails, letters or other correspondence. This will provide useful evidence for your portfolio.

Be able to understand communication techniques and methods

There are many different ways to communicate and it is important to understand the various communication techniques and methods available for you to use. This section identifies the specific types of communication commonly used in the workplace. It also looks at the importance of choosing the most appropriate method to suit each circumstance. By understanding the different techniques and methods available to you, you will be able to communicate in the most practical and effective way, which should ensure that the information and knowledge you communicate is received and understood by the relevant persons.

Identify what techniques and methods can be used to communicate information and knowledge

Communication is happening all of the time within every organisation and some of the main methods of communication are shown in the table below.

Type of communication	Method
Written	Emails Letters Reports Memos Agendas Newsletters/journals Posters/notice board Suggestion schemes
Verbal	One-to-one communication Team meetings Appraisal meetings Team 'away-day' meetings Small group presentations Seminars Conferences Large formal presentations Project/improvement groups
Other methods	Body language Telephone/mobile phone Data/voice recordings DVD or television communication Video/telephone conferencing Internet and intranet

Table E11.1 Methods of communication.

Portfolio Task 3 30 minutes

Links to LO2: Assessment criterion 2.1

Identify the main ways that you communicate in your organisation. Write a short personal statement to describe the techniques and methods that can be used to communicate information and knowledge to different people.

> **PLTS**
>
> By describing the ways in which you communicate, you will be demonstrating how you include your team in effective participation and how you form collaborative relationships with your team (TW; SM).

Clear and appropriate communication

In written communication it is important to use accurate grammar, spelling and punctuation. You should understand the principles of how to formulate meaningful sentences that will be understood correctly by the recipient. Poorly constructed letters and reports with grammatical errors and spelling mistakes can create a negative image of you and your organisation.

It is important to communicate in a professional way that the reader will be able to understand. If English is not your first language or you struggle with punctuation, spelling and grammar, this is something you may need to address.

Do not overcomplicate communications with technical words or words that may be difficult to understand. Do not use jargon or abbreviations unless you are sure that the other person will know what they mean.

Finally, when you present information, you should ensure that it is in the right format, layout and presented in your organisation's house style.

> **Checklist**
>
> When communicating make sure you:
>
> - write letters or reports in a way that meets the needs of the audience and in the agreed house style
> - correspond using the correct format, e.g. formal for an external customer
> - use the correct agreed format or house style for team meeting minutes and agendas
> - use your signature box if you are communicating by email.

New communication methods and technology

The business world is constantly changing and all organisations need to think up new and innovative ways of working. An example is technological changes, where it is important to update relevant processes and procedures to utilise new technologies that may be available. For example, it may be appropriate to communicate by a web camera link through a conference call. The benefits of introducing new ways of working are that they could make the organisation more efficient, more profitable and provide a better service to your customers.

Selecting the most appropriate communication technique and method

You may be familiar with the acronym **KISS**, which stands for 'keep it short and simple'. This is an essential requirement in a business environment, both in terms of verbal and written communication.

> **Key Term**
>
> **KISS** – Keep It Short and Simple – a useful acronym to remember in verbal and written communication.

The basic principle of this approach is to use:

- fewer words
- shorter words
- pictures, graphs or charts where possible.

It is important to identify the most appropriate method of communication to meet the needs of the recipient. Also, it is important to use the correct level of detail. By doing this, you will communicate more effectively and you are likely to make people feel valued and enhance working relationships. Always remember that communication should be specific to meet the needs of the recipients.

PLTS

This task will need you to be a creative thinker, independent enquirer and self-manager. To be able to collect examples of how you communicate with your team you will also need to show that you are a team worker (CT; IE; SM; TW).

Portfolio Task 4 60 minutes

Links to LO2: Assessment criteria 2.1, 2.2

Explain how you select and use the most appropriate communication technique and method.

Collect examples of all of the ways that you communicate with your team, for example, through formal methods, such as appraisals or target setting and through more day-to-day methods, such as emails and team-meeting minutes. These will provide useful evidence for your portfolio.

Encourage contributions from others

Verbal communication is a two-way process where information is sent from one person to another, who then interprets the information and continues the conversation by responding. As we have stated previously, effective communication can be achieved by:

- using the right language and level of detail to fit the occasion
- using the right medium – email, letter, verbal, etc.

You will interact with your team members all of the time and you may feel that your methods of communication are effective. However, it is important to gather the views from your team members as this will enable you to challenge your methods and make improvements in the future. One way that this can be achieved is by encouraging contributions and suggestions from other team members to identify how improvements can be made. This has the advantage of motivating team members and will make people feel more valued. A team meeting is a good time to discuss these issues. Perhaps you could raise the issue at your next team meeting to open a discussion on how effective the team is at communicating and if any improvements could be made in the processes or types of communication used.

Portfolio Task 5 90 minutes

Links to LO2: Assessment criteria 2.1, 2.2

At your next team meeting, put an item on the agenda to ask for suggestions and contributions from other team members on how the team can communicate more effectively. It might be possible for your assessor to observe this team meeting. If not, after the team meeting either write up a summary of the issues raised and or ask a team member to complete a witness statement relating to the meeting.

Discuss the meeting with your assessor. You will need to prepare for this discussion by looking over your work and making sure that you can explain the information that you chose to include. Be prepared to answer questions from your assessor.

PLTS

By involving your team in ways to encourage innovation and embrace change, you will be taking a proactive role in generating creativity and also enabling your team to participate in the development of their own performance and progress (TW; CT; IE; EP; SM).

Functional Skills

If your assessor asks you to take part in a discussion about this portfolio task as part of the assessment for this learning outcome, you may be able to count it as evidence towards Level 1 or Level 2 English Speaking and Listening.

Be able to communicate information and knowledge using appropriate techniques and methods

When communicating, remember to:

- use the right language to fit the occasion
- use the right medium – email, letter, verbal feedback, etc.
- get the attention of the people you are communicating with
- get your message across as you want it to be received – reduce the potential for misinterpretation or confusion
- maintain eye contact and observe body language for verbal communication
- allow people to respond
- listen to what is being said to you
- be prepared to discuss issues.

Communicate to target audiences using the appropriate techniques and methods

Verbal communication is happening all of the time in every business. It can take several different forms and examples can include:

- one-to-one verbal communication in person
- one-to-one verbal communication through a device, for example, telephone or video conferencing

- informal verbal communication between small groups of people, for example, a conversation between two or three people in the office
- more formalised verbal communication in small to medium-sized groups, for example, at a team meeting
- formalised verbal communication between one or more people, for example, at a committee meeting or a formal presentation.

Verbal communication over the telephone makes the language used all the more important as there is no use of body language.

Verbal communication is a two-way process. Information is sent from one person to another, who interprets the information and continues the conversation by responding. The communication is then in a perpetual loop until one or both parties agrees to end the discussion.

Verbal communication is not just concerned with actually speaking and listening – there are other more subtle factors to consider, such as:

- eye contact – positive eye contact is a good thing, but staring can be threatening to some people
- negative body language – negative body language traits include a blank stare, crossed arms, avoiding eye contact, looking at your watch and leaning back in your chair
- positive body language – good eye contact, smiling and taking interest, nodding encouragement where relevant, open arms/stance and leaning forward
- physical gestures – can include using arms to explain an issue or simply putting your thumbs up.

Remember

Verbal communication is not a luxury, it is essential.

Barriers to communication

You need to be aware that even if you plan your communication well, things can still go wrong because of barriers to communication. Often these are elements that are outside your control, but as long as you are aware of the issues, you have a better chance of managing any potential problems. The table below outlines some examples.

Barrier	Specific examples
Environmental factors	Background noise in the office makes it difficult for both parties to hear
Psychological factors	The receiver may have limited perception or selective listening
Physiological factors	The receiver may have disabilities or poor memory retention
Barriers to understanding	The information being communicated is taking too long or it is too complicated for the receiver
Barriers to acceptance	The receiver does not respect the other person and has a poor attitude
Technological factors	The email system crashes or an email is sent to the wrong person

Table E11.2 Barriers to communication.

It is worth noting that technological issues are fairly infrequent. It is much more likely that you would have a discussion with someone and they do not fully understand what you are saying to them or perhaps just not listening properly to what you are saying.

Have a look at the following two examples of techniques and methods. As you communicate on a day-to-day basis, you will need to use your judgement to select the most appropriate method.

Scenario 1

Imagine that you have to communicate some issues to your team in relation to a possible change to the structure of the organisation.

Your target audience is your team. You are known to all of your team members and they are likely to be comfortable communicating with you. In this scenario, the most appropriate method would be to arrange a meeting to explain the issues to your team face to face. You will need to prepare well and be tactful and professional during the meeting. It will be important at the end of the meeting to reiterate and summarise what you have communicated and also to check that all team members fully understand what you have communicated to them. It may also be appropriate to follow the meeting up with a written record of the discussion (minutes) and possibly to write to each person individually to summarise what was discussed and what the next stage of the process is.

Checklist

The following checklist should help your verbal communications to be more effective in the future:

At the planning stage you should:

- identify who you are communicating to – a client, your manager, your team or a group of people?
- identify any potential barriers
- think about whether your audience will be shy, nervous, aggressive or receptive towards you
- decide what method to use – face to face, telephone or formal presentation?
- decide if it is more appropriate to communicate by letter or email.

At the action stage you should:

- be tactful, polite and professional at all times
- actively listen to what is being said to you
- clarify what is being said and question any elements that you are unsure about
- summarise at the end of the conversation and agree 'who is doing what'.

Scenario 2

Imagine that you have to communicate with an outside organisation to check up on the progress of a delivery from a supplier.

Your target audience is your supplier. Your supplier will know your organisation, but they may not know you as an individual. Also, they may have a large team dealing with delivery issues, so it is important to understand that you may not be able to communicate with the same person every time you contact them.

In this scenario, the most appropriate method would be to make an initial contact by telephone to discuss the issue and to then follow up what was agreed by email. By sending an email to clarify what was discussed, you have created a written record of what was agreed and how the issue will be resolved.

These two examples show the importance of identifying your target audience and using a variety of methods to communicate. Also note the importance of following up what has been communicated to give clarity and assurance to both parties.

Using electronic forms of written communication in a business environment

Email is a fast and inexpensive way of delivering communications and information. It can be sent globally and once you click the send button, an email will be delivered in seconds. Emails also have the advantage of being able to distribute information to large groups of people quickly and the recipients then have the opportunity to respond, print, save or forward information in their own time.

When communicating by email, plan what you are going to say first and apply a common-sense approach to what you say.

Remember to take care when writing and sending email. Emails are a proper and accepted form of communication and in that respect they are no different from communicating through a letter or verbally. Just the same as any other form of communication email must be professional, meaningful and accurate.

Would you write anything in a letter to a customer that may cause offence?

Would you say anything offensive or inappropriate to your manager?

If you send or forward an inappropriate email to other people, then there may be serious consequences and you could be disciplined. Most organisations have an 'acceptable use policy' to cover email and internet use in the workplace. Check if your organisation has one and make yourself and your team familiar with the contents.

There is a generally accepted etiquette for communicating by email in a business environment, as shown on the following page.

- Set up and use your email signature box with your job role and contact details.
- Plan what you are going to communicate in the same way as you would if you were writing a letter.
- Write a subject line or title on the top of the email.
- Use a polite and professional tone.
- Start the email with the name of the person you are communicating with. 'Hi' is acceptable for informal emails.
- Use short sentences, paragraphs and bullet points as this will make it much easier for the recipient to understand.
- Remember that specific legislation and internal policies cover what you send by email. Do not send anything that may cause offence or breach any other type of legislation.
- Be aware that you must protect any personal information about yourself, colleagues or customers. Do not forward any information onto third party organisations without the express consent of the person and do not share your user ID or password with anyone.

There are also some things it is useful not to do.

- Don't forget to lock your computer when you are away from your desk.
- Don't forget to put your out-of-office reply on when you are away from work.
- Don't write in capitals or red typeface as it is the equivalent to shouting.
- Don't forward chain emails to other people.
- Don't send sensitive or confidential information by email.
- Don't write aggressive emails or say something that you might later regret.
- If you receive an email that has upset you, don't respond straight away, take time to consider your response.

> **Activity** 30 minutes
>
> Think about how you would write an email to your manager, your team, a new supplier and a close friend. How will they be different? Think about how you start and end the emails and what sort of language you might use. Discuss your thoughts with your assessor.

Delivering verbal presentations

It is good to get used to talking to people in a group on a semi-formal basis. An example of this could be leading a team meeting. By doing this on a regular basis, you will build up your confidence to potentially deliver a more formal presentation to a larger group of people.

Formal oral presentations can prove daunting if it is something that you have never done before. However, don't panic if you have been asked to deliver a presentation – as with most things in business, if you prepare well, you will succeed. The following section will help you to prepare and deliver a presentation.

Successful presentations need to be planned thoroughly.

Activity 3 hours

Ask your manager if you can undertake a formal presentation to a group of people. Either ask your assessor to attend to observe you, or ask your manager to write up a witness testimony. You may also want to write up a personal statement to reflect on the experience and explain what things you can improve on for next time.

PLTS

By planning and delivering a presentation to a group of people, it will require you to think creatively and also plan and research what you are going to deliver. In addition to this, following the presentation, you will also be able to gather feedback and reflect on how you can aim to improve your presentation skills in the future (CT; IE; RL).

How to plan and deliver successful presentations

Before the presentation:

- check the presentation brief – what is the purpose of the presentation, what do you need to cover?
- check the practicalities – format, timings, resources, equipment to be used etc.
- decide on what you are going to say and complement the presentation with pictures, graphs, video clips or hand-outs as appropriate
- decide how you will learn the presentation and prepare some notes to assist you
- practise the presentation on your own or with a colleague and ask for some feedback.

During the presentation:

- make sure that you are well prepared and are ready to go
- wear smart clothes and have a good positive posture, don't be static, but don't move around too much either
- stay calm, relaxed and confident
- before you begin, take a couple of deep breaths and start slowly with your opening line – and smile – that will relax you and the audience
- at the start, communicate the housekeeping arrangements such as fire exits, break times, etc.
- create an opener that will get everyone's attention, such as a fact, quote or question, for example 'Did you know that…'
- explain the outcomes of the presentation after your opener, for example, 'At the session today, we will…'
- work closely with the audience and be aware that you will need to make transitions between different topics or issues. Changing the pace of the presentation can help to grab the audience's attention back. Pausing for a few seconds can help you to achieve this
- end the presentation well by summarising all of the issues and linking them back to the initial outcomes that you set at the beginning of the presentation
- be ready to deal with any questions at the end of the presentation.

After the presentation:

- ask your colleagues for some feedback – how did you do?
- evaluate the feedback and identify any improvements for next time.

Explain how the target audience has received and understood the information communicated

In some situations you will be able to gauge straight away if your audience has understood the information that you have communicated. For example, in a formal presentation scenario, the audience will be able to ask questions to clarify any issues they have. If you were in a meeting with colleagues from another part of the organisation, again, your colleagues would be able to question you on a particular issue to clarify their understanding of what is being discussed.

However, communication within your own team is much more subtle and complex and you will need to be especially careful to communicate issues in a timely manner, clarifying everyone's understanding of what has been discussed and agreed. Ultimately, a team operates on a day-to-day basis based on a number of factors including:

- your own management style
- the dynamics of the team members including the skills, knowledge and motivations of individual team members
- your interaction with other teams and the interaction that takes place with your customers
- the resources in place and the objectives that you need to achieve with these resources
- your ability to manage performance, linking it to organisational objectives
- individuals' understanding of their job role.

You will need to manage how you communicate information within your team and ensure that everyone's understanding of the issues is the same. Try to communicate important information verbally and be consistent in your approach by having regular briefings or team meetings and treating team members equally and fairly. Also put in place a process for briefing team members about issues if they are away. For example, you could have a five-minute chat with your colleagues on their first day back to work after a holiday or sick leave.

Communicating effectively with your team on a day-to-day basis should help to improve the overall performance of the team. This is because by communicating issues to your team they will understand and act on that information and as the team leader you will be empowering them to motivate and support each other. It is likely that team members will start to take an active role in shaping the team.

By trusting and supporting your colleagues, they can become more efficient and should strive towards achieving excellence. By working closely with your team and communicating effectively you will develop their skills, knowledge and career aspirations. You can do this by:

- providing training, which will develop their knowledge, skills, and competencies

- providing positive and constructive feedback on their performance
- involving team members in the decision-making process and agreeing objectives collectively
- coaching team members on a one-to-one basis and supporting their individual development
- creating a friendly environment where team members feel that their input is valued and welcomed
- creating an open door policy making yourself available to all staff at all times
- communicating effectively with your team, making sure that all team members know what is happening all of the time.

Once you have all of these practical elements in place, it is very likely that communication will be effective and your team will be empowered and motivated on a day-to-day basis.

PLTS

By researching relevant communication methods, you will be exploring issues and methods from different perspectives and you will be able to analyse and judge the methods and choose the most appropriate ways to communicate in different scenarios (TW; IE; CT).

Functional Skills

If you carry out research involving reading texts including work-related documents as well as internet research in order to complete your portfolio task, you may be able to count this as evidence towards Level 1 and 2 English Reading. Remember to keep records of all of the documents, handbooks, guidelines that you study, along with the websites you visited, as you will need to document the reading research you carried out.

Portfolio Task 6 30 minutes

Links to LO3: Assessment criterion 3.1
Research the different ways that you can communicate to different audiences. Describe two examples of communication to different audiences and explain for each why you would use that particular communication method and what the audience's needs are.

Portfolio Task 7 30 minutes

Links to LO3: Assessment criterion 3.2
Give a recent example of something that you communicated and explain how you know that the target audience both received the information correctly and understood what was being communicated to them.

Techniques and methods of assessing the current knowledge of your team

A useful way to assess the current knowledge and abilities of your team is through asking yourself a number of questions. This will help to see if your own work and the work of the team overall is as effective as you think it is and it will also help you to identify any areas where communication is ineffective and knowledge is inadequate.

Working through the following elements should help to identify any potential issues or areas for improvement.

- Team effectiveness – Do team members trust each other? Are you all open and honest with each other? Do team members support each other? Have any recent changes affected performance?

- Knowledge and skills – Are all team members competent in their roles – do they have adequate skills and knowledge? Do they need additional support? Are there any skills that the whole team lacks? Is the team ready for any future challenges?

- Team communication – Do your team members lead by example and communicate information and knowledge to each other? Are team members **motivated**? Can the team continually improve?

- My communication skills – Do I lead by example? Are team members effective communicators? Are team members involved in regular formal communication with each other, for example team meetings? Can the team continually improve its methods of communication by sharing information and knowledge to develop areas of good practice?

- Review the issues and ask yourself:
  - Do the team receive adequate and regular information?
  - If we have failed to communicate information and knowledge in an effective way, what went wrong?
  - Did we plan activities well and do I manage performance effectively?
  - What would we do differently in the future?

All of these issues will need to be managed on an ongoing basis and the way in which you communicate and interact with your team will be critical if you want to manage information and knowledge effectively and strive to improve the efficiency of your team.

Be able to adapt communication techniques and methods according to target audience response

When developing your communication techniques, be prepared to challenge your current methods and ask yourself the following questions.

- Am I using the right language to fit the occasion?
- Am I using the right medium? – email, letter, verbal feedback etc.
- Am I getting the message across and do the people that I'm communicating with understand what I've communicated to them?
- Do I review my communication techniques to take account of any feedback that I have received?

You should be aware that you may need to adjust your communication methods from time to time. It may only be a slight change, but by challenging your current methods and by acting on any feedback that you receive you will be able to change things, improving your communication in the future.

Explain how to modify communication techniques and methods in response to verbal and non-verbal feedback

From time to time, you may need to modify your communication techniques. Listening carefully when you are communicating is an important part of this process. It will enable you to identify if the information and knowledge that you are communicating is being received and understood. If it is not being understood, by listening carefully you will be able interpret what is going wrong and then present the information in a more appropriate language or medium.

For example, if you are communicating some information from a written report to your team members, but by listening to their responses it is clear that they are not quite sure what you are saying, you will have to adjust your method accordingly. This could be as simple as explaining the issue in greater detail, using less complex language and technical terms or presenting the information in a different format, for example in a graph or a chart. These skills will develop with practice.

Listening skills

In order to fully appreciate how you can adapt your communication skills, you also need to be able to develop your listening skills. This will help you in terms of checking to see if the information you are communicating has been understood and to listen more carefully if you receive any feedback from your manager, a colleague or customer. Don't forget if you receive some feedback, you will need to listen and interpret that feedback and implement it for future communications.

Listening might sound straightforward, but it is not that easy and needs practice. It is easy to hear what is being said, but is something completely different to understand, interpret and then act upon what has been said to you. Also, it is easy to listen to someone speaking and to either finish off their sentence for them or think in your own mind what you want them to say rather than actually listening to what they do say.

Always actively listen to what is being said to you; this needs concentration and practice. Try to make sense of the information being communicated and listen with intent. Then apply the information to the situation and context of the discussion to reach a more detailed understanding of the issues being discussed.

Remember

Listening is essential if you are going to communicate successfully, but it is an often overlooked communication skill.

Purpose and benefits of giving and receiving feedback

Generally speaking, feedback of any type is useful. Good feedback should always be **constructive**. Receiving feedback from your team members and other people, then acting upon it, should help to improve your communication techniques in the future.

The most common formal feedback that you are likely to receive is through reviews or appraisal meetings with your manager.

Most organisations have a process in place to allow for meetings between individual employees or teams and their managers to review performance and capability. At these meetings, you can discuss the:

- achievements for the previous year
- specific goals or objectives for the forthcoming year
- training and development needs
- way to give and receive positive and constructive feedback.

Try to be objective in your evaluation of any feedback that you give or receive and try to learn from your mistakes. By identifying any issues, it should help you to improve your communication techniques in the future.

In addition to receiving feedback from your manager or team members it is also good practice to give frequent feedback to your team members as this should help to improve their competence and hopefully their communication techniques.

> **Key Term**
>
> **Constructive feedback** – meaningful feedback of some value that can be understood and used to modify behaviour for the better.

Communicate information and knowledge Unit E11

Checklist

How to give feedback to your colleagues.

- Feedback has more impact when it is immediate – don't wait to give feedback at a later time, as you will both forget the detail.
- In order to motivate your team, you need to be positive. You may have some issues to address, but be positive and tactful.
- Always give praise openly and freely when it is due.
- Get to the point quickly and focus on the issues not the person.
- Give clear specific examples to support what you are saying.
- Be objective, don't judge the person – look at the specific issues and then feedback.
- Don't expect your colleague to agree with everything you say – actively listen to their response and work out a way forward.
- Check that you both agree with the outcome and any agreed action at the end of the discussion.
- Treat all colleagues equally and fairly by giving them all an equal amount of feedback and support.
- Give feedback at the right time and avoid feedback overload.

Checklist

How to accept and value feedback:

- Listen to what people have to say about you.
- Avoid overreacting and let people have their say; don't let your emotions get in the way.
- Pay attention to what is being said; clarify what the issue is or what you need to do to improve your communication methods in the future.
- Be prepared to respond and explain what action you might take.
- Take the feedback on board and if it is valid and constructive, follow it up with some positive action.
- Make sure that you feed back to the person at a future date, to let them know what you have done.

Ways of obtaining feedback on the success of verbal communication

For feedback to be of some value, you need to be able to understand it, accept it and take action on it to improve your performance in the future. You may receive some positive feedback and there may not be any action required from you as a result of such feedback. The important thing is to ensure that you understand what all feedback means and how to put this into context in relation to your whole job. If you receive some feedback from a customer or a colleague and you are not sure what it means, then ask them to clarify what they are saying.

By accepting feedback from your colleagues and customers, it should help you to improve your own communication skills and overall performance. By improving your performance, you should become more efficient in your role. If all of your colleagues are also doing the same, then the whole organisation should improve and become more efficient.

Finally, don't forget that you can always ask someone for some feedback on your performance.

The purpose and benefits of using feedback to further develop your communication skills

Feedback can be formal or informal. An example of informal feedback might be a customer saying to you 'You dealt with my problem really well, thank you.' This is obviously positive information and if you are doing something well, just carry on doing the same.

Sometimes, you will get more formal feedback. This may come from your line manager or a colleague that you work closely with. Other sources of formal feedback are from customers or from other organisations that you work closely with. If you have received some positive feedback from a customer, for example an email thanking you for assisting them, print this out as it will be a valuable piece of evidence for your portfolio.

Remember that feedback is a two way process: you can give feedback and you will receive feedback.

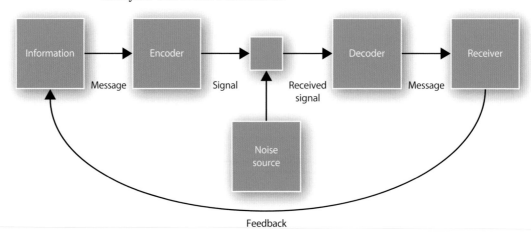

Figure E11.2 It is important to give and receive feedback when communicating at work.

Developing your communication skills

Always think of feedback as a positive thing. Try to be objective in your evaluation of any feedback and try to learn from any mistakes that you have made. Put plans in place to make sure that you improve your communication skills next time. If you have received some negative feedback, you need to assess it logically and realistically. Ask yourself the following questions.

- Am I still learning the systems, processes and ways that the organisation communicates? If so, it may take time to be fully competent: set a target!
- Can I ask for support or advice if the same situation occurs again?
- Perhaps I was not given enough time or the correct resources were not in place to allow me to communicate effectively?
- Do I need to write a procedure or note for myself and the team to make sure that I/we can communicate more effectively next time?
- Have I got a specific development need or do I need some training?
- Was the problem or issue outside of my control?

By working through these questions, you will start to identify how you can improve in the future and possibly make changes to your working methods to become a more effective communicator. You can also use these questions with your colleagues to identify any relevant issues.

Portfolio Task 8 — 60 minutes

Links to LO4: Assessment criterion 4.1

Explain how you modify your communication techniques and methods in response to verbal and non-verbal feedback.

Try to think of an example where you have received some verbal or non-verbal feedback on some ineffective communications. An example could be an email that you have sent to your team members, which you know has not been read by all of them. Another example might be if you are communicating something verbally to your team and they are clearly not interested as they are looking at their watches, yawning and looking around.

Explain a specific example and detail how you dealt with the situation, learnt from the experience and put in place a system or process to ensure that this type of thing does not happen in the future. You may want to write this as a personal statement or you may wish to conduct a professional discussion with your assessor to explain it. Pull together any relevant evidence for your portfolio.

PLTS

By reviewing communication methods, you are evaluating your experiences and looking for ways to improve your techniques in the future. Receiving constructive feedback is really useful (RL; SM).

Team talk

Susan's story

I'm a team leader in a specialist outdoor clothing company in Cumbria. I manage a team of four full-time staff and three part-time staff. One of my main tasks is to ensure that we have an efficient process for rectifying any quality issues on the products before they are despatched to retailers.

Occasionally during the quality control process, we find some products that are not stitched correctly. However, recently there has been a significant increase in faulty products and it is becoming more difficult to resolve them.

We have recently employed new staff and have also found that new machine parts have been faulty. I think these issues may be causing some of the problems.

My manager is aware of the quality problems and has asked me to find out what the issues are and then bring a report to a meeting to discuss with the directors. I prepared a detailed list of all of the issues and then I began to draft out my report. In the first section I explained the issues, in the second part of the report I identified the options to solve the issues and then in the last part I put forward a recommendation. Based on my findings the recommendation suggested replacing the faulty parts and delivering training to the new staff on operating the equipment.

Top tips

Susan could have also spoken to her colleagues to ask for their input or opinions on why there were so many quality problems. By doing this, she could have found out about any other problems or issues. Susan did well to write down a list of all the issues before starting to write the report. This demonstrated that she had thought about everything and by preparing a list, she was starting a structured process to try to resolve the issues. Can you think of anything else that Susan could have done better?

Ask the expert	
Q	I have to formulate a report for a meeting, what do I need to do?
A	Gather as much information as you can and make sure that you understand exactly what is being asked of you so that you can plan your report. You need to: ■ be clear on the objectives for the report – what do you want to achieve? ■ prepare the report in a format to meet the audience's needs – in the right language, the right level of detail and in the 'house style' if required ■ agree a specific date for completion ■ structure the report with a beginning, a middle and an end which includes a proposal or a recommendation ■ make sure that there are no barriers to your communication method. If you think a written report is not the most appropriate method, then think of an alternative.

What your assessor is looking for

In order to prepare for and succeed in completing this unit, your assessor will require you to be able to demonstrate competence by:

- describing the purpose and benefits of effective communication
- describing the various methods, structures and processes used to communicate both in writing and verbally
- contributing to discussions and listening actively
- planning communication and presenting information in the most suitable format and the right level of detail
- demonstrating effective communication in both written and verbal form
- demonstrating how to use feedback to further develop your competence.

You will demonstrate your skills, knowledge and competence through the eight portfolio tasks in this unit. Evidence generated in this unit will also cross-reference to the other units in this qualification.

Please bear in mind that there are significant cross-referencing opportunities throughout this qualification and you may have already generated some relevant work to meet certain criteria in this unit. Your assessor will provide you with the exact requirements to meet the standards of this unit. However, as a guide, it is likely that for this unit you will need to be assessed through the following methods:

- One observation of relevant workplace communication to cover the whole unit.

- At least one witness testimony to be produced.
- A written narrative, reflective account or professional discussion.
- Any relevant work products to be produced as evidence.

Work products for this unit could include:

- emails, letters or other communication methods that you have used
- copies of any team meeting agendas and minutes
- any feedback that you have received on your performance, e.g. your appraisal
- any formal communication that you have completed, e.g. a presentation.

Your assessor will guide you through the assessment process as detailed in the candidate logbook. The detailed assessment criteria are shown in the logbook and by working through these questions, combined with providing the relevant evidence, you will meet the learning outcomes required to complete this unit.

Task and page reference	Assessment criteria
1 (page 66)	1.1
2 (page 67)	1.2
3 (page 69)	2.1
4 (page 70)	2.1, 2.2
5 (page 71)	2.1, 2.2
6 (page 78)	3.1
7 (page 78)	3.2
8 (page 83)	4.1

05

Unit D5 Plan, allocate and monitor work of a team

Working as a team can provide enormous benefits in terms of productivity, achievement of business goals and creating good working relationships. Teams can achieve work goals that would be impossible for individuals working alone. However, the key to successful teamwork lies in how well its activities and tasks are planned and allocated to the different team members. Good monitoring and management of teamwork processes are also essential in the achievement of the team's work goals.

In this unit, you will investigate some of the best ways of planning teamwork objectives and managing your team effectively to keep on target. You will also look into the issues you need to think about when allocating tasks to the various members of your team. Individual skills, current workload and personalities are all vital elements that you will need to take into account when scheduling and allocating tasks to team members.

What you will learn:

- Be able to plan work for a team
- Be able to allocate work across a team
- Be able to manage team members to achieve team objectives
- Be able to monitor and evaluate the performance of team members
- Be able to improve the performance of a team

Links to the Technical Certificate

If you are completing your NVQ as part of an Apprenticeship Framework, you will find the following topics are also covered in your Technical Certificate:

- Motivating the work team to perform
- Planning and monitoring work
- Team performance

Be able to plan work for a team

Effective planning is a vital first step in scheduling the work of a team so that it can then get on with its tasks efficiently. Working well together and being organised are also central to the achievement of your team's goals. When you plan the work of your team, you will need to think about how to ensure the team members work together in the most effective manner possible and how they can be best organised to get their tasks completed.

Agreeing team objectives with your own manager

Before working out a plan or a schedule for your team's work objectives, you first need to set and agree the objectives with your own line manager. This is the very first step in the objective setting process. It is important because the objectives and targets of your team need to be a good fit with the overarching aims and strategy of the business. This ensures that the individual tasks and activities of each and every team member contribute towards the overall achievement of the business's goals.

Aligning team objectives to the wider business goals

Your line manager will be fully briefed on the wider plans and goals of the business and is therefore well placed to oversee the team objective-setting process. Securing the agreement of your line manager in this respect ensures that together, you are establishing team objectives that are aligned to the wider business goals.

Figure D5.1 Work objectives must fit within the wider goals of the organisation.

Negotiating with your manager

A key element of any successful meeting with your manager to set out your team's objectives will involve you having to negotiate effectively with them. This will mean that you have to be **assertive**, stand your ground and defend your team where, for example, your manager has perhaps overestimated the possible work rate of the team or underestimated the equipment costs or numbers of staff required for a particular task. This is all part of good business communication, which is a critical skill for you to develop to become an effective manager.

Never be afraid to speak up if your opinion on some aspect of your team's work differs from that of your manager. Your manager is, after all, one step removed from the day-to-day workings of the team, whereas you have more direct, hands-on knowledge.

Negotiating problems or issues in situations such as these can be a very good opportunity for you to demonstrate your professionalism and management skills. You should present your issues to your line manager along with carefully considered alternatives. This way, you are giving your line manager both the problem and a range of possible solutions.

If you fail to flag up any unrealistic expectations on the part of your manager during your objectives setting meetings, you will only be creating problems for yourself and your team members further down the line. This is why it is essential to have any such issues aired at the outset and more realistic solutions found.

Developing a plan for a team to meet agreed objectives

Once you have agreed your team's objectives with your own line manager, you know exactly what is expected of you and your team. The next question is 'How are you going to make it happen?'

The key to your success lies in careful and well thought out planning and in establishing clear work targets that can be easily understood by your team members. In this section, you will look at the planning process, the benefits of careful planning and the various planning tools you can use.

The planning process

During the planning process you will need to think about issues such as:

- the number of team members available to you
- the specific skills and expertise needed and those available
- equipment requirements
- the available budget
- any training or recruitment requirements

Key Term

Assertive – speaking up for yourself and stating your opinions firmly but not aggressively.

Activity 15 minutes

Write a brief summary describing the key areas that you would need to discuss with your manager in an objective-setting meeting. Which, if any, of these areas might you be likely to disagree on and why?

PLTS

Reflecting on and evaluating your experiences of meetings will help you to develop your skills as a reflective learner (RL).

Unit D5 Plan, allocate and monitor work of a team

Key Terms

Bottlenecks – areas where progress slows or stops due to one part of a process becoming overloaded.

Contingency plans – backup plans in case your main plan has to change.

Milestones – key stages within a project.

Proactive – thinking ahead and initiating events rather than waiting for things to happen.

Remember

A good planning process helps you to:

- co-ordinate activities for maximum effectiveness
- allocate tasks and resources in the best way
- identify 'what if' scenarios and work out how best you would deal with them.

Activity 15 minutes

Identify one of the current business aims for your organisation that will impact on the work of your team. How would you go about translating this business aim into practical work targets for the team? Sketch out some plans on paper and discuss them with your assessor.

- the schedule and any key **milestones**
- any possible **bottlenecks** or hold-ups which may arise along the way – and how you could deal with these.

Taking time out at the beginning to plan your team's work objectives also means that:

- you are less likely to overlook important aspects of the work
- you can think about 'what if' scenarios and build in **contingency plans** to allow for these
- you can apply a **proactive** approach to your planning, rather than merely reacting to – and firefighting – events as you go along.

Essentially, time to plan allows you clear thinking space, so that you can prepare well and manage your team to the best of your ability.

Breaking down plans into clear work targets

Suppose that your organisation had the overall plan of increasing your team's sales by 15 per cent over the next twelve months. What would you do to translate this business aim into individual work targets for each of your team members? Assume that you have exactly the same number of staff as the previous year and that recruiting additional team members is not an option for you.

One approach could be to examine individual sales achievements for the previous year and work out exactly how many additional sales each team member needs to achieve per annum in order for the team to meet this 15 per cent improvement. Once you have worked out this annual figure, you can then break it down into monthly, weekly and even daily sales targets for each individual.

For example, if the previous year's sales amounted to 120,000 units, then the new target for the following year is 120,000 + 15%, which equals 138,000 units. If you have ten team members, then each person must achieve 13,800 unit sales over the year in order for your team to achieve the new target. Further dividing this figure down, you can see that each team member must achieve 1,150 sales per month, or 57.5 sales per day.

Breaking down the figures in this way allows your team to clearly see what they are expected to achieve on a daily basis. They can also easily measure their own achievements against this figure.

Stages of the planning process

A standard business planning process might look like the one shown in Figure D5.2. It consists of a series of steps or stages, which ensure that all of the essential elements of planning are undertaken.

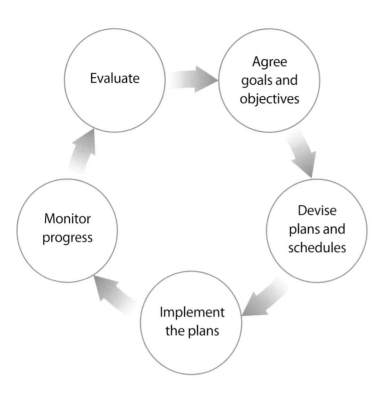

Activity 30 minutes

Look af Figure D5.2 showing the stages of the planning process. For each of the five stages, list the things that you currently do – and any additional actions that you could implement in the future – to manage each stage of the planning process.

PLTS

Reviewing your current actions and exploring new solutions will help you to develop your skills as a creative thinker (CT).

Figure D5.2 Why do you think it is important to use a framework for the planning process?

Capacity and capabilities of the team

It is essential that any work plans that you make for your team take full account of the team's **capacity** and **capabilities**. This means thinking about how much work the team can realistically get through (its capacity), bearing in mind any existing work commitments, as well as examining individuals' specific skills and abilities in different areas (capabilities). There is little point in setting work plans that are unachievable, so a careful and honest assessment of the team's strengths and weaknesses is critical at this stage. It may also throw up useful indicators of:

- recruitment needs for the team, either now or in the future
- training needs for certain team members, including possibly multi-skilling to create a more **versatile** team
- resourcing problems, such as a lack of adequate equipment.

Any issues that come to light may need flagging up to your line manager to identify the best options for addressing them.

Key Terms

Capabilities – skills and abilities.

Capacity – availability to take on further tasks.

Versatile – capable of carrying out a variety of different tasks.

Unit D5 Plan, allocate and monitor work of a team

Useful planning techniques

You can start your planning very simply by sketching out your team's work plan on a piece of paper. However, it is recommended that you also keep a computer-based copy of your plan in some form, as this will be useful, will appear more professional when presenting to higher management and is very easy to update and amend when required.

There is a variety of different planning tools you can use, such as:

● critical path analysis
● flow charts.
● Gantt charts.

Trying out different tools will help you to decide which is most convenient and useful for you for the type of planning work that you need to carry out.

Critical path analysis

Critical path analysis (CPA) is a very useful tool for planning larger or more complex projects. Its key benefit, as the name implies, is that it identifies the **critical path** through your project – in other words, the key activities and the deadlines by when each must be completed for the project to come in on time.

Figure D5.3 shows a series of numbered circles, or nodes, representing each task. Each node gives the earliest and latest start and finish times for that task. Where the earliest and latest times are the same, this is where there is no slack at all in the project and gives you your 'critical path'. Tasks that have different earliest and latest start and finish times are the places where there is slack time (sometimes also called float) and some capacity for delays in beginning specific tasks, without impacting the final completion date of the project.

One drawback of CPA is that it looks quite complicated and technical, so it is potentially more difficult to understand than a Gantt chart. A critical path analysis is not normally appropriate for smaller projects.

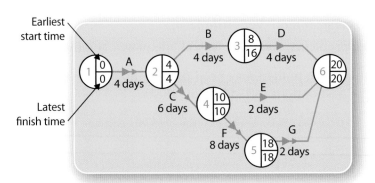

Figure D5.3 Critical path analysis.

Flow charts

A flow chart is a simple diagram showing all the steps required in a process in the order they need to be completed. Flow charts consist of two different types of steps – actions and decisions. Actions are shown in oblong boxes and decisions in diamond boxes. The start and finish points are shown in rounded boxes. The example in Figure D5.4 shows the process by which receptionists should route incoming calls to a business.

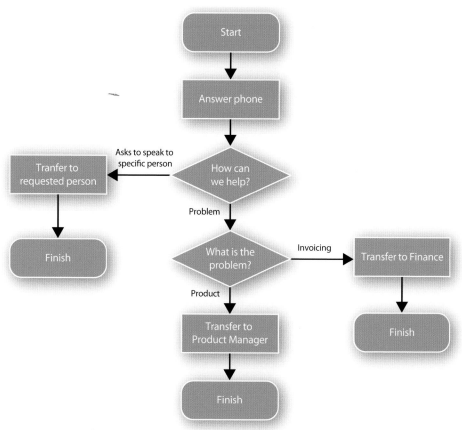

Figure D5.4 A flow chart.

Gantt charts

A Gantt chart is a very widely used method of charting a project. It allows you to list each main task, along with the time needed for it to be completed. It also shows which tasks must be completed before others can begin. Dependency is when one task cannot begin until another has finished. For example, if you are making a cup of tea, you cannot pour the water into the cup until you have boiled the kettle, so pouring on the water is dependent on having first boiled the kettle! A Gantt chart gives you a very good visual overview of the whole project, along with a clear picture of the key milestones along the way. Time is usually plotted along the x-axis and the tasks are plotted along the y-axis. Gantt charts are commonly used to present project plans to senior management and clients. You can easily put together a simple Gantt chart using Microsoft® Project or other similar software. An example can be found on page 23.

PLTS

Analysing and evaluating the different planning tools which you could adopt for your job will help you to develop your skills as an independent enquirer (IE).

Activity 30 minutes

Carry out research to find more information on at least three planning tools and techniques. You can research the techniques mentioned in this section, or you can find out about others if you wish. Write a brief, one-paragraph summary on each of the techniques which you research. Some useful websites you could visit for information include www.businessballs.com and www.mindtools.com. Ask colleagues at work if they use any specific planning techniques that may also be useful for you.

Portfolio Task 1   1 hour

Links to LO1: Assessment criteria 1.1, 1.2

1. Describe the reasons why it is important to agree team objectives with your own manager. Give an example of an occasion when you have done this and include any relevant work documents to support your answer. If you have not yet agreed team objectives with your manager, say what you think would be the key issues to cover and why.

2. Describe the steps involved in developing a plan for a team to meet agreed objectives, taking into account capacity and capabilities of the team. Show how the development of your plan fits into the stages of the planning process model outlined in this section. You will also need to show that you understand what is meant by the terms 'capacity' and 'capability' and outline how you have accounted for these elements in your plan.

Your assessment could take the form of a written narrative or a professional discussion with your assessor. It could also include the production of workplace evidence, work-based observations or the use of witness testimonies, as appropriate.

Functional Skills

Taking part in a professional discussion with your assessor as part of your assessment will allow you to practise your Functional English Speaking and Listening skills.

Be able to allocate work across a team

The way in which you communicate your plans with your team will have a huge influence on how motivated your team are about them. Openness, enthusiasm and a positive approach on your part will be more likely to result in a successful start to your team's project. Allocating work according to individual team members' skills and aptitudes is also a critical consideration in determining the success of the team's work.

Discussing plans with your team

It is important that you take the time to brief your team on your plans for their work. The better the communication process, the more likely your team are to:

- understand what is required of them
- be committed to the team's goals
- feel involved and motivated.

Remember, your team cannot hope to perform well if they have not been told clearly the overall goal which they are working towards. Give them the big picture and this will help them to understand specific work objectives.

Effective team briefing helps your team understand their work goals.

Briefing meetings

Set up a briefing meeting with your team to tell them about the plans. Make sure you are well prepared for your meeting by collecting together all of the information that you will need beforehand. Produce a **meeting agenda** and circulate it to your team in advance to give everyone time to read it. Give yourself time to think about how you will present to your team and practise your delivery in a warm, open and informative way.

Communication

Remember that you need to establish two-way communications with your team so they feel able to speak up, ask questions and give their own suggestions. **Participation** increases motivation!

Key Terms

Meeting agenda – a list of the main points to be discussed in a meeting.

Participation – actively taking part.

Checklist

The golden rules for successful team meetings are:

- be very clear
- encourage participation
- set out team rules and processes
- check everyone understands.

Commitment

Aim to get 100 per cent agreement on – and commitment to – the team's plans as early as possible. Allowing your team to have input into this process helps to give them ownership of it, which is a great method of increasing motivation.

Clarity

Most of all, you need to remember to make the briefing meeting as clear as possible, so that everybody understands what is going on and can see how their individual contribution to the team is valuable. This is also a perfect opportunity for you to assert your skills as team leader and set out the ground rules and working guidelines for the team's processes.

Activity **15 minutes**

How well do you handle team briefings? Look at the following list and make notes on whether you do the following and things that you could do in the future to improve your team communication skills.

- I always set a clear purpose for my team meetings.
- I aim to get full agreement on team goals.
- I actively encourage contributions from each of my team members.
- I listen to my team.
- I establish the ground rules on how team processes will work.

Agreeing work allocation and SMART objectives with team members

Allocating the work tasks to your team members is an area requiring skill and judgement. On one hand, you need to assign tasks in such a way that the work can be completed efficiently, on the other, you also need to think about being seen to be fair. Questions that you need to consider include the following.

- Do your team members have the required skills to complete the work you are allocating to them – or will additional training be needed?
- Are the team happy with the tasks allocated to them? If not, you need to address this issue quickly to keep morale from dropping and to prevent conflict arising.
- Has the workload been allocated evenly to each of the team members? Have you taken into account the time, effort and skill-set involved in each task?
- Is there a dependence on certain team members to complete key tasks? Can you deal with this by coaching or training other team members?

Once you have agreed the work allocation among your team, you should have a list of who will do what and by when. You may have this information in the form of a rota or schedule. Make sure to recap the task assignments to the team once they are finalised and use this as an opportunity to take questions and clarify any points needing explanation. Once the final amendments are complete, remember to circulate the schedule to the team.

	Monday	Tuesday	Wednesday	Thursday	Friday	Saturday	Sunday
Sophie	Kitchen 8–1	Kitchen 8–1	Kitchen 8–1			Kitchen 8–1	Kitchen 8–1
Charlie	Kitchen 10–7		Kitchen 10–7	Kitchen 10–7	Kitchen 10–7	Kitchen 10–7	
Marcus	Kitchen 1–9	Kitchen 1–9		Kitchen 1–9	Kitchen 1–9		Kitchen 11–7
Rhys		Bar 9–3	Bar 9–3	Bar 9–3		Bar 5–11	Bar 5–11
Olivia	Bar 5–11	Kitchen 10–7	Bar 5–11		Bar 5–11	Kitchen 1–9	
Stephen		Bar 5–11	Bar 5–11	Bar 5–11	Bar 9–3	Bar 9–3	
Ashleigh				Bar 5–11	Bar 5–11	Bar 12–7	Bar 9–3
Deena	Bar 9–3			Bar 12–7	Bar 12–7		
Sanjay	Bar 12–7	Bar 12–7	Bar 12–7			Bar 5–11	Bar 12–7
Gabriela	Bar 5–11	Bar 5–11	Kitchen 1–9	Kitchen 8–1	Kitchen 8–1		

Table D5.1 A staff rota showing a team's work allocation for the coming week.

Delegation

By allocating tasks to your team members, you are delegating work to them. **Delegation** is a vitally important management skill and it is essential that you do it well. When you delegate work to a team member, you are assigning work – and authority – to them, although you retain ultimate responsibility for the overall completion of the task. Delegation is a necessary activity for the simple reason that you cannot do everything yourself. That's why you have to employ management skills such as delegating tasks to others.

Benefits of effective delegation

Effective delegation has many benefits: it is central to improved team performance, better productivity and increased motivation as staff enjoy being given more responsibility. Staff are also given the chance to experience new and challenging tasks and to develop additional skills. This is of great benefit to the team and even to the business as a whole, as it will ensure smooth **succession planning** with suitably skilled and experienced staff moving easily into more senior positions when they become available in the future.

Key Terms

Delegation – assigning tasks or responsibilities to someone else to complete.

Succession planning – planning for future staffing requirements.

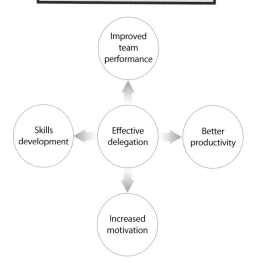

Figure D5.5 Delegation.

Establishing your level of delegation

It is possible to delegate in different ways. Suppose, for example, that you ask one of your team to research an issue for you so that a decision can then be made. You could:

- make the decision yourself based on the findings
- allow your team member to make the decision
- make the decision together, after discussing the findings with one another.

Whichever approach you decide to take with delegation, make sure that you are absolutely clear about this to your team beforehand. This avoids any misunderstandings and makes sure that everyone knows what is expected of them. Also, be very careful to avoid the common error of **micro-managing** your team once you have delegated a task to them. You simply have to trust them to get it done in the manner they find most suitable.

> **Key Term**
>
> **Micro-managing** – closely monitoring and controlling the work activities of others.

> **Checklist**
>
> The golden rules for effective delegation are:
>
> - delegate as much as you can to your team
> - trust them to get on with the tasks
> - be clear with them on your delegation rules
> - match tasks to team skills and preferences
> - do not keep the best tasks for yourself.

> **Activity** 10 minutes
>
> Look at the following list and think about how good your delegation skills are. List them and identify any areas where you are strong and any areas where you may have development needs. Write a short comment against each of the criteria so that you can show it to your assessor.
>
> - I let my team know clearly the level of delegation which I use.
> - I show my team that I trust them to get on with the work.
> - I consider individual skills and preferences when I am deciding which tasks to delegate to whom.
> - I do not keep the best tasks for myself.
> - I allow extra time for team members doing tasks for the first time.

Agreeing SMART objectives with team members

You are probably already familiar with SMART objectives, as they crop up in many of the units. SMART stands for:

- Specific – exactly what needs to be completed and to what standard (within 24 hours, within three rings, with no more than 5 per cent error rate)
- Measurable – including a number, such as 100 sales, 15 phone calls, 20 customer complaints resolved
- Achievable – objectives need to be achievable by the vast majority of staff, not just the top 5 per cent, so don't set goals that only your best salesman can ever hope to achieve

- Realistic – objectives must be firmly founded in reality
- Time-bound – have a time by when the objective must be completed (this is usually over a relatively short time frame and should always be within 12 months).

Agreeing SMART objectives with your team members breaks down the overall aims and mission of the team into individual, manageable work tasks, complete with all of the information they need to ensure they can achieve them.

Take a look at the following example of an objective for an events co-ordinator role in a marketing company:

Secure at least 500 attendees at the annual national telemarketing conference, which takes place on 30 November. This will be achieved by sending invitations to all registered members of the professional association by 30 June. The list of registered members is available from the administration department.

Look to see how this objective satisfies the SMART criteria:

Specific	– to secure attendees for the annual national marketing conference
Measurable	– 500 attendees is a measurable target
Achievable	– the list of registered members is available
Realistic	– inviting guests in June to attend a conference in November is realistic
Time-bound	– invitations need to be sent by 30 June.

Activity 30 minutes

Make a list of at least three objectives that you have, or could set for your team members. For each one, address the five elements of the SMART acronym to show how your team's objectives satisfy these criteria. If any of your objectives are not SMART, or could be improved, this is a good opportunity for you to develop them.

Agreeing standard of work required by your team

Standards of work refer to the precise performance details that are required in a given task. For example, a customer service agent position may have the following standards:

- answer the phone within three rings
- speak in a polite and friendly manner to all customers
- return calls to customers within 24 hours
- resolve all customer complaints or, where this is not possible, refer them to a line manager before the end of the business day.

Notice in the example above that some standards refer to precise numbers (answer the phone within three rings, return calls to customers within 24 hours), whereas others are more general. Standards with numbers attached to them are sometimes also referred to as targets, although they essentially mean the same thing.

Standards are very important for you to be aware of as a team leader because:

- they provide the guidelines by which people know when they have succeeded in completing a task correctly
- they ensure consistency in work output over time, no matter who is performing a given task
- they help staff to know exactly what is required of them
- they will provide the basis for your subsequent checking and monitoring of work.

Activity 10 minutes

List three examples of work tasks that your team needs to complete. For each one, state the standards that are applied to that task. Explain how team members are made aware of these standards. If there are no existing standards in place, devise new standards of your own and say how these will be communicated to staff.

Negotiating with team members

A key part of agreeing the standards of work required by your team will involve negotiating with them – either individually or as a group. Negotiations will most likely concern the allocation of tasks to be completed.

For example, what if one of your team members had a particular preference for one task over another? How would you go about securing their agreement and commitment to their work? One approach could be that you decide to switch task allocation around to other members to accommodate preferences. A note of caution here – remember to be seen to be equally fair and accommodating to all of your team if you do this. You cannot negotiate with one of your team and refuse to be accommodating to another.

Switching tasks may also be necessary due to the individual skill sets of the various team members. One person may be particularly good at closing sales, for example, but not so efficient at the administration side of things. Allocating tasks according to skill sets is an effective way of improving team efficiency, especially in the short term.

Portfolio Task 2 2 hours

Links to LO2: Assessment criteria 2.1, 2.2, 2.3

1. Explain the reasons why you think it is important to discuss team plans with your team. Write a short checklist, which could be used to train new team leaders, showing the essential 'dos and don'ts' relating to such team discussions.

2. Explain how you would go about agreeing work allocation with your team members. What issues might you come across during this process? Say how you would deal with these.

3. State the reasons why you should always agree SMART objectives with team members. Include examples of work-based SMART objectives which you have, or could have, set for your team to demonstrate how you might go about this process.

4. Give reasons to explain why it is essential to agree standards of work required by your team. If possible, show evidence of standards which you could use with your team.

Your assessment could take the form of a written narrative or a professional discussion with your assessor. It could also include the production of workplace evidence, work-based observations or the use of witness testimonies as appropriate.

Functional Skills

If you produce a written report as part of your assessment, this will allow you to practise your Functional English Writing skills.

Be able to manage team members to achieve team objectives

Management involves many different skills and activities, such as leading, delegating, co-ordinating, checking, monitoring and evaluating. In this section, you will investigate how you can apply your management skills to ensure that your team achieve their objectives and operate as a high-performing unit.

Supporting team members to achieve objectives

Providing support to your team members will be an ongoing responsibility for you as team leader. Supporting team members helps keep everybody on track and can bring a halt to any issues that are slowing down productivity.

Providing support involves:

- coaching
- providing timely one-to-one feedback
- conducting regular group update meetings.

Coaching

Coaching is the provision of support and guidance in order to help people to improve their performance. It is an informal process where a person with more experience helps new and inexperienced team members to become fully competent in their job. Coaching is an **on-the-job** process, which is based on good relationships and a caring approach.

As team leader, if you notice that one of your team is struggling with a certain aspect of their job, you should consider coaching as an effective approach for performance improvement and one that provides very quick results. The main drawback, however, is that it is an expensive and potentially time-consuming technique, especially as only one person is being coached at a time.

If you do not have the time to coach others yourself, you could consider nominating other, suitably experienced, members of your team as coaches to help newer members of staff. This can also be an excellent way of building good relationships among team members.

Providing timely one-to-one feedback

A key ingredient of providing effective support to your team involves giving **timely** one-to-one feedback. There are two reasons for this. First, your team members value their one-to-one time with you, as this is a good sounding board for discussing things they may not like to mention in front of the whole team. Second, keeping your team informed about their current progress on a regular basis is vital, so that they have up-to-date knowledge about how they are doing. Imagine if someone was regularly making errors in their work without knowing it for months. Issues such as this are easily and quickly fixed by having a one-to-one feedback schedule in place and sticking to it. These feedback sessions need not take long, nor should they be at all formal.

Conducting regular group update meetings

The key to supporting your whole team is providing them with regular information on the team's overall progress with a focus on collective, rather than individual, contributions.

A short, weekly meeting is often suitable for this purpose, although the frequency will depend on your particular company or industry.

Regular group update meetings are an excellent forum for recognising team achievements, reinforcing the team purpose and encouraging contributions and thoughts from each of your team. They are also a good source of identifying any issues and addressing them before they are allowed to continue and cause damage to the team's morale and its productivity.

Key Terms

On-the-job – taking place while doing the job, i.e. not away from the workplace, for instance in college.

Timely – something which occurs exactly when it is needed.

Activity 15 minutes

Do you employ coaching, either yourself, or via more experienced members of the team? If so, give examples of the types of coaching that occur in your team. If you do not currently use coaching, talk about whether and how it could be used as a skills development method in your team.

Activity 15 minutes

What types of useful information would you be able to obtain from your team by having regular meetings with them? Make a list of some of the key issues relevant to your team or department.

For example, in a retail store, you would be able to get instant feedback from the shop floor sales team on how well a new product was selling, which products your customers most prefer or which products were being regularly returned to the store.

Remember

Even if there are no issues to discuss and the feedback meeting is just to say that everything is fine, it is still important to keep feedback regular. It is also a good opportunity to recognise successes.

Regular team updates keep everyone informed on progress against targets.

Portfolio Task 3 ⏱ 30 minutes

Links to LO3: Assessment criterion 3.1

Explain why it is important to provide support to all team members in order to achieve team objectives. Give examples of the ways in which you either do, or could, provide ongoing support to your team. Include any relevant work documents to support your answer.

Your assessment could take the form of a written narrative or a professional discussion with your assessor. It could also include the production of workplace evidence, work-based observations or the use of witness testimonies, as appropriate.

Functional Skills

If you use computer-generated documents to provide evidence towards your assessment, this will allow you to practise your Functional ICT skills in developing, presenting and communicating information.

Be able to monitor and evaluate the performance of team members

Performance monitoring is an essential part of effective team management and you will need to have suitable procedures in place to provide you with reliable performance indicators for your team. In this section, you'll take a closer look at how to go about the process of effectively monitoring and evaluating the performance of your team.

Assessing work against agreed standards and objectives

Earlier in the unit, you looked at both objective and standard setting for your team. Together, these objectives and standards will provide the basis upon which you will carry out assessment of your team's work. Conducting your assessment based on objectives and standards ensures **objectivity**, fairness and consistency, so that each member of your team is treated equally when being assessed. It also ensures that the criteria on which you are basing the assessment are directly related to the key outcomes required for the team. In other words, these are the important **performance indicators** on which your team will be judged by senior management. Some examples of performance indicators might include:

- number of outbound calls made
- value of sales made
- number of complaints resolved.

There will be two aspects to your assessment – individual and whole team assessment. We'll begin by looking at individual assessment.

Individual team member assessment

Assessment can be done using a form such as the one on the next page, which is based on the objectives and standards for that role. The example below is for a customer service agent.

Forms such as this are useful ways of assessing individual team member's performance against objectives and standards. Results for all of the team can then be compiled to create a team assessment profile. This will give you a very clear, detailed picture of the strengths and weaknesses of your team.

> **Key Terms**
>
> **Objectivity** – based on facts, neutral and unbiased.
>
> **Performance indicators** – measures that show the achievement of objectives.

Team member assessment form

Team:	Customer service team
Team member name:	Leanne Evans
Role:	Customer service agent
Team Leader:	Brian Fieldings

Assessment rating key:

Unacceptable	Satisfactory	Good	Very good	Outstanding
1	2	3	4	5

Role objectives and standards	Rating
Speak politely and cheerfully to customers	5
Answer the phone within three rings	5
Answer ten calls per hour	3
Keep the call-waiting queue to no more than six	3
Resolve complaints received by phone from customers or, if not possible, refer them to a line manager the same day	5

Key strengths:	Always professional and polite in all dealings with customers. Very efficient at resolving customer complaints.
Areas for development:	Needs to attempt to get through more customer calls per hour. Needs to focus on reducing the call-waiting queue.
Comments:	Overall, a very good performance assessment with strong evidence of outstanding performance in some areas. Leanne has an excellent track record for successfully resolving all types of customer complaints. A focus on increasing the speed of dealing with each case would make for an overall outstanding assessment next time.

Figure D5.6 A team member assessment form.

Team-based assessment

Carrying out the assessment of the team's work will require a combination of:

- ongoing observation of performance
- data collection and analysis.

Activity 30 minutes

What do you think are the key areas on which your team should be assessed? Research any existing assessment documents for guidance or, if there is nothing currently available, put together a team assessment checklist of your own.

Ongoing observation of performance

Ongoing observation of your team's performance will give you immediate information on any gaps where standards are, for whatever reason, not being met. It is your responsibility to provide the necessary support to bring about improvements in such situations. These **performance gaps** can occur for many reasons and the support that you put in place needs to be sensitive to this.

For example, it may simply be that someone has not understood clearly what they were supposed to do. This is a straightforward issue to put right. It may be, however, that someone is having personal issues which are having an impact on their performance. In this type of situation, you would be wise to seek advice from your own line manager before trying to deal with it, especially if you are new to this type of situation. It may be appropriate in such cases to refer the matter to the human resources department within your organisation so that they can refer the employee for counselling or provide other supportive measures.

Key Term

Performance gap – a gap between the current and the required performance standards.

Data collection and analysis

Part of your ongoing monitoring and evaluation will require you to gather data on your team's work output. Depending on the nature of your team and the industry in which it operates, this may include collecting figures for things such as:

- sales made
- complaints resolved
- units produced
- services provided to customers
- commissions earned from sales made.

These figures give you a measurement of the actual work output of your team. You can look at the figures over time to see whether output is increasing or decreasing overall, identify any peaks or troughs in output and any seasonal, monthly, weekly or even daily variations. You can also further break down the figures to identify output per employee.

Activity 15 minutes

Think about what you would do if you encountered a performance gap in your team. Describe what you think is the correct way to deal with this situation.

This kind of analysis helps you to plan ahead for appropriate staffing levels, to avoid the problem of too few or too many staff on certain shifts. It also allows you to plan ahead for the ordering of the correct amount of materials and stock, as well as looking at ways of making the best use of time during quieter periods.

You will also need to collect figures for issues such as:

- usage of materials including wastage
- number of customer complaints
- number of product defects
- error rates
- production **downtime**.

By including issues such as these in your data analysis, you can identify areas where costs can be reduced or downtimes can be improved, to increase the overall productivity of your team.

Using graphs to analyse your figures

The best way to analyse your team's output figures is to put them into graphical format. You can easily do this using a program such as Excel® or other similar software. The longer the time period over which you can collect data, the more meaningful any analysis will be. For example, figures for output for one single month of the year will only provide you with a brief snapshot of performance. However, if you have the figures for the whole of the last twelve months, you will be able to gain very useful information which will help you plan for the following year.

Take a look at the following graph, which shows factory output over a 12-month period.

> **Key Term**
>
> **Downtime** – time lost at work due to machinery or system failure or personnel problems.

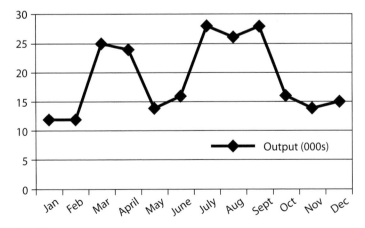

Figure D5.7 Factory output over one year.

If you look closely at the figures over the year, there are two main findings you can draw. The first thing to note is that there are two major peaks in output over the year. The first occurs in March to April and the second occurs in July to September. During these two peak periods, output is almost double that of the other months.

The second key finding is that, overall, you can see a general upward trend in output over the year. You could reasonably expect this general trend to continue in the following year.

You can produce similar graphs to show your team's performance figures for defect rates, complaints and any other aspect of team performance, which you need to monitor. This is also a very good method of identifying improvements against targets over a set period of time.

Identifying and monitoring conflict

Disagreements are inevitable among team members at times, especially when they are under pressure, or feel passionately about something. However, when such disagreements become a permanent feature of working life, or disrupt the ethos of the team, then this is where disagreement has descended into conflict and needs resolving.

Possible sources of conflict

Conflict can arise from many areas, but the following are often key triggers:

- personality clashes among team members
- power battles and overly competitive team members
- team members focused more on their individual goals than those of the team
- hidden agendas
- communication problems within the team
- unclear goals
- low morale among team members.

From your own experience as a team leader, you could probably add more issues to this list.

Monitoring conflict

It is essential for you to keep a close eye on the functioning of your team, including levels of harmony. You need to spot the difference between healthy debate and serious disagreements and conflict in the team. If left unresolved, conflict will ruin the effectiveness of the team and undo all of your hard work and team-building efforts.

Things to watch out for include the following:

- **Tasks** – are there particular tasks or processes that are the source of constant argument among the team? If so, you may need to evaluate your team's current processes and implement new working arrangements which eliminate this issue.
- **People** – are there any particular people who are the source of conflict or aggression? If this is the case, and personality clashes are the root cause of the problem, maybe a change of team membership could be the solution.
- **Behaviour** – is there evidence of bullying, harassment or any other inappropriate behaviour within the team? If so, you must address this immediately and decisively. You would be advised to speak to your human resources department in situations such as these.

Dealing with conflict

The specific way in which you handle a conflict situation will depend on its circumstances and its root cause. However, the following are some principles that are useful in most conflict handling situations.

1. Be assertive.
2. Get all of the facts from the affected parties before you decide on the solution.
3. Try to get agreement from opposing parties on the solution but if this is not possible, use your leadership position to take the decision and implement it quickly.
4. Act decisively.
5. Carefully monitor the situation afterwards to be sure that it has, in fact, been resolved.

Activity 15 minutes

What would you do if you encountered examples of conflict within your team? How do you think you would handle the situation? Find out what the specific guidelines are in your organisation for dealing with such issues. It is important for you to be aware of these to ensure you act in accordance with organisational guidelines if any such circumstances occur.

Ensuring the conflict has been resolved

It is part of the conflict-handling process to make certain that all issues have been resolved and that no **grievances** linger afterwards. Unresolved conflict can escalate into further aggression and even physical violence in the workplace, resulting in serious disciplinary action and even prosecution. This is reason enough to follow up on all such situations and to ensure that they have been dealt with satisfactorily.

Checklist

Remember, when dealing with conflict to:

- identify the problem by fact finding
- speak to everybody concerned
- listen to the issues
- decide on the most appropriate solution
- monitor the situation afterwards.

Key Term

Grievance – a cause for complaint, which can be the result of a wrongdoing or a hardship suffered.

Unit D5

Plan, allocate and monitor work of a team

Organisational policies for managing workplace conflict

Conflict can have an impact on other areas such as health and safety, discrimination, equality and diversity, as well as grievance and discipline, which are all specifically covered by employment legislation. Where an employee raises a grievance as a result of conflict, then the conflict has moved from an informal to a formal position and the organisation must then invoke its workplace policies and procedures for dealing with it.

ACAS recommends that, for this reason, organisations should put in place specific conflict-handling policies that are separate from the grievance and disciplinary procedure. They also recommend including **mediation** as a stage in the conflict-handling process. Mediation is carried out by an independent and impartial person, which could be a member of the organisation, such as a representative from the human resources department, or it could be carried out by an outside body. The aim of mediation is not to impose a solution, but instead to help the individuals or groups involved in the conflict to reach agreement on an acceptable solution.

Consulting with employees

Many organisations have established structures in place for consulting with employees on issues that are often the cause of conflict. These can include working groups, which are temporary groups set up on an ad hoc basis to look at a specific issue, and staff councils, which are permanent groups established to periodically review issues on an ongoing basis.

Dispute resolution procedures

Where conflict cannot be resolved through consulting with employees, organisations can turn to their dispute resolution procedures. These might include:

- written agreements between the organisation and its recognised trade union on the methods which will be used in resolving disputes
- approaching another third party, such as ACAS, to assist in the dispute resolution process.

Identifying causes for team members not meeting team objectives

There are a number of possible reasons why team members may fail to meet their objectives. For example, team members may be completely overloaded with work at a given point and feel unable to live up to the expectations made of them. They may have misunderstood their objectives, or they may have health or other personal issues which

---

Key Terms

ACAS – Advisory, Conciliation and Arbitration Service – a statutory, independent body that offers advice to employers and employees on many workplace matters including grievances and disputes.

Mediation – help from an independent third party in reaching agreement between opposing individuals or groups.

are having an impact on their performance. As team leader, it is your responsibility to identify the reasons for poor performance and to take steps to put them right, if this is possible.

Your first task, having identified an underperforming team member, is to speak to them about it. Point out the issue and see if they can help identify the reasons. They may well have a perfectly valid reason for the underperformance. For example, it could point to a lack of adequate training or a lack of direction. Perhaps the objectives which were set were too complicated or too demanding. Issues such as these are fairly easy to put right, with a little investigation on your part. Other issues, such as personal problems, may require the intervention of the human resources department, as they have expertise in this area and are probably better placed to provide the necessary help and support to the team member.

Portfolio Task 4 60 minutes

Links to LO4: Assessment criteria 4.1, 4.2, 4.3

1. Explain the reasons why it is important to assess team members' work against agreed standards and objectives. Give examples of the ways in which you either do, or could, go about this process as part of your job. Include any relevant work documents which provide evidence of your team assessment activities to support your answer.

2. Describe the steps you could take to identify and monitor conflict within your team. Explain why monitoring conflict within a team is so important. Discuss any work-based rules or guidelines for dealing with conflict situations that exist in your organisation.

3. Identify some of the main causes for team members not meeting team objectives and say how you would deal with each of these issues. If you have experienced your own team members failing to meet objectives, discuss these examples in your answer.

Your assessment could take the form of a written narrative or a professional discussion with your assessor. It could also include the production of workplace evidence, work-based observations or the use of witness testimonies, as appropriate.

Functional Skills

If you produce a written report as part of your assessment, this will allow you to practise your Functional English writing skills.

Be able to improve the performance of a team

In this section, you'll investigate various ways in which you can make your team more productive and effective and the benefits of this. You will look at methods of providing constructive feedback to aid performance as well as investigating how to implement performance improvement measures.

Identifying ways of improving team performance

Improving your team's performance has many benefits, both to the team and the business, including:

- improved efficiency
- increased morale among staff
- reduced waste
- more streamlined processes
- staff are less likely to leave the team.

But however successful your team may currently be, there is always room for improvement. Having a clear focus on certain factors will reap enormous benefits to your team's performance. You could:

- find ways of increasing collaboration
- focus on collective team spirit rather than individual achievement
- set clear and challenging goals and objectives
- encourage participation in decision making
- aim to get 100 per cent agreement to goals and processes
- nurture a positive team culture.

All of these factors aim to increase team motivation as the basis for better performance.

Motivating your team

Motivation is what makes us want to do something. So, how do you make your team want to do something? There are various theories on the subject. We will take a brief look at some of these so that you have an appreciation of the thinking behind certain systems of job design, rewards and bonuses adopted by organisations.

Taylorism

Frederick Winslow Taylor put forward the theory of **scientific management**. This argued that workers were naturally lazy, unwilling to work hard and were mainly motivated by money. From this, he developed a system of paying workers based on their output. This was called a **piece rate** system where, the harder a worker worked and the more they produced, the greater the pay they received. This type of

Key Terms

Scientific management – a theory of management that used science to improve work efficiency.

Piece rate – a payment system where workers are paid per unit produced or per sale made.

thinking is behind many sales pay structures, where salespeople are paid either a basic wage plus a **commission** on each sale made or even paid commission only.

Mayo's Hawthorne studies

Elton Mayo studied workers in a factory in Chicago. He changed various aspects of their working conditions to see what effect this had on their productivity. He found that workers were motivated by:

● working in groups rather than working alone
● greater involvement from management
● better communication with management.

Mayo's work was hugely influential and began the development of personnel or human resources departments in organisations, which had the aim of looking after the interests of employees.

Maslow's hierarchy of needs

Abraham Maslow put forward a theory of motivation with a focus on workers' different levels of need. He argued that there was a hierarchy of five different levels of needs with basic survival at the bottom and **self-actualisation** at the top. He argued that the needs at the bottom of the hierarchy had to be fulfilled before moving up to the next level.

Key Terms

Commission – a monetary reward, often a set percentage of the value involved, paid to an agent in a commercial transaction.

Self-actualisation – achieving your highest career potential.

Activity 15 minutes

To what extent do you think that Mayo's theory of motivation has been adopted by your own organisation? How much are group working, involvement and communication used as motivators by management? Decide whether you think motivation could be improved by increasing the use of these methods and give examples to support your opinion.

Unit D5

Plan, allocate and monitor work of a team

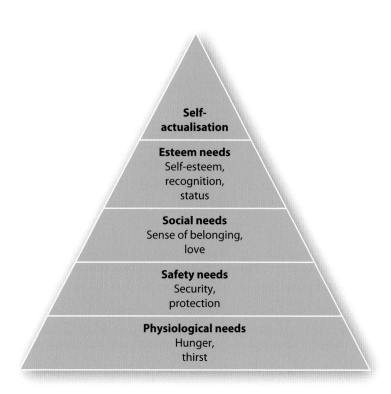

Figure D5.8 Maslow's hierarchy of needs.

So, a worker who was not earning enough money to feed his family and therefore not yet having his basic need for survival satisfied, would hardly be expected to be concerned with matters such as status, recognition and self-esteem. Maslow's theory argues that, as workers progress up each level of the hierarchy their focus moves away from the most basic and onto the achievement of increasingly prestigious aims.

Activity 15 minutes

Apply Maslow's theory to your own organisation. For each of the five levels of need that Maslow identified, think of a way in which your organisation tries to satisfy this need. Use a table like the one below to record your thoughts. Some suggestions are included under the table to help you. The first example has been completed for you.

Need	How my organisation tries to satisfy this need
Physiological needs – hunger, thirst	A basic wage
Safety needs – security, protection	
Social needs – sense of belonging, love	
Esteem needs – self-esteem, recognition, status	
Self-actualisation	

Suggestions: job security, a team culture, benefits such as company cars and bonuses, opportunities for career advancement and self-development.

Herzberg's dual factor theory of motivation

Frederick Herzberg put forward a theory of motivation consisting of two elements:

- motivators – aspects of the job itself, such as opportunities for interesting work, responsibility and promotion, which made people want to work harder
- hygiene factors – not directly concerned with the job itself but with issues surrounding the job, such as pay and safety conditions at work.

Herzberg argued that if hygiene factors were not provided, dissatisfaction would arise. However, just providing these basic elements did not bring about motivation, it just removed dissatisfaction.

Herzberg thought that organisations should therefore focus on designing jobs in ways to bring about motivation at work including job enlargement (providing a variety of tasks for interest), job enrichment (providing increasingly challenging tasks for a sense of achievement) and empowerment (increased responsibility for decision making).

Case Study

Motivation in action

Mel is team leader of the telemarketing team in an employment law consultancy firm. He has been in his job for almost three months and is taking stock of the performance figures for his team of 30 outbound telesales operators for that period. He can't help but feel a little frustrated at the overall picture. There is no immediate disaster but the figures tell a picture of merely average performance. Mel knows from his considerable experience in a similar role that his new team could be doing so much better. He starts to make notes of some of the issues.

There is high turnover of staff in his team. The telesales operators earn a low basic salary and a meagre bonus scheme for achievement of targets, which is seldom paid out to anyone. Commitment is low and there is not much sense of team spirit.

Mel decides to make some changes. He implements a new and improved bonus scheme which he feels would be achievable by the majority of his team. He also decides that each new sale made by a telesales operator should be recognised. He installs a bell in the telesales department, which is to be rung by team members on completion of a new sales deal. The team is to give a round of applause to celebrate each new deal. In addition, Mel starts a weekly team progress meeting where he shows his team presentation slides detailing the sales made each week, as well as sales by individual operator. He awards the title of 'salesperson of the week' to the highest achieving team member.

Within one month of the changes, the team is performing highly, having developed a healthy sense of competitive spirit. They eagerly await their weekly target updates and are regularly rewarded with significant bonuses when they met or exceeded their sales quotas.

Questions

1. What were the key changes that Mel implemented to improve performance in his team?

2. What do you think was the main effect of Mel showing sales achieved per employee in his weekly meetings?

3. How do you think Mel's changes relate to:

   a) Taylor's scientific theory of management?

   b) Mayo's theory of motivation?

Write one or two sentences to relate Mel's changes to each theory.

Providing constructive feedback to improve performance

Constructive feedback is designed to focus on positives and on producing improvements. It is intended to be helpful and not to be personally critical in nature. Constructive feedback can nevertheless be used to discuss both good and bad aspects of performance.

The key to effective constructive feedback lies in its delivery. Negative aspects of feedback are conveyed in a careful and non-offensive way, so that the focus is clearly on how to bring about any necessary improvements and on what help can be given to achieve this. With constructive feedback the performance may be criticised, but never the person. The following are examples of how negative aspects of performance can be dealt with in a constructive way.

'I've noticed that you seem to be having a little trouble getting to grips with the new payroll system. Perhaps some further training would be helpful for you. I can speak to human resources to sort this out for you. How would you feel about that?'

'Your paperwork is sometimes a little late in being completed. Perhaps it would be a good idea to set aside the last hour of each day and use this to complete your forms. Do you think this would be helpful to you?'

The constructive feedback process

The usual process for constructive feedback is as follows:

- begin with a positive area by congratulating an achievement
- mention a less positive area of performance and offer help and support to bring about the required improvements
- end on a positive note, maybe by summarising an overall good performance or by mentioning some positive feedback received from a colleague, manager or customer.

This process is sometimes referred to as a feedback sandwich, or a caring sandwich.

Figure D5.9 Feedback sandwich.

Why do you think it is important to begin and end on a positive note when providing constructive feedback?

Activity   15 minutes

List three performance issues you think you may potentially have to deal with when providing feedback to your team members. For each one, practise the wording you could use in order to raise the issue with them in a constructive way, focused on helping them to improve.

Implementing team performance improvement measures

Team performance improvement measures can be concerned with many different aspects of the team's work including:

- production output
- error reductions
- cost savings and reduction in waste
- team absence and punctuality
- quality improvements to both goods and services.

For example, suppose that you are going to implement a performance improvement measure to increase the quality of your customer service so that 99 per cent of all calls are correctly dealt with within 24 hours.

The following shows one approach to implementing this measure.

1. Hold a team meeting to announce the measure.
2. Get commitment from everyone involved – this could include providing **incentives** such as bonuses for achieving the new targets.
3. Set clear targets for each individual, along with time limits for reaching them.
4. Arrange any training needed by team members.
5. Examine the performance figures as soon as they are available to you and monitor performance improvements against target.
6. Keep the team regularly updated on their progress against targets and make sure you reward achievements.

> **Key Term**
>
> **Incentives** – any items (monetary or otherwise) that motivate a particular action.

Portfolio Task 5   60 minutes

Links to LO5: Assessment criteria 5.1, 5.2, 5.3

1. Identify some of the different ways in which you could go about improving team performance. Explain which specific aspects of team performance would be improved using these methods and the benefits this would bring.

2. Give examples of ways in which you could provide constructive feedback to team members to improve their performance.

3. Describe how you would go about implementing identified ways of improving team performance.

Your assessment could take the form of a written narrative or a professional discussion with your assessor. It could also include the production of workplace evidence, work-based observations or the use of witness testimonies, as appropriate.

> **Functional Skills**
>
> If you take part in a professional discussion with your assessor, this will allow you to practise your Functional English Speaking and Listening skills.

Team talk

Rob's story

My name is Rob Joynson, I'm 26 years old and have been a team leader at Ashley Manufacturing Ltd for nearly two months. I've inherited an existing team of manufacturing operatives and am beginning to worry about their performance. The team has not hit one of its targets since I arrived and morale seems incredibly low. The operatives always seem to be arguing among themselves and nobody takes a pride in their work. Last week, we were meant to have 1,000 pallets of products completed and shipped to a major client in Europe. However, the quality of the finished products was so bad that many pallets had to be recalled and replaced, all of which delayed the order being shipped. This also increased the costs of the project significantly.

I really need to get to the bottom of the problems with my new team before their underperformance starts to reflect badly on me. I am on six months' probation in this position and I need to turn this team around before the end of my probationary period. The trouble is, I don't know where to start.

Top tips

Taking over an existing team, with all of its politics, personalities and legacy issues, can be a daunting experience. In order to begin managing these various factors to mould your team into a high-performing one, you need to assert your role as the new team leader. Talk to the team members, set the ground rules for processes and decision-making, and open up two-way communications. The sooner you get your team working effectively together, the sooner you will have a productive team. Remember, enthusiasm breeds enthusiasm (and vice versa!) so the more you exude positivity, the more it will spread among the team. Set clear roles, objectives and deadlines. Hold regular meetings to measure improvements and have a focus always on celebrating successes with recognition, rewards and praise.

Ask the expert	
Q	I have recently begun a new team leader role but have quickly discovered that my team are not performing well. I do not know how to go about bringing them back on track.
A	You need to implement some team-building and performance-improvement strategies to refocus the team and inject a fresh positive approach. However, you cannot do this until you have the facts on the root cause of the problems. Start by getting the team together for a meeting to ask for their opinions on the problems currently being experienced. You may be surprised by what you find out! Set new performance goals and objectives for your team and make sure team members input into the process and feel a sense of ownership of it. Set regular team meetings for the next three months so that you can keep a close eye on target achievement as well as morale. Take every opportunity to reward achievement and focus on positives.

What your assessor is looking for

In order to prepare for and to succeed in completing this unit, your assessor will require you to be able to demonstrate competence in:

- planning work for a team
- allocating work across a team
- managing team members to achieve team objectives
- monitoring and evaluating the performance of team members
- improving the performance of a team.

You will demonstrate your skills, knowledge and competence through the learning outcomes in this unit. Evidence generated in this unit will also cross-reference to the other units in this qualification.

Please bear in mind that there are significant cross-referencing opportunities throughout this qualification and you may have already generated some relevant work to meet certain criteria in this unit. Your assessor will provide you with the exact requirements to meet the standards of this unit. However, as a guide, it is likely that for this unit you will need to be assessed through:

- one observation of relevant workplace activities to cover the whole unit
- one witness testimony

- a written narrative, reflective account or professional discussion
- any relevant work products to be produced as evidence.

The work products for this unit could include:

- your team's objectives or targets
- your team's work plans, rotas or schedules
- assessments which you have made of your team members' work against agreed standards
- examples of feedback you have given to team members on their performance.

Your assessor will guide you through the assessment process as detailed in the candidate logbook. The detailed assessment criteria are shown in the logbook and by working through these questions, combined with providing the relevant evidence, you will meet the learning outcomes required to complete this unit.

Task and page reference	Assessment criteria
1 (page 94)	1.1, 1.2
2 (page 101)	2.1, 2.2, 2.3
3 (page 103)	3.1
4 (page 111)	4.1, 4.2, 4.3
5 (page 117)	5.1, 5.2, 5.3

Unit B5 Set objectives and provide support for team members

This unit will assist you in developing your skills and knowledge to become a more effective team leader. The unit explains the principles and benefits of improving your team's performance and explores the value of effective communication in your team.

By empowering, supporting and valuing your team, you will be able to motivate and encourage your team members to meet their own work objectives, in turn meeting the overall objectives of the organisation.

The unit will explore different leadership styles and various team behaviours. There is also practical guidance to assist you in managing your team effectively.

What you will learn:

- Be able to communicate a team's purpose and objectives to the team members
- Be able to develop a plan with team members showing how team objectives will be met
- Be able to support team members identifying opportunities and providing support
- Be able to monitor and evaluate progress and recognise individual and team achievement

Links to the Technical Certificate

If you are completing your NVQ as part of an Apprenticeship Framework, you will find the following topics are also covered in your Technical Certificate:

- Principles of team leading
- Developing working relationships with colleagues
- Coaching skills
- Getting results from your team
- Decision making
- Knowledge management in team leading

Be able to communicate a team's purpose and objectives to the team members

In this section we will look at the purpose of team working, how to communicate with your team members and how to set SMART objectives for your team.

Describe the purpose of a team

There are various definitions of what a team is. For instance:

A team is a number of people with complementary skills who are committed to working towards a common purpose, meeting performance goals and are accountable for their actions.

A key thing here is that a team will have a purpose. In a business environment, that purpose will link to what the organisation wants to achieve. Organisations set out their aims in their business plans, goals and objectives. They may also produce a mission statement, which will describe in a few words what they want to achieve. From this, objectives will be set and **strategies** employed to achieve their aims. Within the organisation, teams of people will all work towards achieving individual objectives that feed into the overall mission of the organisation.

Team member behaviours

Members of a team have two distinct roles. First they have to achieve the goals of the team and second they have to maintain an effective working relationship with each other. These two elements are interlinked because if the goals of the team are not met, then it will inevitably put pressure on the day-to-day working relationships within the team.

Through his extensive research in the late 1970s Dr Meredith Belbin devised a world-recognised model for team preferences, which can help us to understand why team members can behave in certain ways. He identified the following specific roles as shown in Figure B5.1. In most teams, individual team members can take on several characteristics. Belbin argued that 'although one person can't be perfect, a team can be'.

The essential characteristics of each team member are:

- the completer-finisher ensures that nothing is overlooked and provides thorough attention to detail
- the specialist will be able to support the team on specialist issues and may sometimes work within a separate team
- the co-ordinator controls the activities of the team and is able to get the team working together as a complete unit
- the team worker promotes team spirit and encourages other team members through their supportive approach

---

Key Term

Strategies – Tools and processes used to achieve objectives.

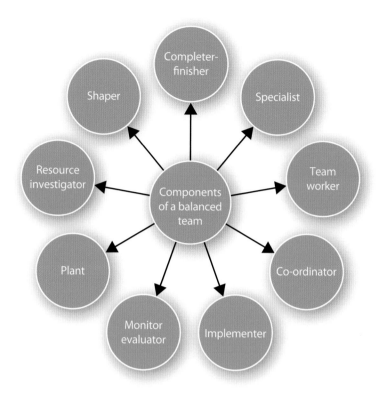

Figure B5.1 Belbin's team roles.

- the implementer translates ideas into plans and breaks things down into tasks and actions
- the monitor/evaluator is a critical thinker, who is objective in their approach and can analyse ideas and suggestions
- the plant concentrates on the big issues and can be a source of innovation and ideas for the team; can be single minded
- the resource investigator harnesses resources for the team and networks with other teams and organisations
- the shaper makes things happen by injecting energy and strong direction.

As you can imagine, not all teams will have all of these types of people and some team members will have more than one attribute. However, these characteristics are all useful elements for a team to become fully effective.

There have been more recent studies by other experts who suggest similar personality types within teams as:

- action person
- caring person
- detail person
- co-ordinator
- creative thinker.

Unit B5 Set objectives and provide support for team members

Again, some team members will have some or all of these attributes and don't forget – you are a member of the team as well.

For a team to be effective the team leader should recognise how each person's individual skills and abilities can help the team achieve its day-to-day objectives.

Portfolio Task 1 — 60 minutes

Links to LO1: Assessment criterion 1.1

Describe the purpose of a team. Consider your own team and check to see if you have any specific gaps, team-member types or characteristics and then try to think of a solution to resolve this. For example, if you don't think that you have many people in your team who think creatively, what can you do to improve this? Maybe you could have a brief creative session in your team meeting from time to time and ask the team to come up with any potential new and innovative ways of working.

Set SMART team objectives with its members

The organisation will set SMART objectives and these are likely to be shown in the mission statement and the overall objectives for the organisation.

Different departments or divisions within the organisation will also set SMART objectives that feed into the overall objectives of the organisation. Different teams or team leaders will set SMART objectives or targets that feed into the departmental objectives.

Individual members of staff will also set targets in conjunction with their team leader to feed into their team's targets or objectives. Figure B5.2 shows how this would work in an organisation.

You and your team may not always realise it, but what you do on a day-to-day basis will link directly into the organisation's overall mission and objectives. If what you are doing does not link into the mission, why are you doing it?

Mission statement and overall objectives

↓

Objectives by section or department

↓

Action plans and targets by team

↓

Action plans and targets by individual staff

Figure B5.2 Linking organisational goals to individual targets.

Portfolio Task 2 — 60 minutes

Links to LO1: Assessment criteria 1.2, 1.3

Describe how you set SMART objectives for your team and explain how you communicate the team's purpose and objectives to the team members.

Your assessment could take the form of a written narrative or a professional discussion with your assessor. It could also include the production of workplace evidence.

Communicate the team's purpose and objectives to its members

Unit E11 covers communication in greater detail, where the acronym KISS is explored – 'keep it short and simple' – which is an essential requirement in a business environment, both in terms of verbal and written communication. The basic principle of this approach is to:

- use fewer words
- use shorter words
- use pictures, graphs or charts where possible.

This approach can be linked to more general principles to ensure that you communicate effectively. Remember that you should:

- use the right language to fit the occasion
- use the right medium – verbal communication, emails or letters
- get the attention of the people that you are communicating with
- get your message across as you want it to be received – reduce the potential for misinterpretation or confusion
- maintain eye contact and observe the body language
- allow people to respond
- listen to what is being said to you
- be prepared to discuss issues
- don't allow team members to dominate team meetings and convince other team members that their opinion is right.

You may need to admit defeat where you are out-voted by your team. Collective decisions that the whole team agrees with are more powerful and more likely to work than decisions imposed by the team leader.

Team leadership and communication

You may have heard the statement that a 'team leader is only as good as their team'. There is some truth in this but in some ways the opposite is also true. A team is only as good as its leader – you. The key to success for the team leader is to shape and manage their team to ensure that the relevant **outcomes** are achieved and also to personally demonstrate behaviours that their team needs to aspire to attain. In simple terms, the team leader must:

- make sure that their team achieves its objectives
- demonstrate professional and supportive behaviours at all times
- lead by example
- communicate clearly.

> **Key Term**
>
> **Outcomes** – the things that have been achieved.

To be an effective team leader, you will need to gain the trust and support of your team. The table below shows some practical ways on how you can do this. It also includes suggestions for evidence, which you can include in your portfolio.

Behaviour	How to achieve this outcome	Possible evidence sources
You create a common sense of purpose	Involve the team in agreeing the goals and objectives	Team objectives or appraisal targets
You clearly agree what is expected and hold people to account	Agree objectives with each team member and manage their performance	Appraisal targets or performance management information
You seek to understand people's needs and motivations	Be sensitive to the needs and expectations of the team	Notes from discussions or personal statements
You make time available to support others	Put time aside to support the team both as a group and individually	Notes from one-to-one meetings or training events
You show respect for the views and actions of others	Involve the team in the decision-making processes	Team meeting minutes or 'away day' events
You develop an atmosphere of professionalism and mutual support	Be professional at all times and encourage team members to perform well and enjoy their job	Witness testimony or achievement of objectives
You show integrity, fairness and consistency in decision making	Foster team spirit and appropriate ethics and values in the team	Team meeting minutes, witness testimony or relevant procedures

Table B5.1 How to gain the trust and support of your team.

The benefits of effective communication

Collaboration means working together, and the key to effective collaboration is effective communication. By working together, team members can share their values and the vision of the organisation, develop a team spirit and absorb the information that they need to work well with each other. Trust, mutual respect and honesty between all team members is vital.

As discussed in Unit E11, the principles of effective communication are to:

- make sure that it is a two-way process
- provide information that is clear, concise and in the right level of detail for the recipient
- ensure that everyone is clear about what is being communicated
- listen carefully to what is being said
- keep people informed on a regular basis, both in relation to general issues and their individual performance.

As a result of applying these principles, you and your team should reap the benefits and be able to work more productively. By building a positive working relationship with your team, you should see:

- less resistance to change
- improved commitment, co-operation and enjoyment of their roles

- increased output, productivity and efficiency
- improved supportive working within the team and across other team boundaries.

Listening skills

Listening is an often overlooked and underrated communication skill. How good of a listener are you? Have a go at the following activity.

Activity 30 minutes

It is easy to hear someone speaking to you, but are you actually listening and understanding what they are saying to you? Complete the following short questionnaire by ticking the appropriate boxes.

When you are communicating with someone, do you:

Your behaviour	Always	Sometimes	Never
Finish off their sentences			
Think that you know the point that the other person is trying to make before they have finished			
Think about what you are going to say next while the other person is still talking			
Jump to conclusions before the person has finished talking			
Interrupt people while they are talking			
Get frustrated and wish that they would get to the point more quickly			

If you find that you have ticked the always and occasionally boxes, then try to identify these issues and set out how you can improve in these areas. If you have a personal development plan, it would be a good idea to include these issues and agree a timescale to complete them in. Set yourself a SMART objective to resolve each issue.

Portfolio Task 3 30 minutes

Links to LO1: Assessment criterion 1.3

Collect examples of all of the ways that you communicate with your team. For example, formal methods, such as appraisals or target setting and more day-to-day methods, such as emails and team-meeting minutes. These will provide useful evidence for your portfolio.

PLTS

By undertaking this task and collecting examples of how you communicate with your team, you will be demonstrating how you communicate effectively with your team and how you manage performance by setting clear goals and objectives (TW; CT; SM).

Be able to develop a plan with team members showing how team objectives will be met

In this section you will learn how to discuss how team objectives will be met and how to ensure team members participate in the planning process and think creatively. This will help you develop plans to meet team objectives and set SMART personal work objectives with team members.

Discuss with team members how team objectives will be met

Once you know the targets for your team as a whole, the next stage is to plan activities in conjunction with your team members. This involves team members agreeing targets and objectives with you and may be done as part of the annual appraisal meeting. If your company does not have an appraisal system in place, you may agree objectives on a less formal basis.

Once the individual targets are agreed, then specific activities can be planned and the resources put in place. Resources include time, manpower and equipment or facilities to do the job.

As the tasks are undertaken, it will be up to you to monitor and review the performance of individuals and the team as a whole. This can be explained by Figure B5.3 and the following worked example.

Imagine that you work for a telecom company and the company's mission is to be the 'number one telecommunications provider in the UK', with their main objective for the forthcoming year being to increase sales by 5 per cent. Other objectives include updating the existing customer database by the end of the year.

You manage part of the customer service team and some of your responsibilities involve updating the customer database for your geographical region. You have been assigned some objectives from your manager, one of which relates to updating the customer database. The objectives are:

- Overall organisational objective 'To update the customer database by 31 December 2012'.
- As the team leader for the Eastern region of sales, your objective, set by your manager, is to complete the work required to update the database for your region by 30 November 2012.

You now need to involve your team in the process and set sub-objectives for your team members to achieve which should link into your objective.

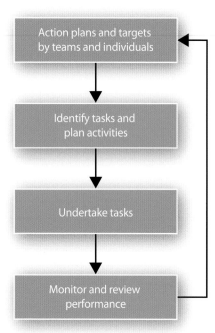

Figure B5.3 Managing team and individual targets and performance.

So, how do you do it?

1. Work with your team and set sub-objectives for some or all of your team members. You may need to formulate a mini project plan to set out what you need to achieve by some agreed dates (milestones).

2. Meet with the team to explain what has to be done. This could be the whole team together, smaller groups or on a 'one-to-one' basis as appropriate.

3. Once you have agreed a plan with your team then you need to manage and monitor their performance to ensure that they are making good progress and can meet your agreed deadline.

Be aware that you are not working in isolation. In this example, other teams from different regions will also be working on their customer databases to ensure that the whole customer database is updated by the agreed date.

This is just one example and it is likely that you will have several objectives to achieve both as an individual and as a team as a whole, so careful planning is needed to ensure that you keep track of what you and your team are achieving.

PLTS

By demonstrating that your team members actively participate in the planning process by setting targets and agreeing objectives, you will be showing how you allow your team to discuss how their objectives will be met. Try to gather any relevant evidence, for example, appraisal documents or minutes of team meetings where you discuss these issues. This will provide useful evidence for your portfolio (TW; IE; SM).

Portfolio Task 4 60 minutes

Links to LO2: Assessment criteria 2.1, 2.2
Describe how you set objectives with your team members and explain how you ensure that team members participate in the planning process.

Ensure team members participate in the planning process and think creatively

In the 1960s and 1970s, Bruce Tuckman developed the team development cycle, which is still widely regarded as the definitive approach in helping us understand the different stages that teams can go through during their development. Most teams are likely to be part way through a team cycle at any given time. Tuckman suggests specific actions and strategies to adopt at the various stages. As a team leader or manager, you first need to recognise which stage your team is at and then adopt the relevant strategies for that phase. Always remember that a team is not necessarily at the performing phase just because it has been together for many years. Also bear in mind that teams who may be performing today, could, because of factors such as a lack of resources or staffing changes, move back to the forming stage at any time. Understanding the stage your team is at and managing them accordingly will help you to encourage their creativity and achieve full participation potential.

The following table shows the various stages, some of the team characteristics that you may experience and some ideas for how you can manage these stages effectively.

Stage	Team member behavioural characteristics	Your role as team leader
Forming	Polite, guarded, watchful, low level of involvement and participation, team members don't know each other	Establish clear objectives; build a supportive and open environment. Clarify the roles and expectations and get team members interacting with each other.
Storming	Difficulties can emerge, some team members opt out, resistance to change, sub-groups develop, different opinions voiced openly	Affirm your role, provide positive feedback, reiterate roles, responsibilities and objectives and manage conflict constructively.
Norming	Acceptance of roles and responsibilities, open exchange of information and opinions, active listening, working together and more co-operation	Encourage communication, tackle any issues, accept feedback, encourage ideas, creativity and innovation.
Performing	Team members are mutually supportive, high performance and increased productivity, give and receive feedback, openness, strong team identity, proud, feel secure and valued; team operating at maximum effectiveness	Encourage flexibility, delegate to and coach team members, leave the team 'to it' – empower and delegate.

Table B5.2 How a team leader may manage different behavioural characteristics.

The benefits of creativity and innovation

The benefits of encouraging and recognising creativity and innovation within a team is that they create an environment where people look at their role and the organisation differently and explore all aspects, not just accepting the status quo as the most appropriate solution.

You can encourage creativity and innovation by organising group sessions. If you get everyone involved in the process, it should ensure that the whole team is on board and no one feels intimidated or uncomfortable.

Activity 30 minutes

Consider your own team and check what stage you are at. Can you develop some of the strategies and actions to maximise your team's performance?

PLTS

By completing this questionnaire, you will be identifying how effective your team is. As you work through each question, you will challenge each element in order to establish where any possible weaknesses may be. By undertaking this task, you will have the opportunity to proactively manage your team's effectiveness (TW; IE; SM).

Creativity in a team could potentially improve efficiency and productivity.

If you hold these types of team events say once or twice a year, your colleagues can come up with new ideas, suggestions and creative ways of working that could potentially improve efficiency and productivity. All ideas should be considered and explored further where appropriate.

As your team develops into the performing stage then innovation and creativity should be more prevalent. A brief checklist on how to encourage creativity and innovation is shown below:

- Your team members will only respond to requests for new ideas and initiatives as long as they are appreciated and never mocked.
- New ideas can involve risk taking and you need to be ready to take them on where appropriate.
- Allow team members time to think about creative ideas, for example, facilitate team events.
- Set up groups to explore ideas in greater detail.
- If an idea is approved and implemented always make sure that you thank your team member and put in place any new resources, training or support required to undertake the new or revised process.

Innovative ways of working should also be encouraged during normal day-to-day operations. Ask your colleagues if they can think of any ways to improve their job.

Portfolio Task 5 30 minutes

Links to LO2: Assessment criteria 2.2, 2.4

Irrespective of the stage of development your team is currently at, how effective do you think that your team is? Complete the following questionnaire by scoring your team from 1 to 5 against each criterion and see if it identifies any issues for you to resolve.

How effective is my team?	Not effective				Very effective
	1	2	3	4	5
The team understands its objectives and targets					
Each team member understands their role and responsibilities					
A pleasant working atmosphere is in place and feedback is given and received by all					
Team members communicate well with each other					
Team members resolve disagreements					
All team members participate in discussions and the decision-making process					

Follow-up: If you have scored 2 or below in answer to any of the questions, it would be a good idea to address these issues.

Develop plans to meet team objectives

As we have explored, teams need a common purpose to ensure that they can link into the overall objectives of the organisation. Individual team members need to be committed to their own job, but at the same time be aware and understand how what they do ensures their team meets their objective, which in turn ensures the whole organisation meets its objectives.

Most organisations have an agreed working culture: this means 'this is how we do things round here'. It is also likely that there will be some **performance standards** in place, which you and your team will need to meet. These may include some specific targets and behaviours that you need to achieve on an on-going basis and also may include some general standards. For example, some general performance standards that all staff would need to meet may be:

- dealing with customers and colleagues quickly, courteously and efficiently
- treating everyone equally and fairly.

Some specific standards that you may set for your team may be on an individual basis, dependent on their current level of knowledge and ability, and these are likely to be linked to their targets and objectives. Your organisation may also have some specific performance targets, for example, to respond to all customer queries within five working days.

It is worth remembering that not all standards will be written down or communicated overtly and there may often be an assumption that all staff will just behave to this standard anyway.

One of the key elements for improving performance is to make sure that you and your team members are **self-motivated** and enjoy your jobs. This will improve your **job satisfaction** and should get you thinking about how you might be able to improve your job role and associated processes to become more efficient.

You and your team members should be accountable for your job and take responsibility for your actions. Adopting this frame of mind enables all team members to plan their work and to start to achieve their objectives.

How to set objectives and provide support

Take a look at these issues and challenge yourself and your team. If you think that you can improve in some of these areas, then plan to resolve the issues.

- Ensure achievement of personal and team objectives – All team members should know what is required of them and you should know how to manage this, through regular reviews, one-to-one meetings or team meetings. You also need to know what to do when things go wrong and staff are not meeting the agreed standards of performance or achieving their targets and objectives.

> **Key Terms**
>
> **Job satisfaction** – enjoying your job on a day-to-day basis.
>
> **Performance standards** – minimum performance standards which need to be met by you and your team.
>
> **Self-motivated** – in work terms, coming into work each day in a positive frame of mind and you are able to complete the tasks by taking ownership of your job.

- How effective is your team? – Do team members trust each other? Are you all open and honest with each other? Do team members support each other? Have any recent changes affected performance?

- Do you have the right resources in place? – You may be encountering problems if you do not have the correct resources in place – time, manpower, equipment, systems, etc. You may need to resolve some issues or investigate if any new technology can be used to improve the efficiency of your team.

- Knowledge and skills – Are your team competent in their roles? Do they have adequate skills and knowledge? Do they need further additional support? Are there any skills that the whole team lacks? Is your team ready for any future challenges?

Review the issues and ask yourself:

- Did we achieve our targets and objectives and if so how well did we do?

- What would we do differently next time?

- If we failed to achieve our targets and objectives, what went wrong?

- Did we spend enough time planning and securing the resources to achieve our objectives?

- Did we plan the activities well and did I manage performance effectively?

Always try to plan effectively. If you plan well, there is less chance of things going wrong.

Set SMART personal work objectives with team members

As part of your job, you will plan your own work and the team's work. For regular and routine jobs, you might prepare a 'to do' list of things that you need to do that day or that week. By prioritising your tasks you will be able to plan your work more effectively. However, as a team leader you will also need to plan resources in more detail for the whole team by identifying the work to be undertaken and then planning how you are going to achieve this with the resources that you have in place.

Use the following checklist to help you plan your tasks effectively.

- Write down all of your team objectives and targets and when you need to achieve them by.

- Highlight any specific deadline dates and try to achieve them by, for example, one week ahead of the deadline.

- For larger jobs, break down the tasks into more manageable elements or formulate a small project team.

- Classify your tasks by deciding how important they are and when they need to be completed by. You can use a system to help prioritise them.

- Identify at the outset any targets that may be difficult to achieve and try to negotiate extra time or resources if required.
- Manage your objectives, resources and the performance of your team through regular consultation and communication with team members, including team meetings and one-to-one meetings.
- Don't worry if a new urgent objective comes up, just slot it into your list and plan the resources required to complete it.
- Think about what you *must* do, *should* do and *could* do.
- Always review your plan at the end of each week.

The planning function of management is an important phase as if you make mistakes by not having adequate resources in place you will not achieve your objectives.

To ensure that you plan your resources effectively, you need to:

- focus on the organisation's mission and objectives
- be clear on your own and your team's objectives and targets and agree these objectives with your team
- identify the resources that you have in place – manpower, equipment, budgets etc.
- schedule your activities and prioritise the objectives
- agree processes and procedures to undertake the activities
- manage performance and budgets.

As the tasks are undertaken, it will be up to you to monitor and review the performance of individuals and the team as a whole. It is likely that meetings with various individuals and groups of people will take place at every stage of the performance management process.

PLTS

By pulling together any relevant workplace evidence, you will be showing how you interact with your team, allow your team to think creatively and independently (TW; IE).

Functional Skills

You may be able to use this personal statement as evidence towards Functional Skills English Levels 1 and 2: Reading and Writing. You need to demonstrate that you have understood the process involved in how you set and agree SMART objectives.

Portfolio Task 6 60 minutes

Links to LO2: Assessment criteria 2.2, 2.3, 2.4

Describe how you encourage your team to think creatively and work with you to develop their own plans to meet the team's objectives.

Gather any relevant evidence demonstrating how you set and agree SMART objectives with your team members. This will provide useful evidence for your portfolio.

Be able to support team members identifying opportunities and providing support

In this section you will identify opportunities and difficulties faced by team members. You will learn how to provide advice to team members to overcome difficulties and make the most of identified opportunities.

Identify opportunities and difficulties faced by team members

Teams are very powerful and as they grow stronger and more effective, they can begin to transform the whole organisation. As a manager, you will need to utilise the strengths and expertise of individual team members, which will in turn make your whole team more efficient and effective. You will need to be able to let go of some aspects to allow your team to develop and grow; this could involve supporting and coaching individuals to further develop their own skills and knowledge. You must harness positive energy in your team and encourage team members to take the lead on certain things. By doing this, you will be:

- developing the skills, knowledge and confidence of your team
- empowering and delegating by allowing team members to control some aspects of their own work
- encouraging team members to undertake other jobs (multi-tasking) by sharing their skills and experiences with other team members
- encouraging the team to take responsibility for their own role.

Delegating

As you plan your team's work schedule for the week, month or year, you will need to identify specific members of your team who will undertake specific tasks. By delegating authority and allowing members of the team to undertake specific tasks, you are giving the team members responsibility over some parts of their job. This can often be a motivating factor for staff as they will enjoy the control over elements of their job and they will like the fact that they can make certain decisions.

Unfortunately, not all managers are good delegators and some managers are unable or unwilling to delegate tasks. Also, some team members do not enjoy having additional responsibilities when a task is delegated to them. These team members may need additional support and reassurance as they learn to take on new tasks and responsibilities.

When you delegate, you need to be aware that it may take your team member longer to undertake the task than it would take you and also that they may not perform the task to as high a standard or mistakes may occur. However, you need to be supportive and build in additional time for your team member to guide them through the process, particularly if they are doing something new for the first time.

Think back to when you were learning something new. An easy option is to think 'I can do that job much quicker, I'll just get it done'. This is not the best option. It is likely that as a team leader you will have a high workload and not enough hours in the day to get the work completed. If you do not delegate, the problem will be compounded and you will just get busier and busier and your team will be less and less effective as you try to control all of the tasks.

Always remember that as a team leader, you can delegate specific ad hoc tasks as well as regular tasks. Ask yourself 'Am I the most suitable person to be undertaking this task?'. Also bear in mind that it is not appropriate to delegate some tasks. For example, if you had some interviews planned and it was important for you to make the appointment yourself, you would not normally delegate this type of task.

Remember

Delegating work shows confidence in your team and frees you up to do other tasks.

Portfolio Task 7 30 minutes

Links to LO3: Assessment criteria 3.1, 3.2

How good of a delegator are you? Complete the following short questionnaire. This will provide useful evidence for your portfolio and might highlight some development needs that you can also include in your development plan.

My behaviour	Agree	Disagree
Some of my team members are not motivated and find their roles mundane		
Some of my team members say that they are not always that busy		
I work really long hours, but I find it difficult to delegate work to my team members		
I don't have enough time available to coach and support my team members		
I'm unhappy if my team members make mistakes		
It is quicker to do the task myself and I can get it right first time without any mistakes		

In summary, delegation gives a person the freedom and authority to undertake certain tasks or elements of their own job without the need to constantly refer issues back to their manager for a decision. They are able to make certain decisions and as a result, they are empowered and able to work more on their own initiative. They are also likely to be motivated, more effective and more productive.

By implementing the elements in Figure B5.4 you are more likely to become an effective delegator.

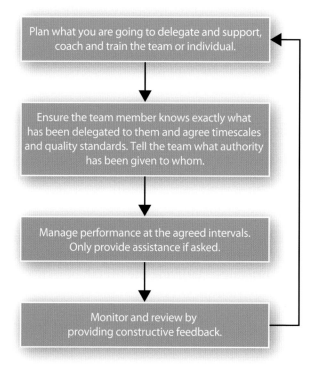

Plan what you are going to delegate and support, coach and train the team or individual.

Ensure the team member knows exactly what has been delegated to them and agree timescales and quality standards. Tell the team what authority has been given to whom.

Manage performance at the agreed intervals. Only provide assistance if asked.

Monitor and review by providing constructive feedback.

Figure B5.4 Effective delegation.

> **Remember**
>
> Always utilise the skills and knowledge of your team. Some team members are likely to have very detailed specialist skills. Encourage and utilise these skills to best effect.

Discuss identified opportunities and difficulties with team members

As a team leader, you will need to be able to provide moral support, for example, if someone has personal difficulties that they need assistance with. You will also be required to provide practical support, for example, if a colleague is struggling to meet a specific deadline.

> **Remember**
>
> Communicate effectively at all times. You never want your team members to say 'We're always the last people to know' or 'We never get to know about anything'.

The level of support required will vary significantly from team to team and also individually. Some team members will require little or no support, whereas other team members may require regular assistance, advice and support. Care needs to be taken here as you need to be clear in your own mind what represents a reasonable level of support. For example, if a person needs regular support in relation to a routine task, then it could be because they are not competent in their role and it may be appropriate in these circumstances to review their capabilities through a formal procedure. However, if a team member needs support in relation to a new task or change in circumstance, then this is perfectly acceptable. Also remember that your colleagues can provide support to each other as specific staff with specialist knowledge may be better placed than you to provide relevant support.

The types of support and advice that your team may need will depend on a number of factors including:

- the type of organisation that you work for and the policies and culture in place
- the rewards and benefits available to staff
- the ability of your team to meet its objectives
- the mix of personalities in your team and the degree of competiveness within the team
- the personal circumstances of your team members.

Be prepared to give time and support to any of your team members as and when they require it. Meet with them on their terms, perhaps at their workstation rather than in your office, and always be sympathetic to their needs.

Don't just think about individual support: you can support the whole team, through team building sessions, specific problem-solving meetings, team briefings, clarifying the overall objectives and planning the work to be undertaken.

Provide advice and support to team members to overcome difficulties and challenges

It is inevitable that you will have to deal with disagreements or conflicts, either within your own team or conflicts between your team and other teams. Generally speaking, these disagreements can be classified into either task-based challenges or people-based challenges.

- Task-based challenges are normally easier to solve than people-based problems as they are less complex. Task-based problems relate to doing the job and examples include meeting tight deadlines, lack of skills, equipment or resource breakdown or staff absences.
- Examples of people-based challenges can include personality clashes, problems over the allocation of roles, lack of support between team members, team members blaming each other or some staff deliberately being disruptive.

Difficulties can also arise in times of uncertainty such as during periods of economic downturn or the reorganisation of a team. During these times, staff may be worried about the security of their jobs and it will be up to you to keep them informed at all times and provide relevant support and advice as required.

While you need to steer your team successfully through these challenges, you also need to recognise that you cannot control everything. As we have discussed earlier, teams are influenced by individual personalities, beliefs, personal feelings and attitudes. You can do your bit, but things which may be outside your control may sometimes go wrong.

Sometimes you may need to impose a decision or introduce a new system or process that proves unpopular. The best way to undertake this is to have an open and frank discussion with all members of the team and explain the reasons for the proposed changes. Listen to the concerns of your team members and take on board any relevant issues. If people know why something is happening and it is explained to them in person, they are much more likely to accept the changes even if they do not agree with them entirely.

Make sure that team members are supported when doing a task they have not taken on before.

Provide advice and support to team members to make the most of identified opportunities

It is critical to ensure that as a team leader you are respected by your colleagues and:

- have a positive attitude
- are an effective communicator
- are competent in your role as a team leader
- able to motivate, influence and encourage the team
- able to harness and develop the skills and knowledge within the team
- know and understand individual team members strengths and weaknesses
- able to link the team goals to the overall objectives of the organisation.

Activity 30 minutes

Think about your team and check if you possess any of the traits listed. If you think that you have any specific areas for development, make a note of them and build them into your personal development plan.

Remember to value your team. In principle, you are only as good as the team that works for you. Your team is your resource to respect, work with and hopefully achieve your objectives. Make the most of any opportunities that may arise. These could include expanding your team, developing new and innovative ways of working, creating more efficient and effective systems and keeping your colleague's skills and knowledge up to date. By doing this, you will be helping to improve the organisation overall, which should assist in providing stability longer term.

PLTS

By describing and explaining the ways in which you interact with your team on a day-to-day basis, you will be demonstrating how you develop opportunities within the team and also how you communicate with your team effectively (TW; IE; EP; SM).

Functional Skills

You may be able to use this personal statement as evidence towards Functional Skills English Levels 1and 2: Reading and Writing. You need to demonstrate that you have understood the process involved in how you support your team.

Portfolio Task 8 90 minutes

Links to LO3: Assessment criteria 3.1, 3.2, 3.3, 3.4

1. Describe what opportunities and what difficulties are faced by you and your team.
2. Describe how you communicate and deal with any difficult situations.
3. Describe how you develop opportunities for your team members and explain the structure of how this works.
4. Think of some recent examples of when you have given support to individual team members or the team as a whole. This could be through a team briefing or maybe during a one-to-one meeting.

Be able to monitor and evaluate progress and recognise individual and team achievement

In this section you will look at how to monitor and evaluate individual and team activities and progress and provide recognition when individual and team objectives have been met.

Monitor and evaluate individual and team activities and progress

Managing performance is critical. You will need to monitor and evaluate individual and team performance on a regular basis. You may undertake this through some or all of the following.

- Gathering and interpreting performance information from the relevant internal systems in your organisation.
- By discussing performance with your team members on a one-to-one basis for example, through individual discussions, more formalised regular performance meetings or perhaps an annual appraisal meeting.

- By discussing performance with your team members in a group environment for example, through a daily 'stand up' ten-minute meeting or a more formalised regular team meeting.

By motivating, supporting and empowering team members, you will be allowing them to take an active role in shaping your team. It is worth remembering that a team is like a living thing: you will be able control most elements but not all, and while you will be able to manage the team to some extent, there are other dynamics in place that you may not have control over. Ultimately the team operates on a day-to-day basis based on a number of factors including:

- your own management style
- the development stage that the team is at (forming, norming, storming, performing)
- the dynamics of the team members, including the skills, knowledge and motivations of individual team members
- your interaction with other teams and the interaction that takes place with your customers
- the resources in place and the objectives that you need to achieve with these resources
- your ability to manage performance and link it to organisational objectives
- individuals' understanding their job roles.

Empowerment is the process of allowing your team members to take control over their work and also become involved in the decision-making process.

By empowering employees, you can assist in preparing the organisation towards long-term success by developing key individuals and teams who may generate a competitive advantage for the organisation. This can be achieved by the organisation having more effective employees as a result of them being more skilled and trained than their competitors.

You will need to have a good understanding of the systems and processes in place in your organisation, as a key part of your role will be to monitor and evaluate performance. Once you have interpreted the information, you will need to know what to do next in order to take the most appropriate action.

Provide recognition when individual and team objectives have been met

By trusting and supporting your colleagues, they can become more and more efficient and should begin to strive towards achieving excellence.

By working closely with your team you will develop their skills, knowledge and career aspirations. You can do this by:

- providing training which will develop their knowledge, skills, and competencies

- providing positive and constructive feedback on their performance
- involving team members in the decision-making process and agreeing objectives collectively
- coaching team members on a one-to-one basis and supporting their individual development
- creating a friendly environment where team members feel that their input is valued and welcomed
- creating an open-door policy whereby you make yourself available to all staff at all times
- communicating effectively with your team, by making sure that all team members know what is happening all of the time.

Once you have all of these practical elements in place, it is very likely that your team will be empowered and motivated on a day-to-day basis.

Motivating your team does not have to cost much. You may be able to offer flexible working or incentive schemes. Discuss ideas with your manager and your team. It is sometimes difficult to give monetary rewards, but think of alternative ways to reward your staff.

Your team members don't just need reward, they also need recognition. You should put time aside to speak with each team member individually to acknowledge any good work they have done and see how you might improve the scope of their role or provide them with additional development opportunities.

Remember

Give praise to your team and thank them when they do a good job.

PLTS

By demonstrating how you manage the performance of your team, you will also be detailing how the team members work together and how they participate in the performance-management process on a day-to-day basis. You may also be able to present any relevant evidence, for example any targets you have set a team member or any reviews of performance that you have undertaken (TW; EP; SM).

Functional Skills

You may be able to use this personal statement as evidence towards Functional Skills English Levels 1 and 2 Reading and Writing. You need to demonstrate that you have understood the process of how to monitor and evaluate progress and recognise individual and team achievement.

Portfolio Task 9 60 minutes

Links to LO4: Assessment criteria 4.1, 4.2

Write a personal statement describing how you monitor and evaluate the performance of your team. Explain what processes you undertake (and their frequency) in order to ensure that performance is managed effectively.

Describe any recent achievements that your team has made and also support this with any relevant evidence.

Team talk

Jodie's story

My name is Jodie and I'm employed as a team leader in a bank in Leicester and I manage a team of eight part-time staff. I've only recently joined the company and it is the first time that I have managed a team. Part of my role is to set and agree objectives with my team and to manage their performance. I agree specific targets with each team member as part of their annual appraisal meeting, but this is something that I have not done before, so I was a little unsure what I needed to do.

I decided to arrange a meeting with my manager to ask her exactly what performance targets we were working towards achieving and how I could manage the process effectively. I knew about some of our performance targets and standards, but I needed everything to be clarified. Before the meeting, I decided that I needed to clarify:

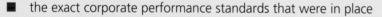

- the exact corporate performance standards that were in place
- the specific targets that were in place for my team to achieve
- when i needed to complete the appraisals by
- how the company dealt with any training requests.

At the meeting, my manager was pleased that I had taken the time to prepare for the meeting and she explained everything to me in detail. I learnt a lot of new things about the company and as a result I was able to structure the appraisal meetings well and set and agree a number of objectives and targets with my team members. I also agreed a process to have a 30-minute one-to-one meeting with each member of my team on a monthly basis to help me manage their performance.

Top tips

Jodie did well to write down a list of all the issues. This demonstrated that she had thought about everything, and by preparing a list she was starting a structured process towards setting and agreeing the objectives and managing the team's performance.

Jodie could have researched the performance targets and objectives in a bit more detail before she met with her manager. By doing this, she would have had more of an overview of the performance standards and objectives that are already in place.

Can you think of anything else that Jodie could have done better?

Unit B5 Set objectives and provide support for team members

Ask the expert

Q	I have to formulate a series of SMART objectives for my team. What do I need to do?
A	Begin by clarifying the team's objectives with your manager and then begin to prepare a list of objectives by considering the following:

- How will your objectives link to the organisation's overall mission and objectives?
- How will you prioritise the objectives?
- Plan your resources – can you complete the objectives alone or do you need any specialist support?
- Agree dates for completing the objectives.
- Consult with your team and finalise the objectives.
- Agree the objectives with the team.
- Manage the process to ensure that you complete the objectives within the agreed time frame.

What your assessor is looking for

In order to prepare for and succeed in completing this unit, your assessor will require you to be able to demonstrate competence in:

- understanding and being able to describe the purpose and benefits of teamwork
- understanding and being able to describe the purpose of communication in teams and how to communicate effectively
- understanding the purpose and being able to plan with team members how objectives will be met
- valuing a team and being able to demonstrate how to respect and support them
- being able to monitor and evaluate team and individual achievement and provide relevant opportunities to support team members.

You will demonstrate your skills, knowledge and competence through the four learning outcomes in this unit. Evidence generated in this unit will also cross-reference to the other units in this qualification.

Please bear in mind that there are significant cross-referencing opportunities throughout this qualification and you may have already generated some relevant work to meet certain criteria in this unit. Your assessor will provide you with the exact requirements to meet the standards of this unit. However, as a guide, it is likely that for this unit you will need to be assessed through:

- one observation of relevant workplace activities to cover the whole unit
- one witness testimony may also be produced
- a written narrative, reflective account or professional discussion
- any relevant work products to be produced as evidence.

The work products for this unit could include:

- your individual and team's objectives or targets
- relevant research that you have undertaken
- emails or other communication methods that you have used in your team
- copies of any team meeting agendas and minutes
- your organisational structure
- any feedback that you have received on your performance
- your appraisal document
- examples of any creative or innovative working methods.

Your assessor will guide you through the assessment process as detailed in the candidate logbook. The detailed assessment criteria are shown in the logbook and by working through these questions, combined with providing the relevant evidence, you will meet the learning outcomes required to complete this unit.

Task and page reference	Assessment criteria
1 (page 124)	1.1
2 (page 124)	1.2, 1.3
3 (page 127)	1.3
4 (page 129)	2.1, 2.2
5 (page 131)	2.2, 2.4
6 (page 134)	2.2, 2.3, 2.4
7 (page 136)	2.1, 2.2
8 (page 140)	3.1, 3.2, 3.3, 3.4
9 (page 142)	4.1, 4.2

Unit C1 Support team members in identifying, developing and implementing new ideas

Creativity and innovation are long-established benefits of team working in businesses. To bring out the best in your team in terms of creativity and innovation, you need to harness the processes involved and develop a team culture where members proactively contribute their ideas and suggestions.

In this unit you will investigate methods of developing the creativity of your team as well as identifying ways in which these ideas can be recorded for future evaluation. You will examine methods of assessing the viability of ideas and look at how you can analyse the benefits and risks associated with ideas for change.

Providing support to your team in submitting formal project proposals for approval will be a key part of your role and you will examine ways in which you can best support your team in this respect.

In the final part of this unit you will look at the process of implementing team ideas. In particular, you will examine ways of monitoring implementation of ideas by your team, as well as methods of communicating progress on implementation to the management team.

What you will learn:

- Be able to develop team ideas and develop the creativity of team members
- Be able to assess the viability of team members' ideas
- Be able to support team members to implement ideas
- Be able to implement team ideas

Links to the Technical Certificate

If you are completing your NVQ as part of an Apprenticeship Framework, you will find the following topic is also covered in your Technical Certificate:

- How to support team members to implement ideas.

Be able to develop team ideas and develop the creativity of team members

To get the best out of your team, ideas and creativity need to flow freely. Team members need to feel able to voice their ideas and opinions and know that they will be listened to. In this section you will investigate some of the methods that you can implement to both encourage and harness this creativity within your team.

Encourage team members to identify ideas

As a manager, you cannot simply order your team to be creative! Instead, you have to take a facilitating approach, which includes protecting your team from the usual constraints, pressures and bureaucracy of the organisation and actively supporting them by allowing them the freedom necessary to be creative.

Protecting your team from organisational pressures can mean giving them a separate physical space in which to be creative and may include allowing them flexibility in working hours and location. You might also need to defend your team to other managers to keep their workload at a level that allows the creative process to flourish. Urgent deadlines and heavy workloads will ruin the creative flow of even the most talented and motivated individuals.

You will need to employ excellent leadership skills to find the most appropriate support that you can give to your team. You will have to inspire them, provide a constant source of challenge and stimulation, allow mistakes and, above all, encourage experimentation. This will allow you to tap into your team's creative energy.

Innovation

Innovation has long been recognised as a vital ingredient in organisational success – it can even make the difference between business survival and collapse, especially where competition is high and new developments are emerging quickly into the market.

Innovation can come about from a variety of sources such as:

- in response to customers' needs – often identified by customer feedback
- by accident – famous examples include Blu-Tack, which was being researched as a possible new sealant that didn't work as intended
- by research and development – most large organisations have their own dedicated research and development departments. Pharmaceutical companies, such as GlaxoSmithKline, and technology companies, such as Apple®, are known for their groundbreaking research and development work.

> **Key Term**
>
> **Innovation** – the creation or improvement of a product, service, technology, process or idea that has a business value.

According to leading economist Joseph Schumpeter, innovation can be concerned with:

- the introduction of a new product or a new quality of product
- the introduction of a new method of production
- the creation of a new market
- the development of a new source of supply
- the reorganisation of an industry.

Some examples of innovations that fall under these categories include:

- the development of wireless technology for computers and laptops
- the development of biofuels as an alternative to fossil fuels
- hybrid electric cars, such as the Peugeot 3008 HYbrid4, which is capable of running on both diesel and electricity
- the production of electricity using wind power instead of burning fossil fuels
- satellite navigation technology
- tablets such as the Apple iPad®, the Motorola Xoom™ tablet and the Samsung Galaxy Tab.

Creativity

Creativity is the generation of original thoughts and ideas. This originality comes from our imagination and allows us to design new and better ways of doing things, such as solving a particular work-based problem, addressing a certain customer need or designing a completely new technology. Creativity can equally arise from combining existing ideas in new ways to produce something better, smarter, quicker or more streamlined. This is why many creativity initiatives in business involve encouraging the generation of as many alternative ideas as possible and not just one or two.

As a team leader, you must understand the immense power that lies in developing and nurturing creativity in your team. Entirely new businesses have even been founded on the results of creativity.

The Wand Company Ltd is an excellent example of creativity and innovation in practice. The company was formed in 2009 by two inventors who came up with an innovative take on remote controls by designing a buttonless, gesture-based control in the form of a wand. This wand can be used to operate various home media, such as TVs, DVD players and stereos, and uses movement to activate and change settings. The two founders of the company achieved fame by appearing on the TV programme *Dragons' Den* and the business has since gone on to achieve huge international business success and multi-million pound turnover. You can find out more about this company by visiting their website at www.thewandcompany.com or watch their business pitch to the Dragons by visiting www.bbc.co.uk/dragonsden/entrepreneurs/richardblakesley.shtml.

Activity · 10 minutes

Map the six examples of innovations listed to one of Schumpeter's categories of innovation.

PLTS

When you are analysing and evaluating information, you are practising your skills as an independent enquirer (IE).

Activity · 10 minutes

Now it's time to think about creativity in your team. List the key factors that you think most affect team members' levels of creativity. Identify whether these factors are positive or negative.

Factors affecting idea generation in teams

Anderson and West developed a theory of group innovation, which states that high levels of creative and innovative performance depend on:

- a shared vision and clear objectives – so that everyone knows the goals of the business as well as what is expected of them individually
- feeling safe within the team – so that there is no fear of negative consequences
- task orientation – commitment from everyone in the team to achieving the highest standards when completing a task
- support and recognition for trying to be innovative.

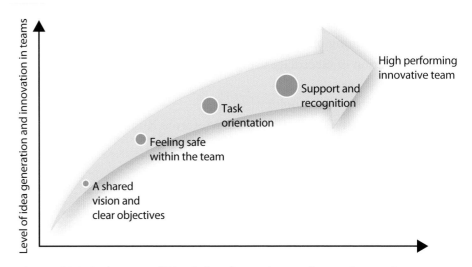

Figure C1.1 Anderson and West's four-factor theory of group innovation.

Your role as team leader is central in building up each of these factors within your team. Think about how you might go about developing creativity and innovation in your team by completing the following activity.

Activity  10 minutes

For each of the four factors identified, mention one way in which you might be able to build up that aspect of the team.

- A shared vision and clear objectives
- Feeling safe within the team
- Task orientation
- Support and recognition

Barriers to idea creation

In many organisations, the free expression of ideas is hampered by issues such as:

- existing work demands and pressures preventing individuals and teams from having the time and freedom to be creative
- the existing **culture** of the organisation discouraging individuals from expressing their ideas openly, especially where there is an old-fashioned management style of command and control
- **politics** within the team, such as rivalry and personality and power clashes, preventing individuals from bringing their best creative ideas to the table.

As team leader, you can help to reduce the impact of each of the issues mentioned above and thus encourage your team to identify ideas. For example, you can help to manage workflow peaks and troughs to avoid excessive work pressures building up. You can also give team members time out away from their normal workplace to research new ideas.

You can encourage an honest, open and trusting climate among your team by asserting your own values and leadership skills, even if this is at odds with the culture in other parts of the organisation.

You can avoid, or at least reduce, the impact of individuals who are at odds with each other by finding ways to make the goals of the team more important than individual successes. In addition, you can arrange the work tasks of the team in such a way as to minimise contact between team members who are at risk of constant clashes with one another. In the long term, where no other solution is possible, a change of team may be the most sensible solution for this type of situation.

You may not yet have specific experience of developing innovation and creativity in your team, but as you gain more experience in your role, you will discover the methods that work best for you and your particular team.

Key Terms

Culture – the existing norms and values of an organisation.

Politics – behaviour within the team, such as unofficial networking, rumour spreading and manipulation of others, which is ultimately designed to achieve personal objectives, rather than for the benefit of the team.

Activity

 10 minutes

List any barriers to creativity that exist in your team and explain what you could do to reduce these. Identify any areas in which you would like training or guidance to help you develop your skills in building creativity in your team.

PLTS

When you are generating ideas and exploring possibilities, you are practising your skills as an independent enquirer (IE).

Checklist

You can build up a climate of innovation in your team by:

- reinforcing goals and objectives to your team regularly, for example, in team meetings and via email
- circulating relevant industry newsletters and emails to the team to encourage them to keep up with developments
- making discussion of industry events and new developments a key part of team meetings
- allowing your team the time to think about new ideas, even if this means time away from their work
- giving your team access to the resources they need to develop their ideas – these could include specialist resources such as software or simply an office space with a flip chart and pens
- providing a forum for presenting back ideas to the team
- praising idea generation
- providing updates on the progress of ideas put forward and explaining the reasons where ideas have been rejected for further development.

Remember

Your team has the potential to generate many useful ideas. Get the best from it by:

- encouraging everyone to be creative
- directly seeking ideas from your team on particular issues
- praising those who put ideas forward.

Lateral thinking

Lateral thinking is a term applied to unusual methods of problem solving and idea generation. The basic idea behind lateral thinking is to approach a problem or a situation from a different angle or a fresh perspective, in order to produce innovative solutions that would not be possible using traditional problem-solving techniques. In fact, the very basis of lateral thinking is to break out of the old habits and patterns created by traditional problem-solving approaches. Often, these very habits create a blinkered view of both the problem and the available solutions and people get stuck in an ideas rut!

Lateral thinking puzzles

Lateral thinking puzzles are a very good way to break people out of traditional modes of thinking and make them approach a problem or a conundrum from a different angle. These types of puzzles can be very effective ice-breakers in team situations, especially ones where you need your team to be creative.

Here are a couple of famous examples of such lateral thinking puzzles. See if you can work out the answers.

1. Coin in the Bottle

   Put a coin in a bottle and then plug the opening with a cork. How can you get the coin out of the bottle without pulling out the cork or breaking the bottle?

   Answer:

   Push the cork into the bottle, then shake the coin out.

2. Doctor

A man and his son were in a car accident. The man was killed but the son was rushed to the emergency ward. The doctor on call took one look at the boy and exclaimed 'I can't operate on this boy. He's my son.' How could this be?

Answer:

The doctor was the boy's mother.

Brainstorming

Brainstorming is a group technique where team members try to come up with as many ideas as possible on a certain topic. Quantity, not quality, of ideas is the goal of brainstorming sessions, so it does not matter how extreme or unfeasible the ideas put forward turn out to be. The ideas generated in brainstorming sessions will later be categorised and assessed. Unworkable ones will be discarded during this process.

Brainstorming generally works best in small groups of no more than about eight. It also requires active participation from everyone in order to work well, so there is no room for sitting back quietly in these sessions. All team members must be willing to contribute. They also need to understand that their ideas will not be judged in any way during the brainstorming process.

Brainstorming can be used in many different situations, such as new product development, where creative solutions are essential to the business.

Mind mapping

Mind mapping is a process where situations or ideas are mapped onto a diagram, beginning with a main subject in the centre, with branches and sub-branches added around it as more links and associated ideas are generated. Mind mapping is generally carried out individually and is used to create as many ideas as possible on a given theme. Colours and images can also be used in mind mapping diagrams to emphasise the different elements and ideas within them.

Record team members' ideas

How can you ensure that you effectively record all the ideas that your team members produce so they are not lost among the huge amounts of information and paperwork generated by the day-to-day requirements of the business?

In order to capture and record team members' ideas, you need to establish documentation procedures in just the same way as for other areas of your job, and preferably keep a log of ideas put forward in date order. This need not be a complicated procedure and can be easily and simply set up. Whatever the format of the notes, they need a central place where they can be filed for later reference. Remember too, to file notes taken during brainstorming sessions, copies of mind maps and minutes of relevant meetings.

Project proposal forms

One approach might be to create a master template of a new project proposal form, which your team can use to explain their ideas, detailing all of the resources needed to be put them into practice. There are many free versions of such forms available on the internet for you to download. You can find examples of these by searching for 'new project proposal form' in a search engine. By using new project proposal forms, all of the ideas suggested by the team will be presented in a standard format and will be easy to store on a shared network drive or intranet. This way, they are easy to retrieve at a later date for assessment and evaluation. Using such a standard form also helps to make sure people complete all of the necessary information.

Staff suggestion schemes

Not all of your team's ideas may be about new projects. Some may be concerned with the smallest of details that could be changed within existing processes to improve some aspect of work. Better tea and coffee facilities, new hand dryers, a new printer or better computer monitors – these types of ideas do not necessarily warrant a full project specification, but do need to be recorded somehow. A staff suggestion scheme could be a good option to use for these circumstances. Such suggestion schemes could be manual, like a box held on reception, or they could be conducted electronically, via an email address such as suggestions@mycompany.com.

Suggestion schemes administered by email are very quick and easy to manage. Suggestions received can be categorised, prioritised and filed simply by using your existing email program to create folders and sub-folders off the main inbox. Suggestions received by email can also be auto-forwarded to more than one individual if required.

Team meeting agendas and minutes

Team meeting agendas and minutes are effective in documenting ideas put forward by team members. Standard agenda items could be subjects such as 'New ideas and suggestions' and 'News from our industry', as below.

Sales team meeting agenda

1. Minutes of last meeting
2. New starters this month – welcome
3. Sales results for the last month
4. News from within our industry this month – what are our competitors doing? Any new product launches? What's been in the headlines in our industry magazine recently?
5. New ideas and suggestions by the team
6. Any other business

Figure C1.2 The team meeting agenda can be used to capture new ideas and suggestions.

The agenda needs to be circulated to all of the team prior to the team meeting, to allow people time to prepare information to present for these agenda items.

Details of ideas generated from team meetings, as well as actions and deadlines, could then be easily documented using the existing team meeting minutes. This is a very effective way of using an existing system to develop new information. As we have seen, ideas and suggestions can come from a variety of sources. It is your job to find a way of storing the information received in a central file, either electronically or manually, so that you can easily access this at a later date to:

- review the ideas received
- ask for further information from your team
- select ideas for further assessment and development.

Portfolio Task 1 60 minutes

Links to LO1: Assessment criteria 1.1, 1.2

1. Explain why it is important to encourage team members to identify ideas. Give an example, if possible, of an idea that was generated within your team and which was either subsequently developed into a project or was the basis of some sort of positive change.

2. State ways in which idea generation could be carried out in your team.

3. Describe some of the different ways in which you could record team members' ideas. Are there any particular methods that would work best in your team? If so, give reasons to explain why.

Your assessment could take the form of a written narrative or a professional discussion with your assessor. It could also include the production of workplace evidence, work-based observations or the use of witness testimonies, as appropriate.

Functional Skills

If you produce a word-processed report as part of the assessment for this learning outcome, you will be practising your Level 1 Functional ICT skills in using ICT systems.

Be able to assess the viability of team members' ideas

Once you have begun receiving ideas and suggestions for improvements from your team, your next task is to assess whether or not they are **viable**. This involves looking at both the advantages and disadvantages of the proposed new idea and making a decision as to whether the advantages of implementation and the benefits it might bring outweigh any negative issues and costs that may arise.

Key Term

Viable – able to work in practice.

A viability assessment is an essential stage in the idea evaluation process. No idea should ever be implemented without a detailed and thorough assessment of its relative advantages, disadvantages, costs and resource requirements, all of which should be backed up by a fully costed and scheduled plan.

Remember, too, that viability should be reassessed even after a project gets under way, especially if it is a long-term project. There are many factors that can change along the way which may make a once fully viable project **untenable**. This can happen where, for example:

- costs spiral way beyond original estimates, making completion of the project too expensive
- new technology becomes available on the market which can provide a better solution for the business much more cheaply
- the needs of the business change, perhaps due to a strategic change in direction, such as a takeover or a merger.

Assess with team members the potential benefits and risks associated with an idea and the resources required

A good approach to assessing new ideas is to involve your team as far as possible in the process. Remember that your team members may make suggestions for new processes and initiatives based on previous experience gained in other companies. This means that they will have valuable experience of seeing the idea work in practice.

This type of experience can be of huge benefit as learning from real experience is better than stepping into the unknown. In this section, we'll use the example of a retail clothing store where the sales team are considering implementing a new process of **cross-selling** their products to customers with the aim of increasing sales per employee.

Analysing benefits and risks

The main benefits of implementing a policy of cross-selling include:

- increased overall revenue for the business
- increased sales per employee – therefore increasing **productivity** for the sales team
- increased customer service levels – as customers are given additional individual attention in the store
- increased customer satisfaction – as customers are helped to purchase an entire outfit, rather than a single item of clothing, therefore reducing the need for them to spend additional time and effort shopping in a number of stores to get the outfit they need.

So far, the benefits of implementing this new idea look compelling. Next, however, you need to take a close look at the possible risks associated with it.

Key Terms

Cross-selling – selling a customer additional products which complement the original product selected.

Productivity – amount of work produced.

Untenable – unworkable.

Some of the possible drawbacks include:

- customers may only actually be looking to purchase a single item
- customers may feel harassed by overly eager sales staff
- it will take up a lot more staff time and may lead to the need for the recruitment of additional staff
- staff will need training in customer contact techniques to help them to accurately assess a customer's needs and to know when to apply cross-selling techniques and when to leave the customer alone. This is a skill which must be developed in order to implement effective, yet not overzealous, cross-selling.

Resource requirements

The key resources needed in order to make this new idea a reality in the example of the retail outlet include:

- training of sales staff – which could be carried out as a whole group training session to keep costs and time required down
- additional displays around the store showing whole outfits being worn, to promote mixing and matching of clothing and accessories
- improvements to the customer changing rooms to include more attractive lighting and placement of mirrors, ambient music, more room space and call buttons, so that customers can easily request assistance without having to leave their changing room.

Involving staff in displays and using their skills will help to make them more aware of the cross-selling policy, potentially helping it to be more successful.

Another area where training may be useful is in development of product knowledge, especially in the selection of suitable additional clothing and accessories that complement the customer's original purchase. If staff have a keen eye for creating whole outfits around the selection of a single item, then they will have a far greater chance of success in maximising their sales by cross-selling.

Costing and scheduling resources required

All of these additional resources will obviously require time and money. The financial requirements should be detailed in a project-costing document, where the costs of each separate item are detailed and further explained, if necessary. The time requirements should be detailed in the form of a schedule. As dates for implementation are probably not yet known, the schedule could be presented in the form of 'Week 1, Week 2', etc.

PLTS

When you are generating ideas and exploring possibilities, you are practising your skills as an independent enquirer (IE).

Activity 15 minutes

Think of a new idea that could be implemented in your team. Now consider how you might assess this idea for viability. Give three benefits and three risks of your chosen idea and decide, based on your analysis, whether it would be workable in your team.

Checklist

All new ideas have potential benefits and risks. Assessing the viability of ideas is essential in order to:

- look at the idea from a number of angles including that of the customer, the team and the business
- produce an objective view of its overall positive and negative aspects
- establish anticipated costs and schedules
- decide whether to accept or reject the development of the idea.

Ways of involving the team in the assessment process

An effective method of getting your team actively involved in assessing the viability of new ideas is to use specially designed team meetings, held away from the main work area or even at an external location. Ask one of your team to be the facilitator for the meeting – this will increase team ownership of the process. They can be responsible for asking for feedback as the meeting progresses and for noting down comments received onto a flip chart or whiteboard. Brainstorming, mind mapping or role playing could be good techniques to adopt in getting the team motivated to contribute to the session.

You can use the session to explore all of the issues presented by the new idea. In particular you need, as a team, to answer the following questions:

- What will the introduction of this new idea bring to the team?
- What will it cost us to implement it?
- What else will we need in order to successfully implement the new idea?
- How do we all feel about the idea?
- How can we win support for our idea from all of the relevant stakeholders?

Reasons for rejecting ideas

Unfortunately, not all ideas will progress beyond the viability assessment stage. There are many reasons why an idea may be rejected including where it is:

- too expensive to implement – the idea itself may well be excellent, however the financial position of the business may not be capable of supporting it at the moment. Ideas such as this may well be shelved until a later date, rather than rejected outright
- considered too radical and does not fit in with senior management's own ideas for the team or the organisation
- not practical to implement because of staffing, operational or logistical barriers
- not properly understood by those with the authority to approve or reject it. This can occur where, for example, senior management are remote from the team and do not have direct involvement with them on a day-to-day basis. They then fail to appreciate the true benefits of the idea to the team.

Portfolio Task 2 60 minutes

Links to LO2: Assessment criterion 2.1

1. Explain why assessment of the viability of new ideas is essential.

2. Describe the processes involved in assessing, with team members, the potential benefits and risks associated with an idea, and the resources required.

Your assessment could take the form of a written narrative or a professional discussion with your assessor. It could also include the production of workplace evidence, work-based observations or the use of witness testimonies, as appropriate.

Functional Skills

If you take part in a professional discussion with your assessor as part of the assessment for this learning outcome, you will be practising your Level 1 Functional English Speaking and Listening skills.

Be able to support team members to implement ideas

Implementing new ideas requires following the correct organisational procedures in order to obtain official approval from those authorised to provide it. You will investigate how you can support your team members in following these procedures in this section. You will also look at issues that your team may experience in the implementation of new ideas and at how you can help them to overcome these.

Explain how to support team members in submitting formal proposals for approval

Providing support to your team is vital to ensure that they are competent in following the correct procedures for submitting formal proposals for approval. This is important because the way in which the proposal is presented to management will effect how it is viewed. Poor punctuation and grammar, or incorrectly completed paperwork, for example, will make the proposal look unprofessional. This, in turn, will make it unlikely to be taken seriously – or even to be read. Imagine the wasted effort where a proposal for a potentially excellent new idea remains unread by the people who count, for the simple reason that its poor spelling and grammar was so off-putting.

The process of submitting proposals

Your job as team leader will involve making sure that each proposal for a new idea gets to the correct manager in a suitably professional manner and in whatever format is suitable for the situation. A project proposal could be submitted in the form of a project proposal form, a report or a presentation. You need to make sure your team is aware of:

- how to access the correct project proposal form, if there is one, or the report or presentation template and any other documents that may be needed
- how to complete the form, write the report, or put together the presentation
- how to structure and present the contents of the proposal
- to whom the proposal should be sent (such as the Operations Director), as well as anyone who should be copied in (such as the Personal Assistant to the Operations Director)
- any attachments that should be included, such as diagrams, research findings, costing information or other supporting documentation.

Quality control

You can play a valuable role in quality control by reading and checking the contents of draft proposals from your team before they are sent off to senior managers. This will involve checking that any forms and documents have been completed correctly and that there are no errors or incomplete parts. You will also need to ensure that all the necessary additional attachments are included with the paperwork.

Things to include in a new project proposal

The key things which should be included in a new project proposal are:

- a project cover sheet – including contact information and a short project summary
- the background to the problem or opportunity – including an analysis of the situation, along with how the proposed project can be of benefit

Checklist

Senior managers are always very busy. If your team wants to get their attention with a proposal for a new idea or project, you need to make sure that all proposals are:

- correctly completed including all parts of the required paperwork
- completed using correct spelling and punctuation
- addressed to the correct manager(s).

- the proposed goal and objectives of the project
- the implementation plan – including a schedule detailing how and when the project will be put into practice
- details of all resources needed
- a budget – clearly stating how much the project will cost and how this is broken down into specific item costs
- a list of attachments.

How to identify and overcome barriers to implementing an idea

Unfortunately, the process of implementing a new idea, no matter how excellent it may be, may not always run according to plan. There are various potential barriers that can prevent ideas from becoming a reality. For this reason it is good to know at the planning stage what these potential barriers could be. This way you will be better prepared for dealing with them if and when they do occur. You may also be able to modify project plans to avoid, or at least reduce the impact of, some of these identified barriers or put forward contingency plans.

Kurt Lewin's Force Field Analysis model of change

Kurt Lewin put forward a model of change that shows forces driving the change and forces resisting it. According to this model, where the driving and opposing forces are equal, no change will occur. The driving forces must be greater than the opposing forces in order for change to take place.

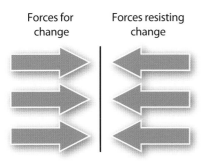

Forces for change   Forces resisting change

Figure C1.3 Lewin's Force Field Analysis.

This model is useful in identifying exactly what, or who, the driving and opposing forces may be in your team. You can develop this line of thought to help in identifying how to deal with those opposing factions in order to turn around this feeling of opposition into creating support for the change.

Barriers to change

Resistance to change is part of human nature. We are essentially creatures of habit and quickly become accustomed to – and comfortable with – the way in which things are done in our organisation. Consequently, we do not wish these familiar ways of doing things to be disturbed or radically altered. The prospect of change can make us uncomfortable simply because it involves moving from the known to the unknown. Some of the more typical barriers to change include:

- self-interest
- insecurity
- fear of losing one's job
- fear of the unknown
- stress – for instance feeling too busy or overworked to be able to cope with change
- inability to understand the reasons for the change
- worries about the introduction of new technology and having to learn new skills.

Overcoming barriers

Many of the barriers to change that might manifest themselves are, in fact, the result of lack of knowledge, which leads to increased fear of the unknown. Barriers such as this can be removed by good management and leadership skills including:

- communication
- involvement
- transparency.

Communication

Devising and deploying a good, clear communications strategy can ultimately make the difference between employees being supportive or unsupportive of the changes. The way in which the change is conveyed is pivotal to how it is perceived by them. Key essential issues to be communicated to employees include:

- the reason for the introduction of the change – so that they can understand the need for it
- the underlying goals of the change – what it is trying to achieve
- how the changes can benefit employees – to gain support from and win over individuals who may have been fearful of the effects of the change
- how these changes will be implemented and what employees can expect along the way.

Involvement

Involving your team in the change process is an excellent method of creating a sense of ownership of it. Asking for suggestions from your team on how best to implement the various aspects of the change – and following their suggestions as far as is practicable – means that the team will all be acting as positive driving forces for the change.

Transparency

Transparency means being open and honest with your team, providing clear and accurate information and not being misleading about any aspect of the change. Being seen to be transparent is critical for gaining the trust of your team – something that you will need if you want to ensure smooth implementation and acceptance of the change. If your team suspects management of being underhand or dishonest with them, this could lead to a whole host of issues, including mistrust and even hostility, which could present huge barriers to the planned change.

Change-management programmes

Change-management programmes are a means for managers and team leaders to increase trust and support for the change being introduced. They are based on good practice and effective leadership of the change process.

Portfolio Task 3 60 minutes

Links to LO3: Assessment criteria 3.1, 3.2

1. Explain the different ways in which you can provide support to team members in submitting formal proposals for approval. Include any work evidence that shows your competence in providing such support.

2. Give examples of some of the barriers which your team may encounter when trying to implement a new idea. For each example, outline how you would advise team members to overcome these barriers.

Your assessment could take the form of a written narrative or a professional discussion with your assessor. It could also include the production of workplace evidence, work-based observations or the use of witness testimonies, as appropriate.

Functional Skills

If you produce a word-processed report as part of the assessment for this learning outcome, you will be practising your Level 1 Functional ICT skills in using ICT systems.

Be able to implement team ideas

Good initial ideas, supported by careful and thorough planning, provide a firm basis for successful implementation. However, the implementation phase itself requires careful execution followed up by monitoring and provision of support and help to the team as and when needed.

Monitor the implementation of ideas by own team

When new ideas are put into practice, you will be responsible for overseeing and monitoring their progress. This will involve asking such questions as the following.

- Are there any technical issues?
- Has the team training in new processes been adequate, or will further training be required?
- What has happened to team productivity since the change was implemented?
- What has been the effect on staff morale?
- Have any unforeseen problems occurred and how can we deal with these?
- Has the planned change progressed as expected?

Looking for the answers to the above questions will provide a good basis for monitoring the key aspects of progress development and will enable you to build up a picture of the success of the implementation phase. You will also be able to quickly identify any areas requiring attention and should make immediate arrangements for these to be dealt with.

Depending upon the specific nature of the idea or change that has been implemented, it may affect your team in different ways and to a greater or lesser extent. For example, the introduction of new technology in a food-processing factory to electronically monitor **inventory** would represent a huge change from the perspective of the business, massively speeding up the collection of accurate real-time inventory data. However, from the operative's point of view, such a change may not represent a radical change in job requirements. In fact, it will certainly make the task of inventory monitoring and controlling stock levels much easier and less time-consuming, as all stock will now simply be scanned with a barcode scanner upon arrival at the factory, and scanned again when it is moved at each stage in its production. Similarly, finished products are scanned and electronically counted instead of this being done manually. The only new skill requirements for staff involve undergoing training in the correct use of the electronic barcode scanners and associated software.

Key Term

Inventory – the total amount of goods in a factory including raw materials, works in progress and finished goods.

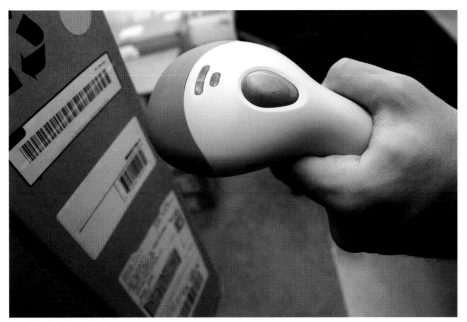

Introducing an electronic inventory control system removes time-consuming manual tasks.

Checking progress by walking around the team work area

Probably the best way to gain a good understanding of the progress of implementation is to walk around the team's work area and to ask your team members how they are getting on. Watch the new processes being carried out and see for yourself how they are operating. Better still, work alongside your team and experience first-hand the true state of progress. Are all staff using the new methods or processes? Is anyone sticking to the old methods or refusing to co-operate? Is your team generally happy? Do any team members report issues or seem unconvinced of the new processes? The more time you spend with your team, the more you will learn about how well, or otherwise, the new ideas have been implemented.

Holding regular team progress update meetings

It is important to use all possible methods of monitoring progress after the implementation of any new changes to your team. Holding regular team progress meetings is a particularly good way to gather information. These should be run in an informal way, which encourages two-way communication. After all, it is you who needs to hear back from your team to establish how well the implementation is progressing. Holding a formal meeting in the boardroom, for example, would not be likely to produce much in the way of useful team feedback, as your team may feel inhibited by the formality of the setting. You need to consider the timing, the location and the agenda of your progress update meetings to get the most out of them.

Activity | 15 minutes

List at least three ways in which team performance could be measured in your team.

PLTS

When you are generating ideas and exploring possibilities, you are practising your skills as a creative thinker (CT).

Checklist

Monitoring the implementation of ideas by your team can involve:

- checking progress by walking around the work area
- holding regular team update meetings
- monitoring team output against targets.

Key Term

Sales scripts – scripts which sales staff must read out to customers.

Monitoring team output

Monitoring the work output of your team after the implementation of some form of change is a good way to measure the benefits of the new idea in concrete terms such as:

- increase in sales
- increase in units produced per employee
- increase in team output
- reduction in faulty goods produced
- reduction in customer complaints
- increases in customer satisfaction levels, as measured by customer feedback surveys.

These are just some of the measures that can be used to monitor changes in team output following implementation of a change in the way the team works. The actual measures that you choose to monitor should reflect both the specific work carried out by your team and the objectives of the changes implemented.

Milestones

The implementation of ideas by your team will take time. This is because the implementation phase needs time to bed in and become established and this requires learning and skills development by team members. People need an adjustment period, where they gradually become accustomed to new ways of working, new technology or new processes.

Because of this time requirement, milestones and interim targets should be set for monitoring of progress. These could be set per day, per week or per month after initial implementation of an idea, depending on the change that has been implemented, as well as the learning and adjustment time realistically needed by your team.

For example, suppose that in the telephone sales department of an insurance company, an idea was implemented to get rid of **sales scripts** in an attempt to improve the relationship between sales staff and customers and to free up the staff to speak as they felt appropriate, use their own initiative to offer incentives to create more sales and to develop a better understanding of their customers' insurance needs.

The ultimate aim of this idea was to increase sales per employee by 15 per cent. This increase cannot realistically be expected to occur immediately and will need a little time – and staff training – to take effect. Therefore, it makes good business sense to establish key milestones for the achievement of this overall aim by breaking it down into weekly or monthly performance targets.

The following table gives an example of how this could be done. The incremental set of milestones can stack up to achievement of the overall aim of the change. This could also be presented graphically.

	Month 1	Month 2	Month 3	Month 4	Month 5	Month 6
Target increase in sales	2%	5%	8%	10%	13%	15%

Table C1.1 A possible plan to follow if profit were to to be raised by 15% over six months.

Communicate the progress of implementation to relevant others in own organisation

The key purpose of communicating the progress of implementation of change is to inform senior management and any other key stakeholders as to its level of success in business terms, such as cost reductions or reduced manufacturing times. Implementation of any change initiative represents a significant cost to the business in terms of both time and money. For this reason, the management needs to see a return on this expenditure in some way, for instance increased sales or production, reduction in complaints or faults, or some other tangible measure of business performance. This is the means by which they can evaluate the success of the change.

Producing a progress report

One of the main ways of communicating progress to your management team would be to produce a professional business report, which would then be sent to all relevant senior managers to demonstrate changes in key performance measures over time.

It is important that the report relates the progress on key performance measures back to the original objectives of the change. This will help to underline how the new processes have successfully addressed the key objectives and are aligned to key business goals.

As we saw in the previous section, measuring performance over time is an important consideration too, as you cannot expect to have 100 per cent perfection immediately after implementation of a new way of working. Changes take time to come fully on-stream and your performance targets could be set over a number of weeks or months to reflect this. For example, after one month, 25 per cent of all customers will have been contacted via the new customer relationship management (CRM) system. After three months, this figure will be 75 per cent and so on.

Producing your report

When preparing your report, remember that it is going to be read by senior managers in your company. It is therefore very important that you produce a professional and well-presented document, containing all of the key information required in a clear and logical structure.

Standard headings normally included in such a report might include:

- Introduction – details of the idea or change implemented and the reasons why it was introduced.
- Summary of progress to date – a brief paragraph summarising the contents of the report.
- Details of key changes implemented – to be listed in the report as Item 1, Item 2, etc, with a brief section on the progress against targets of each item.
- Schedule of completion of implementation and progress against deadlines.
- List of attachments.

You should also make sure that you include a combination of text, tables of figures and graphs in order to convey your key points visually as well as in written form. This will make your report easier to read and to understand. Ensure that you keep your text brief and to the point. Never mention any team members by name in your report. If you wish to raise an issue, you could do so in the form of, 'It was felt by certain team members that …'

Make sure that your graphs and charts are clear and correctly labelled so that they do not cause confusion or conflict with the text in your report. If you are not confident in your report-writing ability, get another colleague to read over your report to check it for grammar and spelling before it is sent off to the management team. A second pair of eyes is always a good option, especially when it is an important document.

Making a presentation of progress updates

You may be required to make a formal presentation to the relevant management team on the progress of implementation of a change. You should spend time carefully preparing such a presentation and make sure to include:

- an electronic slide presentation containing all of the key points you wish to demonstrate
- handouts of any supporting information to be distributed during the presentation
- the originals of any internal progress monitoring statistics, in case they are needed to resolve queries by the management team.

Practising your presentation

You will need to spend time rehearsing the delivery of your presentation before you present the real one. This is especially important where you may not have much experience in making formal presentations to senior management. It can be quite a daunting experience even for more senior staff, therefore, the more practised you are and the better you know your content, the more confident you will be when delivering the final presentation. You will also need to practise using the electronic slide-presentation software and ensure that you know how to advance (and reverse) the slides when you need to. Remember also to rehearse the timing of your presentation. This is particularly important as either over-running or stopping too short of the allocated time slot will be uncomfortable and will certainly not make a good impression on the management team.

Checklist

When making a formal presentation, you need to consider:

- the content of your presentation
- effective use of electronic slide-presentation software
- inclusion of handouts and other useful supporting documents for your audience
- the timings of the presentation.

Portfolio Task 4 60 minutes

Links to LO4: Assessment criteria 4.1, 4.2

1. a. Give examples of activities you could carry out to monitor the implementation of ideas by your own team.

  b. Provide evidence in the form of work-related documents to show how you have done this.

2. a. Explain why it is important to communicate the progress of implementation of ideas to relevant others in your organisation. Give two examples of people to whom you might need to communicate such progress.

  b. Provide evidence in the form of work-related documents to show how you go about communicating progress of idea implementation.

Your assessment could take the form of a written narrative or a professional discussion with your assessor. It could also include the production of workplace evidence, work-based observations or the use of witness testimonies, as appropriate.

Functional Skills

If you take part in a professional discussion with your assessor as part of the assessment for this learning outcome, you will be practising your Level 1 Functional English Speaking and Listening skills.

Team talk

Lucy's story

My name is Lucy Bremner and I am 29 years old. I have been working as a team leader in a retail organisation for four months. I have been asked by senior management to get my team to offer suggestions for new ideas for performance improvements. My team are bright and intelligent, have a wealth of industry knowledge and are very capable in their roles. Despite this, however, the responses to my requests for new ideas to improve our team performance remain largely disappointing. I am beginning to wonder what more I can do to generate enthusiasm among my team to offer suggestions and ideas.

I have tried various approaches, ranging from sending emails to asking people individually for suggestions.

I am worried that my own manager will see this lack of success as a bad reflection on my performance as team leader. I have two more months left of my probationary period and I would like to be able to show my manager some evidence of idea generation before this probationary period comes to an end.

Top tips

Team meetings are a great forum for generating ideas and also provide a good opportunity to praise those who come forward with suggestions. Making idea generation a weekly topic in team meetings, coupled with a renewed focus on the team's goals and vision, will be an effective way to kick-start the process of idea generation in your team. Remember also to praise ideas and suggestions that are made.

Ask the expert	
Q	I have been trying to get my team to contribute their ideas for performance improvements but nobody seems keen to put forward their ideas. What can I do to encourage more idea generation in the team?
A	Firstly, you need to find ways of letting your team know that their ideas will be valued and that they too will be valued for coming forward with suggestions. They also need to have a keen awareness of the overall goals of the team and to be committed to these.

What your assessor is looking for

In order to prepare for and to succeed in completing this unit, your assessor will require you to be able to demonstrate competence in:

- developing team ideas and developing the creativity of team members
- assessing the viability of team members' ideas
- supporting team members to implement ideas
- implementing team ideas.

You will demonstrate your skills, knowledge and competence through the learning outcomes in this unit. Evidence generated in this unit will also cross-reference to the other units in this qualification.

Please bear in mind that there are significant cross-referencing opportunities throughout this qualification and you may have already generated some relevant work to meet certain criteria in this unit. Your assessor will provide you with the exact requirements to meet the standards of this unit. However, as a guide, it is likely that for this unit you will need to be assessed through the following methods:

- one observation of relevant workplace activities to cover the whole unit
- one witness testimony may also be produced
- a written narrative, reflective account or professional discussion
- any relevant work products to be produced as evidence.

The work products for this unit could include:

- documentation used for recording team members' ideas
- a project viability assessment
- examples of formal project proposal documents
- meeting minutes or emails relating to the development of new ideas, especially those evidencing the support provided by you to your team
- progress reports relating to implementation of new ideas.

Your assessor will guide you through the assessment process as detailed in the candidate logbook. The detailed assessment criteria are shown in the logbook and by working through these questions, combined with providing the relevant evidence, you will meet the learning outcomes required to complete this unit.

Task and page reference	Assessment criteria
1 (page 155)	1.1, 1.2
2 (page 159)	2.1
3 (page 163)	3.1, 3.2
4 (page 169)	4.1, 4.2

Unit D10 Manage conflict in a team

As a team leader you may encounter conflict with your team members or others from both inside and outside of your organisation. This unit will give you the opportunity to explore some of the main causes of conflict and the steps you can take to minimise them.

You need to understand the importance of supporting your team members and how effective communication can be key to helping you manage and resolve conflict situations. You will learn about strategies for dealing with conflict and some of the techniques that you can use to encourage team members to resolve their own conflicts.

Policies and procedures are likely to exist within your organisation to assist you when managing conflict and this unit examines the importance of these along with the necessity of maintaining complete, accurate and confidential records of conflicts.

What you will learn:

- Be able to support team members' understanding of their role and position within a team
- Be able to take measures to minimise conflict within a team
- Be able to understand how to encourage team members to resolve their own conflicts
- Be able to understand legal and organisational requirements concerning conflict

Links to the Technical Certificate

If you are completing your NVQ as part of an Apprenticeship Framework, you will find the following topics are also covered in your Technical Certificate:

- Roles of a team and stages of team development
- Why it is important to be professional and encourage team participation
- Adopting a positive approach and resolving work related difficulties
- Dealing with conflict within a team
- Understanding self managed teams

Be able to support team members' understanding of their role and position within a team

Your team members will feel more confident in their working environment if they are clear about what is expected of them. Their work roles and responsibilities must be communicated to them in an appropriate format, such as job descriptions, rotas and work schedules.

It is important that your team members can approach you with any concerns they have and that you show you will support and guide them through any difficulties.

Effective two-way communication is necessary if morale and motivation is to be maintained, so you need to examine how you communicate and which techniques you should use in particular circumstances.

Communicate standards of work required

Productive working relations with your team members largely depend upon your ability to communicate effectively with them. The **standards** you expect your team to work towards must be made clear – if you don't explain to your team members exactly what you expect from them, you can't expect them to achieve what you want them to.

The purpose of setting standards with your team is to:

- make sure everybody is working towards the same quality standard
- ensure the customer or end user receives the same quality level.

In order for this to happen the standards required must be effectively communicated.

During team meetings, supervision meetings or one-to-one discussions, you may find opportunity to communicate your expectations regarding standards of performance and behaviour. As a follow up to face-to-face meetings, you could reinforce the importance of working to these standards by:

- sending group emails, informing the team where they might find policies, procedures and standards expected electronically (for example, on the organisation's intranet)
- pinning copies of policies and procedures on notice boards to be read
- signposting the team to hard copies of policies, procedures and standards – perhaps kept in lever-arch folders on shelves in an office where they can be easily inspected.

In addition, these documents may form part of the organisation's **staff handbook** and might also be contained in the induction file that each employee receives when they start their job in your organisation.

Key Terms

Standards – rules used as a basis for comparison or judgement.

Staff handbook – information pack for employees containing the organisation's policies and procedures.

It may be necessary to allocate time – perhaps during an induction day or a team meeting – for each team member to read through the index of policies and procedures that the organisation has, and then to read the contents of those you consider most applicable to the work of your team (for example, the health and safety policy, dress code, fire procedures). It is a good idea to produce a form for each employee to sign and date that they have read and understood the contents of the policies and procedures you consider important and appropriate.

Policies and procedures need to be revised from time to time to meet changing demands of industry customers and the economy. It is important that you keep your team members updated of any reviewed policies, procedures and standards. A useful time for you to do this is when you conduct staff appraisals (see Unit A1 on PDRs) with your team members.

It is important that you communicate to your team members a list of the policies and procedures that exist in your organisation, what their purpose is and where they can be found.

In some industries, organisations adopt an approach to standards which identifies them as:

- standard costs – this is the desired cost of producing an item or providing a service
- standard time – this is the desired time an employee takes to complete a given task when producing an item or providing a service.

The standard time can be multiplied by how much per hour an employee working on a task is paid, which results in a total labour cost for that task.

The standard – or desired – costs and time can later be compared to the actual costs and time taken, to establish how well the organisation or team, is performing. These results should then be communicated to the employees and any difference between what was expected and what actually happened can be discussed in detail.

The process of quality assurance serves to ensure that quality standards will be met. These standards should be discussed and agreed with your team members with a focus on customer or end-user satisfaction. For this purpose you may use a team meeting as a vehicle to brainstorm ideas from the team. This is an opportunity for you to let the team know that views and ideas are welcomed and that all opinions are equally valued. In turn, team members may feel more motivated, which could automatically increase workflow and output for which they should receive recognition, praise and perhaps reward. Then as morale increases further so will output, and a positive cycle of workflow can be sustained.

Clear channels of communication and using the right methods and techniques at the right time, can help to keep your team informed and updated of what is expected of them and what has been achieved.

Checklist

Don't forget to communicate to your team the following:

- changes to policies and procedures
- the purpose of the policies and procedures
- where they can be found e.g. intranet, notice board.

Remember

It is not enough for employees to just know that policies and procedures exist – they should all be encouraged to read and understand them.

Remember

When discussing expected standards and targets with your team, build in milestones, so that progress towards completed tasks can be measured and communicated at intervals through the process.

Encouraging good communication and standards of behaviour

By making your team members fully aware of the standards of work and behaviour that is expected of them, you can go some way to helping to reduce the possibility of conflict situations occurring.

The behaviour you expect from your team members must be made clear. How they behave in the workplace can have an impact on meeting targets and expected standards of quality.

In your role as team leader, you must communicate effectively and stress to your team members that it is important for them to communicate effectively with each other too! Doing this can encourage a **holistic** approach to meeting targets and standards, and can promote a positive team spirit and complementary behaviours.

Failure to communicate in the right way and at the right time, may lead to negativity in the team and in particular:

- confusion
- mistrust
- distress.

These factors can adversely effect team dynamics and behaviours.

In your organisation, standards may apply to work performance and behaviour. You may be able to identify policies and procedures in your workplace that relate to behaviour. A policy informs employees what senior management consider acceptable, or not acceptable, behaviour or actions (for example an equal opportunities and diversity policy). Procedures however, can be described as sets of step-by-step instructions to follow when undertaking specific tasks. This ensures that everyone carries out these tasks in exactly the same way, resulting in a consistent approach towards achieving recognised and expected standards. There may also be a code of conduct and even a dress code in force to guide employees.

> **Key Term**
>
> **Holistic** – looking at all parts of the team's efforts so that individuals work closely together to achieve the same overall goals of the team.

> **Remember**
>
> Effective communication means getting the right message to the right people at the right time, and obtaining feedback.

> **Activity** 45 minutes
>
> Research the purpose of the policies and procedures listed below and identify your own definition of each:
>
> - Equal opportunity and diversity
> - Bullying and harassment
> - Unacceptable behaviour
> - Health and safety
> - Grievance
> - Disciplinary
> - Code of conduct (if appropriate)

Culture and communication

Culture is often referred to as 'the way we do things here' and this is often influenced by the attitudes and behaviours of employees at all levels and the policies and procedures that are in place.

If you reflect upon the culture you work in, you may establish that it is, for example, a pleasant working culture in which everyone gets on well with each other. Alternatively, it is possible that you may work in a negative workplace culture (for example, a blame culture).

The team that you lead may, in turn, develop its own culture and the attitudes and behaviours of each team member will play a part in the development of this. As part of its own distinct culture, teams may adopt their own way to operating (their 'norm') in an effort to achieve standards and targets. They may also develop their own use of language and jargon within the team and perhaps create nicknames for each other. An advantage of this is to create a strong team identity and a culture that is supportive of team members, but a disadvantage might be a tendency to become inward looking and exclusive and a reluctance to accept new members into the team.

 Portfolio Task 1 · 20 minutes

Links to LO1: Assessment criterion 1.1
Explain to your assessor how you communicate the organisation's standards of work to your team and outline the behaviour that is expected of them. Provide examples of methods of communication where you are setting out the standards of work. Examples of these could include minutes of meetings, emails, appraisal documentation.

How team members can work together and support each other

Encouraging effective team working and bonding has many benefits. These include increased levels of morale and motivation and mutual respect between team members. Team members should be given the opportunity to share ideas and best practice during team meetings as this will encourage a holistic approach. The more that people feel part of the team and have a sense of belonging, the more likely they are to support each other on a day-to-day basis, but particularly during difficult times in the workplace.

For various reasons, team members will display behaviours that may be of a positive or negative nature. Negative behaviour might be associated with their work role or their working environment (for example, disagreements with other team members) while positive behaviour might be associated with job satisfaction and clearly defined job roles.

PLTS

Through discussions with your assessor, you will generate ideas and explore opportunities that will enable you to communicate standards you expect your team to work towards (CT1; EP 2).

Activity 30 minutes

1. Reflect on your team members and identify whether there are any behaviours you think could be changed (or reflect on own behaviours – what would you like to change?)

2. How often do you think you should make time in meetings or get your team together to discuss behaviours at work and how things can be changed for the better? Give reasons for your responses.

Discuss your responses with your assessor.

Team members' behaviour

Your observation of your team members' behaviours may enable you to categorise each of them as one of the following:

- Passive – a person who feels their opinions are not as important as those of other people in the team.
- Assertive – a person who accepts that everyone in the team is entitled to an opinion that is no more or less important than any other team member.
- Aggressive – a person who thinks that their opinions are more important than anyone else's in the team.

Within your team you may find personality clashes because of different attitudes, mind-sets or ways of thinking. If such clashes are not managed effectively they can sometimes escalate to potentially damaging conflict situations. It may help to be aware that in any workplace there is likely to be a mix of:

- 'can't do' people – these people want to perform well, but are currently not capable of doing so, until they receive further support, training or guidance
- 'won't do' people – these people simply don't want to be at work and their motivation is solely to receive their pay at the end of the month. Regardless of capability or support, they have no interest in performing well.

As a team leader you can support, guide and encourage your 'can't do' people but your 'won't do' people will be harder to manage. By being aware of 'won't do' people in your team you can take steps to intervene when, for example, other willing team members are having to compensate by trying to do their own work and take on some of the work that the 'won't do' person should be doing. As you might imagine, if you don't intervene to prevent escalation of bad feeling, then conflict between team members may arise. Further, your team members may not feel they are getting the support they should from you, potentially creating conflict between you and them.

Douglas McGregor's Theory X and Theory Y

In the 1960s Douglas McGregor, a management theorist, carried out some research into types of workers. He identified two different categories, which he called Theory X and Theory Y.

Theory X workers are considered to be lazy and are only motivated by earning money rather than job satisfaction or the challenge of working as part of a team. They often need to be supervised closely and generally respond to detailed directions and instructions. Theory Y workers are committed to the work of the team and enjoy the challenge of working towards targets and objectives. They seek responsibility and enjoy problem solving to improve the work of the team.

Activity — 20 minutes

Write a statement saying whether you think these different types of people need managing in a different way. Explain your reasons and discuss your thoughts with your assessor.

Remember

When dealing with difficult situations, be aware of your own limits of authority. It is not a weakness to advise your line manager of difficult situations and seek support when you feel you need to.

Activity — 60 minutes

Conduct some research into Douglas McGregor's Theory X and Theory Y workers and discuss your findings with your assessor.

To promote a holistic approach to work and to the meeting of targets, it is important that you encourage your team members to work well together and support each other in every way possible.

To achieve this this, consider to what degree you:

- empower your team members to take the lead
- praise individuals for working well
- praise the team for working well
- encourage creative thinking and formulation of ideas in the team
- advise your team members, as soon as possible, of difficulties or changes that will affect them
- agree and negotiate different ways of doing things with your team.

If your team is armed with up-to-date information relating to targets and expectations, then members can take steps to organise themselves and focus on supporting each other. There will be times when team members are emotional or angry over something that has happened in the workplace or at home. In situations like this it may well be fellow team members who intervene and offer support in the first instances.

Because you will have already communicated the expectations and targets for the team, your team members will realise that by supporting each other during difficult or challenging times, they are more likely to achieve what is expected of them.

A culture of support is likely to develop in the team if members:

- are prepared to listen to each other's concerns
- step in to help a teammate who may get overloaded or behind with their work
- build rapport and trust in the team (e.g. encouraging openness)
- respect everyone else's views
- ask each other for honest feedback
- communicate effectively with each other
- share team problems and difficulties
- respect diversity in the team (See Unit B11 for more information).

> **Remember**
>
> The way team members interact and communicate with each other is likely to affect how supportive the team culture is.

Management theorists Andrew Leigh and Michael Maynard conducted research into team development and suggested that a team will work through six development stages.

1. Starting – integrating new team members and building relationships.
2. Sorting – there may be conflict as members compete for a position in the team.
3. Stabilising – the team adjusts to accept the workplace culture and adheres to rules and regulations. At this stage, members usually agree the best way for the team to do things.
4. Striving – the team starts to perform well and aims to meet its targets.

5. Succeeding – the team achieves its objectives, meets targets, standards and expectations and examines way to enhance performance

6. Stopping – members of the team leave, are promoted or transferred, or perhaps a one-off project is complete. Team members may be saddened by these events.

Refer also to Unit D1 to also examine the work of Bruce Tuckman and Meredith Belbin in relation to teams and team building. Tuckman, for instance, came up with a similar idea of stages in team development, naming them Forming, Storming, Norming, Performing and Mourning.

Leadership styles

For team members to support, respect and value each other, it is necessary for you as the team leader to promote the fact that you are part of the team. Team members need to understand and respect that you are the leader, but this doesn't stop you taking turns with unpleasant tasks to muck in with the team occasionally and supporting them when things get difficult.

Kurt Lewin, a management theorist, identified the three following styles of leadership.

- Autocratic – people do things your way only. Useful in times of a crisis, but some people find this style demotivating.

- Democratic – you allow people to be involved in the decision-making process and value their opinions. You however will make the final decisions.

- Laissez-faire – you trust the capabilities of the team, so that you can stand back and leave them alone to get on with the work.

Being aware of your preferred leadership style can help you to reflect on to what degree you empower your team to make their own decisions and support each other. The term 'preferred leadership style', is used because you may from time to time change your style to suit circumstances as they happen, for example a machine breakdown needs urgent action – you may become autocratic.

Portfolio Task 2 20 minutes

Links to LO1: Assessment criterion 1.2

Having your team members working together and supporting each other is important for an effective team. Using your own workplace examples, explain to your assessor how your team members work and support each other. Your evidence to support your discussion could include examples of minutes of meetings where your team agree their roles and responsibilities.

Be able to take measures to minimise conflict within a team

Being able to identify a potential conflict situation can give you the opportunity to step in to take action that will prevent it from escalating further. Knowing what to look for isn't always easy, but having an understanding of some of the factors that can lead to conflict between your team members can help you to take measures to minimise the possibility of it happening.

How organisational structures, systems and procedures can give rise to conflict

On a day-to-day basis the activities that your team members undertake can be the cause of conflict. For example, your organisation's policies and procedures may be outdated and need reviewing, which may result in team members ignoring them and working in slightly different ways. People may begin to argue over the best way to approach a task which can lead to conflict.

Similarly, the way your organisation is structured can lead to conflict if, for example, communication is ineffective or if it is not clear who should report to whom or who has the authority to make decisions.

Organisational structures

Very often, the way an organisation is structured can influence how effectively people communicate with each other. Poor communication can lead to situations of conflict and some examples of this will be discussed later in this unit.

Organisational structures are not static. As a business operation expands its range of products or services, its structure will evolve. This may be due to an increase in demand from the market place, the result of a merger or takeover, or perhaps because new contracts have been won. Whatever the reason, as the business grows the structure may change accordingly. If not managed properly, such change can result in conflict.

Depending on the nature and type of business activity, the number of staff and the number of customers, organisations are likely to be structured in one of the following ways:

- hierarchical (or pyramid)
- geographical
- product
- matrix.

These different types can best be illustrated by an organisational chart, a pictorial or visual method of communication to inform staff of who does what in the organisation and who reports to whom. The chart shows how many managers there are working at different levels in different departments, and how many operatives there are in each department.

Hierarchical (pyramid): this is the most common type of structure found in many organisations, as seen in Figure D10.1. It is develops over time as an organisation grows larger with layers of employees at different levels. Authority and decision-making power increases up the pyramid.

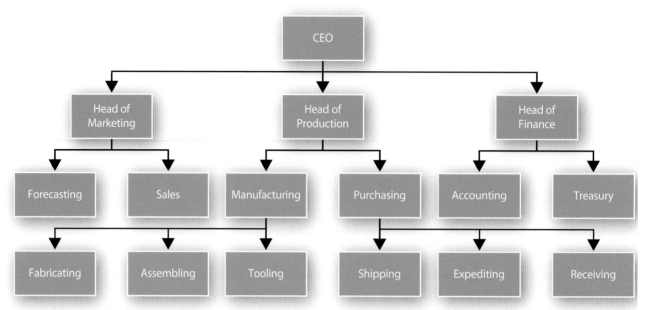

Figure D10.1 Example of a hierarchical structure.

Geographical: often used by large retailers who have many branches in many different regions of the UK (for example, Tesco or B&Q), as seen in Figure D10.2.

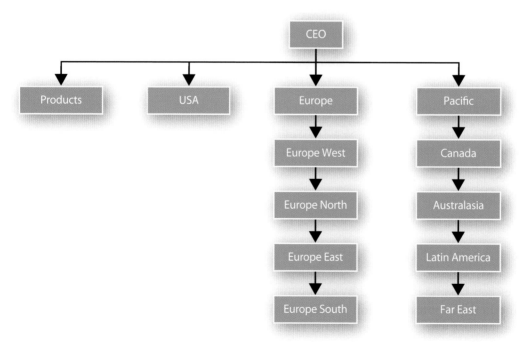

Figure D10.2 Example of a geographical structure.

Product: likely to be used by an organisation that makes a variety of related products. For example, a pharmaceutical organisation may produce different types of specialist medicines, vaccines and sterile supplies. For more information, see Unit D1 page 38.

Matrix: often used for one-off projects such as motorway bridge building or perhaps a car manufacturer producing a limited edition.

As a team leader, you need to know and understand the structure of your organisation and exactly how many team members should report to you. Everyone should know how many layers of management exist and what the other departments are in the organisation. Sometimes, the boxes used in a chart will show names of employees working in their positions, other times, the chart will show only the job title and perhaps how many positions are held (for example, '21 × sales representatives' might be written in one box.)

Consider that a sales manager has a meeting with their team leaders to discuss sales targets. The manager will expect the team leaders to convey this information down the hierarchy to their team members. Remembering that in the first place the sales manager would have been instructed by their own manager to increase sales, this is known as the **chain of command**. The sales manager cannot be expected to manage the workload of each sales assistant in each team. Therefore, the sales manager will only be concerned with managing each team leader and in turn each team leader will be concerned with managing their own team members.

Chain of command

If a chain of command is too long and there are too many layers for messages or instructions to travel through, then difficulties with channels of communication can occur.

- Messages can be distorted as they go either up or down the chain of command. Each person in the chain might interpret the message differently and repeat it to the next person in a slightly different way.

- The more people in a chain of command then the longer the person who sent the original message may have to wait to receive a reply; this might ultimately affect staff morale or customer expectations.

- It may be easier for someone in the chain to hold on to bad news, complaints or a problem, hoping they can resolve it themselves before others in the chain find out about it and consider that person unable to do their job properly.

> **Remember**
>
> Someone in the organisation must be given the task of regularly updating the structure chart otherwise, due to people leaving, being promoted or new people joining the organisation, it can quickly be out of date.

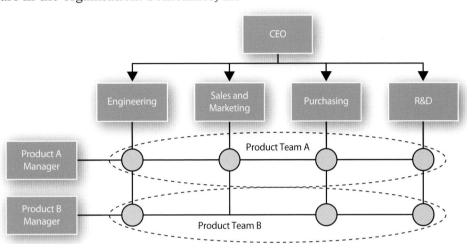

Figure D10.3 Example of a matrix structure.

> **Key Term**
>
> **Chain of command** – the line of authority.

Unit D10 Manage conflict in a team

These examples illustrate how easily workers can become dissatisfied, frustrated and demotivated if communication is poor in the chain of command. In extreme cases, conflict can arise and some organisations may restructure themselves in an effort to de-layer their organisational structure, reducing the length of the chain. This means that middle managers will often be removed (either redeployed or their positions made redundant). Teams may be empowered or organised into self-managed teams, meaning that the need to retain all supervisors and team leaders will be reduced.

Portfolio Task 3 30 minutes

Links to LO2: Assessment criterion 2.1

Give examples to your assessor of possible issues with organisational structures, systems and procedures that have or could cause conflict in your team. Provide examples of policies, procedures, structures and/or minutes of meetings which explain the main cause.

Copies of your minutes of meetings, organisational structural charts, policies and workplace procedures will provide evidence for your portfolio.

The importance of policies and procedures

Ignoring procedures can be dangerous and harmful and may also lead to conflict between team members. If one team member cuts corners, to get a task finished quickly then not only can this adversely affect the quality of the product or service, it could put other workers at risk.

It is therefore vitally important that you emphasise the importance of following procedures, for instance, in your team meetings. If procedures are not followed by a minority, the rest of the team may become frustrated and feel let down by their colleagues. These situations may begin by the perpetrators being jokingly chastised by the rest of their colleagues, but if the consequences of not following the procedures are serious – affecting the whole team – then conflict in the team may occur.

It may be useful to examine the procedures you and your team use. If they have not been reviewed recently it may be time to rewrite them, as changes in your industry and equipment you use may warrant this. Your team members should be involved in this **process**, after all they are the ones doing the tasks you are reviewing.

This can only be good for morale, as team members will appreciate that you value their opinions. It can also help to minimise the risk of conflict in your team as you should obtain 'buy-in' from members.

The ownership they have of their procedures should encourage everyone to abide by them and the importance of this should be reinforced during the one-to-one discussions and staff appraisals you conduct with each team member.

Identifying potential causes of conflict

Generally, conflict can occur as a result of:

- organisational problems – the workload may be too challenging or perhaps not challenging enough. This may lead to frustration or boredom and some team members may be tempted to take their frustration out on others. Ineffective communication and unfair working practices can also be problematic between team members.

- structural problems – insufficient reward and recognition may cause some members of your team to question 'Why do I bother?'. They may withdraw from their usual effective way of working resulting in their team colleagues resenting them as they are prevented from meeting targets. Experiencing abuse of power from others and generally not enjoying their job may also trigger situations of conflict in the team.

- personal problems – your team members may be experiencing bullying, harassment or be on the receiving end of constant teasing from others in the team. Perhaps colleagues are inflexible towards them when they try to encourage a holistic approach to meeting targets. These circumstances can easily escalate to conflict situations.

Being aware of potential conflict situations between team members. You may need to intervene and quickly put corrective action in place to remedy the situation before morale and performance is affected.

Conflict can occur for many reasons. You may have experienced or witnessed some of the following examples:

- Not respecting others' values or beliefs.
- Disagreeing on how tasks should be carried out.
- Resources not being shared out fairly.
- Regular absences of a team member, with others having to cover their work on top of their own.
- Inadequate procedures to follow.
- Favouritism towards a team member(s).
- Unclear job roles/no job description.
- Confusion over work roles – who should be doing what?
- People in the team feeling their work is more important than others'.

Add to the list, poor communication, not involving team members in the decision-making process and personality clashes, and its easy to understand how conflict can arise between team members. In addition, the culture of the team or workplace cannot be overlooked. For example, managers creating an unhealthy blame culture or an 'us and them' culture can be damaging to team spirit and lead to conflict.

Remember

When 'change' occurs, for example a restructure or a new shift pattern, employees can become demotivated and frustrated leading to conflict unless the reasons and details of the change are communicated effectively.

Team members exposed to conflict will look to you, as team leader, to take steps to rectify these situations. Failure to do so may result in you losing the faith your team have in you and you may lose their respect.

Be aware of the limits of your authority when dealing with conflict situations. You may need to inform your manager if the situation is becoming serious or if you need support. It's always a good idea to keep your managers fully aware of any situations.

Team morale versus conflict

Allowing conflict situations to continue can damage team morale. Even those team members not directly involved may find the atmosphere difficult to work in or may even find themselves being encouraged to side with one party or another. This can result in sub-groups forming in your team, seriously affecting morale, motivation and performance. If standards and targets are not being achieved as a result, questions will be asked of you, and your manager will want answers. Perhaps worse, customers' expectations may not be met and they may find other suppliers for their goods and services placing the job of everyone in the team at risk. This highlights the importance of managing conflict in a team.

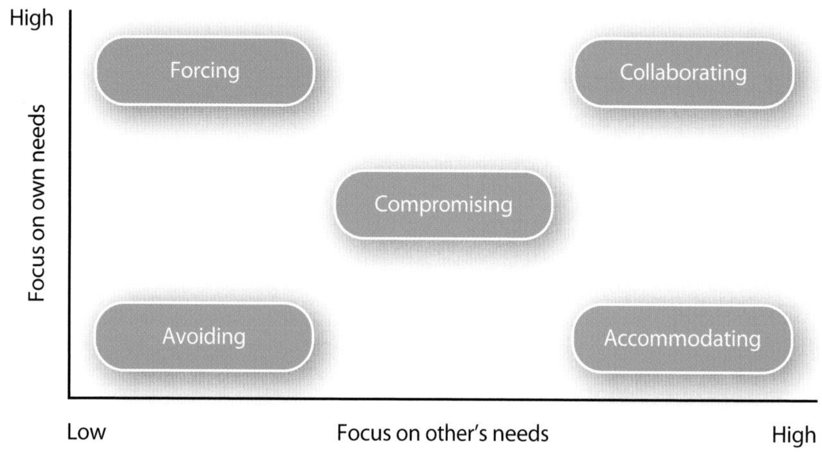

It may be useful to take a step back and analyse how you deal (or think you might deal) with conflict in your team. Perhaps everyone does react differently, but being aware of your own management style and aiming to develop your own approach may be useful.

Examine D10.3. Management theorists Kenneth W. Thomas and Ralph H. Kilmann devised this model in 1974 to recognise stages of conflict that can occur.

Figure D10.4 Stages of conflict.

Conflict management

In 1983, theorist M. A. Rahim carried out some research into conflict management. Rahim suggested that five conflict-management strategies can be considered when attempting to resolve a conflict situation:

- Integrating – exchanging information, examining differences and exploring alternatives to satisfy the parties involved.
- Obliging – minimising differences and examining commonalities to satisfy parties concerned.
- Dominating – at the expense of ignoring the needs of one party involved, the other party sets out to win over the situation and emerge with satisfaction.

- Avoiding – one party not only fails to satisfy their own needs, but also fails to show any concern for the needs of the other party. A lose-lose situation.
- Compromising – both parties agree to give and take and resolve the issue so that there is a win-win situation.

Rahim claims there isn't a best-fit approach to manage conflict but that the five strategies listed above give possibilities for parties to consider either concern for themselves, concern for others or perhaps a combination of both (compromising).

Team members' personality traits

In the 1970s psychologists working in the area of stress and conflict reached a conclusion that generally, people will fall into one of two personality traits as described below.

1. Type A Personality – this person is prone to anxiety and is easily stressed by situations that occur. Being very restless, this person can easily become involved in conflict situations.

2. Type B Personality – this person is generally more laid back and relaxed. Being easy going this person is less prone to stress and less likely to enter into conflict situations.

Your awareness of these two personality traits may lead you to identify which of your team members are most likely to become involved in conflict situations. This may help you to monitor team members in given situations, possibly enabling you to prevent conflict situations before they actually happen.

You may have heard of the 'fight or flight' syndrome. This suggests that in a stressful situation, people are likely to either stand their ground and fight back or they will choose to walk (or run) away from the situation. Those that select the option to stand their ground are more likely to create or fuel conflict in the workplace.

Think of the saying 'seeing red'. It is interesting to note that when stressed a person's brain receives a rush of additional chemicals as the body tries to deal with the stressful situation. As these chemicals reach the brain, a person may very quickly say something which is later regretted or even become aggressive. However, after about six seconds experts suggest the chemicals settle and the person calms down.

Take a close look at how your team members operate. Can you identify **rivalry** in any form? This could be between individual team members, or perhaps between two teams in your organisation. While competition can be healthy and productive, resentment can easily build up between competing teams or individuals, when reward or praise reaches some, but not all. Watch out, too, for acts of discrimination. Some team

Key Term

Rivalry – competition between individuals or teams.

members may be on the receiving end of discriminatory practices and may initially try to ignore what is happening to them. Over time they can become more and more frustrated until they eventually retaliate leading to a conflict situation (see Unit B11 on equality and diversity).

Given that conflict can lead to lowered morale, motivation and performance, taking action to avoid it can be particularly beneficial. When conflict occurs, workers may not have such an enthusiastic approach towards their work because the atmosphere is tense. This can prevent important and relevant information being passed from team member to team member, ultimately affecting the completion of tasks and the achievement of goals.

All of this can result in higher stress levels, leading to:

- more absenteeism (for example, people don't enjoy work and take unofficial days off)
- a higher sickness rate (for example, stress-related illnesses)
- increased staff turnover (for example, people leave to find a more relaxed working environment).

Bad publicity travels fast! Friends and family of your team members may tell other people outside of your organisation of the perceived poor working atmosphere. This, in turn, can damage the image and reputation of your whole organisation, potentially affecting future business opportunities and the job security of everyone.

Taking action to avoid conflict becomes increasingly important if the working relations of the team and indeed the reputation of the whole organisation are to be protected and safeguarded.

Avoiding, managing and resolving conflict

Back in 1976, management theorist Kenneth W. Thomas developed five approaches to managing conflict. It will be beneficial to analyse each of these approaches and consider which you believe is the best one!

- Forcing – you intend to get your own way at any cost and defeat the parties involved.
- Avoiding – you decide to wait and see what will happen and you don't address the reasons for the conflict.
- Compromising – your aim is to get things back to how they were, as quickly as possible. You may do this by moving things forward through bargaining and negotiation.
- Accommodating – you worry about upsetting anyone, so you simply accept what is being said to you and go along with what the other parties want.
- Collaborating – you aim to resolve problems so that all parties concerned feel they've been treated fairly. You aim to do this, by discussing ideas together.

Now consider, if you:

- avoid dealing with conflict or are too accommodating, your behaviour may be considered to be passive by nature
- compromise or collaborate when dealing with conflict, then your behaviour may be considered to be assertive. This is because you are not being passive by not reacting, but neither are you being aggressive by using actions that will make sure you win at any cost.

When you are dealing with situations in the workplace that you think may lead to conflict if not resolved, structure a discussion with the parties involved (in a suitable quiet and private environment), that enables you to:

- obtain relevant information from the parties concerned
- identify exactly what the dispute is about
- get the parties involved to agree there will be different views
- aim for a win-win situation (all parties have a positive outcome)
- negotiate a fair outcome for all.

It is worth noting that negotiation is a particularly useful strategy for resolving conflict. For this process to work, be clear in your own mind exactly what you want to achieve. Run through your mind, or write down on paper, what the best possible outcome might be and what the worst possible outcome might be. Do this before your discussions with the parties concerned. When negotiating to achieve a fair outcome, be open, honest and ask for explanations of anything you're not sure of. It's very important to listen well, be assertive and have relevant information to hand.

To avoid conflict escalating, this simple measure of calming the affected person or persons down can help. To calm someone, you should:

- find somewhere private and quiet to take them – invite them to sit down
- reassure the other person that their concerns will be addressed
- give them time to tell you their problem (get it off their chest)
- not interrupt – let them finish, but show you've listened
- be aware of your body language and don't appear threatening
- speak slowly and softly when you do respond.

It is important to consider that the way you and your team members respond to situations can seriously affect your working life. As a team, you may feel from time to time that you have unreasonable demands placed upon you when, for example, objectives and targets from others are not SMART. Your external customers may make your life difficult too, if they are constantly changing their minds or perhaps complaining.

Remember

Being aggressive is unacceptable behaviour and will never resolve a conflict situation.

Activity 30 minutes

If one of your team members approached you to complain that a colleague is leaving early at the end of his/her shift, what actions would you take? How would your responses differ if:

1. the team member leaving early is generally a very good worker
2. initially you have no proof that the team member has been leaving early, but you later find out that it is true and others have been covering for them.

Remember

Sometimes conflict can actually be good! There may be slight disagreement over the way a task is being carried out, or perhaps the writing of new procedures. Providing the process is carefully managed, everyone's views can be accepted and agreed upon, actually improving the way things are done.

Activity 30 minutes

The table below offers examples of causes of conflict and suggested remedies. NB Awareness of remedies and implementing them promptly can be sufficient to avoid conflict happening in the first place!

The causes and remedies in the table have been mixed up. Your task is to examine each cause and then decide which remedy should sit in the table alongside it. Rewrite the table correctly with the causes and their remedies and give a brief reason why the remedy is appropriate.

Cause of conflict	Suggested remedy
Personality clashes in the team	Ensure team members are involved in the process and offer clear reasons why the change will happen as early as possible before it actually does. Provide regular communication updates to the team.
Competition for resources between team members	Ensure all team members are aware of your organisational structure (show them the organisational chart). Is everyone clear of the chain of command, reporting remedies and accountability?
Issues over authority	Examine communication methods used. Where and when are discussions between you and team members held (e.g. team meetings)? Ensure procedures are easy to follow and regularly reviewed.
Misunderstandings between team members	Investigate your budget allowance for purchasing adequate resources with your manager. Examine procedures and rotas to examine how resources can be shared out and their use monitored effectively.
Change in the workplace	Consider separating team members from each other and examine the possibility of job rotation. Offer assertiveness training to team members involved in the conflict.

Remember that family and friends may unwittingly place pressure upon you to do things and eventually you may become too busy both in and out of work unless you monitor situations carefully.

You may become stressed and frustrated in these circumstances and so can your team members if the wellbeing of your team is overlooked, perhaps even the person passive by nature can be prone to conflict.

PLTS

This task will give you the opportunity to reflect on how you have managed a conflict situation and to evaluate what you have learnt from the experience to inform future progress (RL2, 3, 5; EP2, 3, 4).

Functional Skills

By preparing a 500-word document you will be practising your Functional Skills English Level 1 in writing. You will practise your grammar and punctuation skills, and structuring of your sentences.

Portfolio Task 4 45 minutes

Links to LO2: Assessment criteria 2.2, 2.3

1. Give examples to your assessor of potential conflict between your team members.

2. Explain the strategies you agreed with your manager or team members to resolve the potential conflict.

3. If you were to manage this situation again, would you do anything differently?

4. Reflect, in a maximum of 500 words, on the actions you undertook to try to avoid this potential conflict.

Advisory, Conciliation and Arbitration Service (ACAS)

There is also help outside your organisation to resolve conflict. The Advisory, Conciliation and Arbitration Service (ACAS) offers support to organisations in industrial relations. With regard to conflict, it advises that the actions in the table below can be of benefit:

Type of conflict	How it can be addressed
A personality clash or one-off minor disagreement	The manager or team leader has a one-to-one discussion in an informal manner
A persistent and ongoing situation	The team leader/manager has informal discussions with those involved to identify the root cause of the conflict
An employee uses the organisation's grievance policy to take action against another employee	This is a more formal case. The team leader/manager should follow the internal procedures to deal with this and make sure that human resources is notified
An employee wishes to pursue a claim and take the case to an employment tribunal	The team leader/manager and human resources should suggest mediation with ACAS wherever possible before action for a tribunal case goes ahead

Table D10.1 How to address conflicts.

Be able to understand how to encourage team members to resolve their own conflicts

Involving your team in the identification and resolution of their own conflicts empowers them and gives them input into their own situation. It may not always be appropriate for team members to solve their own conflicts, but making it known that they are encouraged to take responsibility for them can have a very positive effect on morale and ultimately the success and effectiveness of the team.

Team members identifying potential problems

There may be occasions when your team members identify potential problems or conflicts and report them to you. If this happens, you must act quickly to resolve any issues before they become more serious.

The difficult situations and sources of current or potential conflict that team members may identify could be due to a variety of causes, for instance human error, a system failure or faulty equipment, unacceptable behaviour or simply a shortage of resources that are needed. It may be that procedures to address the way work is done need to be updated, additional training is required, and the way resources are allocated needs to be reviewed.

Activity 20 minutes

Think of an example when your line manager encouraged you to resolve a problem or potential conflict that you had identified. Write down what the issue was, how you resolved it and how your line manager monitored your actions and evaluated the outcome.

Remember

Rather than spending time trying to resolve a problem or conflict situation, it's better to take steps to make sure difficult situations don't happen in the first place.

Whatever the cause, there is a knock-on effect to these problems, because they can lead to:

- increased conflict, absenteeism and perhaps good people leaving the organisation
- increased risk of accidents and incidents
- backlog of work and therefore unhappy customers as deadlines are not met
- more complaints from internal/external customers
- quality standards not being met and projects/tasks taking longer to complete
- equipment and machines not used effectively due to more downtime.

All of the above can lead to additional costs for the department/ organisation, but can also greatly increase the risk of conflict between team members.

Identifying potential conflict areas or problems before they occur or when they are still at the early stages is obviously desirable. It is therefore prudent to encourage your team to be aware of potential problem areas and nurture a culture where they are encouraged to come to you as soon as possible if they foresee a problem.

Team members resolving their own difficulties

In some instances it may be better for you to encourage your team members to resolve their own problems or conflicts. This will depend on your team members and how serious the situation is or could become. You must use your judgement to decide whether to empower your colleagues to resolve the issue themselves, or whether you intervene.

Remember that encouraging your team members to resolve their own difficulties, within reason, can motivate them as they will recognise that you trust them and respect their judgement. You can encourage your team to take the initiative in this way in team briefings, through other public channels such as notice boards, or even specially timetabled meetings or workshops where you discuss with your team how problems can be resolved.

Consider this process that you can share with your team.

- Decide exactly what the problem or difficulty is.
- Collect information about the difficulty to understand why its happening.
- Think about how many alternative solutions there may be.
- Evaluate how effective each alternative solution might be (for example, costs, health and safety impact, customer service impact, impact on colleagues).

- Choose the best solution and implement it.
- Evaluate the outcomes to see whether your chosen solution worked.

You can reinforce this step-by-step approach to resolving difficulties by making reference to it in the PDRs/staff appraisals you conduct with your team.

To resolve problems, inform your team that there needs to be a balance between the needs of the organisation, the team members and ultimately the customers.

Make your team members aware that when resolving difficulties between themselves they need to listen to each other and respect each other's views and opinions. Failure to do this can result in additional conflict situations arising.

Your team should be encouraged to:

- avoid arguments between themselves and others in the organisation
- be assertive, but not aggressive
- be flexible in their approach
- acknowledge how others are feeling and include everyone in the problem-solving process
- avoid negative criticism
- use voice control (soft and quiet tone, no shouting)
- avoid sarcasm
- be aware of their own body language
- be aware of their own behaviour patterns (for example, don't intimidate others in the team).

The team must fully understand what it is that needs to be resolved and the consequences of not resolving it. There may well be obstacles to prevent them resolving a situation in the way they would like to, such as costs or perhaps new laws, such as health and safety regulations.

As team leader, you should monitor the actions your team members are taking to resolve their difficulties. Having empowered them, you still need to be mindful that time taken to resolve something means they may be distracted from their day-to-day tasks affecting the achievement of your targets. You could help avoid this by issuing a deadline for them to resolve the difficult situation.

Through training demonstrations, or team briefing opportunities, you may wish to familiarise your team members with the following conflict resolution tools.

> **Remember**
>
> Always examine the risks to the organisation of implementing your chosen solution in terms of cost, images and reputation.

Unit D10 Manage conflict in a team

Fishbone diagram

This tool is also known as an Ishikiwa diagram or cause and effect diagram.

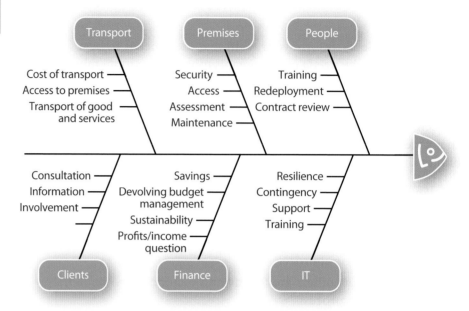

Figure D10.5 An example of a fishbone diagram

Using this diagram, the team can brainstorm ideas, working backwards through the bones of the fish. Suitable headings can be placed on the main bones and responses written in as the discussion progresses.

Five whys model

Another useful tool is the five whys model, which aims to find the root cause of a problem. This is done verbally by asking 'Why?' five times.

Consider the example below:

Q: Why has the customer complained?
A: Because her delivery wasn't made as promised.

Q: Why wasn't the delivery made?
A: Because the order wasn't picked in the warehouse.

Q: Why wasn't it picked in the warehouse?
A: Because the new member of staff didn't follow procedures.

Q: Why didn't the new member of staff follow procedures?
A: Because she didn't receive the correct training to do her job.

Q: Why didn't she receive the correct training to do her new job?
A: Because her induction process was insufficient.

Root cause is that the induction process needs reviewing to incorporate sufficient training to do work effectively and efficiently.

Helping your team resolve conflict

Reinforce with your team members that when resolving difficult situations themselves, they should:

- pool their expertise, recognising each other's strengths and weaknesses
- discuss ideas with someone else, perhaps in another team, who has had similar difficult situations to deal with
- explore how useful an action plan will be so everyone knows who is doing what and by when
- obtain permission from you before making any major decisions
- communicate with each other effectively, and you as team leader, so that everyone is kept up to date at all times.

Portfolio Task 5 30 minutes

Links to LO3: Assessment criterion 3.1
Using examples you currently use in your department, explain to your assessor how you encourage your team members to identify and resolve their own problems and conflicts. Explain any techniques you find successful and any that you find are unsuccessful. Give reasons for your comments. Your assessor will record this discussion as evidence for your portfolio.

Checklist

Remind your team members to try to resolve their own difficult situations by:

- sharing each other's knowledge and skills
- discussing and sharing ideas
- setting out an action plan if suitable
- seeking permission if making changes
- communicating and sharing the changes with everyone involved.

Developing respect within your team

Respect emerges from a process of understanding. In other words, respect has to be earned. Mutual respect between team members can minimise the risk of conflict situations arising and solidify the team's approach to fulfilling its obligations and meeting its objectives.

By politely and promptly challenging each other's inappropriate behaviour when and as necessary, and by talking through difficult situations calmly, rapport can be built and maintained. This largely depends upon the culture that the team works within. You might imagine that a blame culture, for example, would not easily lend itself to a culture of support, rapport and respect.

Given that respect must be earned, examine whether team members have:

- full commitment to business objectives
- open and effective communication
- a reliable approach
- honesty, transparency and openness
- trust.

Key Term

Respect – listening and valuing other people's views and opinions.

Unit D10 Manage conflict in a team

Keeping promises, promoting fairness and taking a genuine interest in others can lead to respect. Showing concern, keeping confidence and admitting to mistakes can further develop respect.

When you respect someone it can result in a feel-good factor for both you and the person to whom you show respect. This improves morale and motivation, and ultimately performance. The feel-good factor will sooner or later ripple throughout the team, helping to minimise the risk of conflict.

Checklist

You should lead by example and if you want your team members to respect you, you should:

- be consistently polite and courteous
- never make promises, unless you know you can keep them
- involve your team in decision making
- always be fair when allocating work
- show genuine concern for the well-being of the team
- always try to be positive – even when things appear difficult (this can rub off on your team)
- be honest in your approach (it's no good saying yes just to keep someone happy when you should be saying no)
- be reliable and dependable and keep to your word
- keep up to date with latest trends and techniques – the team will look to you to share best practice
- show your team that you are content to receive negative criticism – as long as it is constructive. That's how everyone learns!
- conduct yourself with professionalism – don't swear, keep to the company dress code etc.
- not be afraid to express your own opinions – don't just agree with others to keep the peace.

Remember

To be respected you have to respect others!

It may be useful to share some or all of the points in the checklist with your team, perhaps in a team meeting, explaining the importance of these for a good team spirit.

Portfolio Task 6 10 minutes

Links to LO3: Assessment criterion 3.2
Explain to your assessor what techniques you currently use to develop and maintain respect between team members. You should produce a personal statement that will provide product evidence for your portfolio.

Be able to understand legal and organisational requirements concerning conflict

Rights and obligations with regard to conflict

In any organisation both rights and obligations have to be considered. You could say that the organisation has obligations placed upon it and that employees have rights. But also, there are certain obligations placed upon the employees, and organisations too have rights.

For example, an organisation has an obligation to pay wages on time for services and skills provided by the employee. The employee has the right to work in safe conditions. Similarly, the organisation has the right to dismiss an employee for serious misdemeanours, such as **gross misconduct**, while the employee has an obligation to turn up for work on time.

When dealing with conflict, there are obligations and rights for both managers and team members to consider.

Key Term

Gross misconduct – serious act by an employee, such as theft or fraud, leading to instant dismissal.

Conflict management	
The organisation's obligations (examples)	**The employee's rights (examples)**
– To provide a safe and healthy working environment – To provide adequate working conditions – Not to allow bullying and harassment – Not to allow discriminatory practices – To ensure everyone knows what's required of them	– To be free from victimisation – To be treated equally and fairly – To be free from unsafe and hazardous working practice – To receive written details of the contract of employment – To have sufficient facilities
The employees obligations (examples)	**The organisation's rights (examples)**
– To exercise appropriate behaviour – To give a fair day's work for a fair day's pay – To meet the organisation's SMART objectives – To use resources and share fairly with each other – To carry out reasonable requests – To respect colleagues and customers	– To control staff behaviour – To receive work of a good standard – To have its plans, mission and goals met – To expect employees to use resources sensibly – To have reasonable requests carried out – To expect employees to attend training to raise standards

Table D10.2 The obligations and rights of the organisation and employees when dealing with conflict.

With rights and obligations in place and clearly understood, conflict situations can be reduced.

Organisational policies and procedures to deal with conflict

Your workplace is likely to have policies, procedures or codes of conduct in place that can deal with conflict in your team. These will describe what to do or what should happen when conflict situations arise. These might include:

- bullying and harassment policy – this policy will explain what rights employees have and the obligations placed upon the organisation if employees claim they are being victimised in some way
- grievance procedures – this informs employees of their rights should they wish to complain about inappropriate behaviour of a manager or colleague or have any other grievance
- disciplinary procedure – if employees are deemed guilty of misconduct, then this will outline what action the organisation can take
- capability policy – this will suggest actions that can be taken with regard to an employee's capability to carry out tasks allocated to them. Are they not pulling their weight or do they need support guidance and training to help them?

ACAS can advise on disciplinary and grievance procedures and the government recommends that organisations adhere to the code of practice that ACAS has in place for following these procedures.

Maintaining records

If situations of conflict are allowed to continue over time and perhaps an employee feels they have to leave their employment or is dismissed as a consequence, they may take action against the organisation, even after they have left. For example, they may claim wrongful or constructive dismissal and at a tribunal hearing the organisation will be asked to demonstrate what support was given to employees to prevent or minimise the risk of conflict. Also, once conflict has been identified, what actions were taken to support those involved. In order to be able to do this, the organisation must have full and accurate records of what took place.

It is therefore important to keep records of discussions, responses and actions put in place when conflict situation have arisen. For example dates, times and details of any incidents of conflict, records of verbal and written warnings and evidence that appropriate support was provided. Examples of support might be:

- counselling – referring of parties involved, particularly victims of conflict, to a professional counsellor to assist them
- health and safety – involvement of the health and safety officer and application of the organisation's health and safety policy if accidents or incidents occurred as a result of a conflict situation.

Key Term

ACAS – Advisory, Conciliation and Arbitration Service – an independent organisation who will provide advice and support and a number of employment issues such as disciplinaries and grievances.

Remember that if there is a prolonged situation of conflict, someone's health may suffer. They may feel stressed, leading to illness, absenteeism and further problems between the employees, the organisation, and perhaps yourself as a team leader. There may be a case for your team member in such circumstances, to bring a claim that your organisation has been in breach of the Health and Safety at Work etc. Act 1974 or associated regulations. Further, there is a possibility that a civil claim may be made against the organisation for negligence.

For a negligence case to be proved, the employee would have to demonstrate:

- a duty of care was owed by the organisation
- there was a breach of the duty of care owed by the organisation
- injury or damage occurred as a result of that breach of duty.

If these can be demonstrated then there can be a successful claim for negligence and the organisation may be sued for compensation. An example would be that a conflict situation was allowed to persist without intervention or support from the organisation leading to stress-related illnesses, which in the eyes of the law may be referred to as 'injury'. It is vital, therefore, to keep accurate records so that the claim can be accurately judged.

Activity — 60 minutes

Talk to your manager or your human resources department to find out what legal and organisational policies or procedures are in place to deal with conflict in your organisation.

Then consider what external sources of help exist that can advise both employees and organisations when situations of conflict arise.

Portfolio Task 7 — 30 minutes

Links to LO4: Assessment criterion 4.1

Provide a 500-word document that outlines the legal and organisational requirements in relation to conflict in your team.

Maintaining accurate and confidential conflict records

It is very important that records of discussions, actions taken and support given in relation to conflict are **confidential** and kept safely and securely.

When you record details of conflict situations, make sure you don't miss out any information, no matter how trivial it may seem at the time. The records you keep should be accurate and complete. They should relay exactly what has happened and what action has been taken.

Functional Skills

By preparing a word-processed 500-word document you will be practising your Functional Skills in ICT and English at Level 1. You will practise entering, developing and refining information for your ICT Functional Skills and presenting information in a logical sequence using appropriate language, format and structure for your English Functional Skills.

Key Term

Confidential – kept secret, or shared only among a limited number of people on a need-to-know basis.

Unit D10 Manage conflict in a team

Data Protection Act (DPA) 1998 – an act that specifies how personal information should be gathered, used, stored and shared.

Remember

Any reports or documents you have produced when dealing with your team members should be labelled 'CONFIDENTIAL' before you file them away.

Remember

You should make a note of any discussions you have with team members. You should record the date, who was involved and exactly what the problem was. You should also record what was agreed and what you advised should happen next.

Confidentiality of records

Be aware of the **Data Protection Act (DPA) 1998**, and make sure all records you keep are stored safely and securely. The DPA ensures that individuals are protected from their confidential details being shared with others without their knowledge or permission.

As with any type of record held about an individual in the workplace, any discussions you have with a colleague regarding a conflict situation must be kept confidential with records stored securely and safely. There are eight principles to consider. Records should be:

- processed fairly and lawfully
- obtained for specified and lawful purposes
- adequate, relevant and not excessive
- accurate and up to date
- not kept any longer than necessary
- processed in accordance with the data subject's (the individual's) rights
- securely kept
- not transferred to any other country without adequate protection in situ.

Some records you should accurately complete as evidence of support given in times of conflict include:

- reflective accounts you may have written up after informal discussions with the parties involved (make sure you put a date on these when you write them)
- more formal reports produced by you when conflict situations are more serious. Perhaps you have had to consult with your own manager in these types of cases and this too should be in your report; make sure it is signed, name printed and dated by everyone involved
- staff appraisal (PDR) records that show when you have discussed conflict situations with team members and actions you have agreed
- entries in accident books
- revised risk assessments and other relevant health and safety documentation
- copies of communications with ACAS when, for example, you have sought up-to-date advice
- copies of action plans developed to resolve conflict situations with your team members, weekly target-setting documents, used to seek improvement and records of team members' actions
- documentation leading up to and including disciplinary action such as warnings.

It is important to record the outcomes of your discussions with parties involved. For example, you may have agreed an action plan with a team member. This will show that as a result of your intervention, appropriate action has been taken.

Portfolio Task 8 30 minutes

Links to LO4: Assessment criterion 4.2

Discuss with your assessor the importance of maintaining complete, accurate and confidential records of conflict and the outcome of the conflict situation. Describe what types of records you would keep and how you would store them to ensure you comply with the Data Protection Act and your organisation's confidentiality policy.

Your assessor will record this discussion to act as evidence for your portfolio.

Team talk

David's story

Hi, my name is David and I have been a team leader at a supermarket for five years. I have a good relationship with my team and I believe that all of them can come and talk to me about anything at any time. I have an open-door policy and I remind them of this during our team meetings. Generally, every team member has been working hard to meet our objectives, but recently I have noticed that Jim, an older member of the team, has been a lot quieter than usual. He doesn't contribute as much in meetings and he doesn't turn up to after-work team bonding nights any more. But his standard of work is still high and he meets all of his deadlines.

I was concerned to find out what was upsetting Jim, so reminded the team again during our weekly team meeting that my door is always open and if any of them have any problems or concerns, that they should come and speak to me. Eventually Jim came to talk to me and confided that he was being bullied and harassed by a new, younger team member.

Top tips

David should take time to discuss the situation with Jim in more detail to find out exactly what has been happening and for how long. David will need to take detailed notes of the discussion and should, in confidence, inform his own line manager and/or his human resources manager of the situation. He should reassure Jim that he will investigate the situation thoroughly without attracting too much attention, which could, of course, make things worse.

David should offer as much support as possible to Jim and keep him fully informed of the outcomes. David will then need to speak to the younger member of staff on an informal basis initially, to make sure he finds out both sides of the story.

In consultation with his line manager, David should make both parties in the conflict situation aware that the organisation's bullying and harassment policy will be referred to for guidance. If it is the case that Jim is being bullied, then David will need to advise Jim that he may need to revert to the organisation's grievance procedures.

Ask the expert	
Q	How would you deal with a situation where a team member tells you they are being bullied by another team colleague?
A	You should treat any claims in confidence and make sure that you: ■ inform your line manager of the situation as soon as possible ■ keep detailed records of everything you discuss with both parties involved ■ don't make any decisions or take action until you know what has actually happened (until you know the accusations are founded) ■ offer as much support as possible to the injured party and record this ■ store all documents safely and securely ■ make both parties aware of the location of the organisations bullying and harassment policy and grievance procedures ■ keep both parties updated with progress of the investigation ■ after a conclusion has been reached, monitor and evaluate the situation to assess whether it has been resolved or whether any further action needs to be taken.

What your assessor is looking for

In order to demonstrate your competency within this unit, you will need to provide sufficient evidence to your assessor. You will need to provide a short written narrative or personal statement, explaining how you meet the assessment criteria. In addition, your assessor may need to ask you questions to test your knowledge of the topics identified in this unit.

Below is a list of suggested documentation that will provide evidence to help you to prove your competency in this unit.

Work products for this unit could include:

- minutes of meetings with your team where you highlight support available

- examples of emails/minutes of meetings where you remind your team of the standards of work and behaviour expected of them

- organisational charts showing reporting and communication lines

- your organisation's bullying and harassment policy

- your organisation's grievance and disciplinary procedures

- records of informal notes taken during initial discussions when there is a claim of a conflict situation.

Your assessor will guide you through the assessment process as detailed in the candidate logbook. The detailed assessment criteria are shown in the logbook and by working through these questions, combined with providing the relevant evidence, you will meet the learning outcomes required to complete this unit.

Task and page reference	Assessment criteria
1 (page 177)	1.1
2 (page 180)	1.2
3 (page 184)	2.1
4 (page 190)	2.2, 2.3
5 (page 195)	3.1
6 (page 196)	3.2
7 (page 199)	4.1
8 (page 201)	4.2

Unit E12 Manage knowledge in own area of responsibility

Knowledge management is concerned with information relating to your products, services, customers and your market and with how you can find ways to firstly capture, and then utilise this information to find better and smarter ways of operating. Better products, faster response times and better service provision – all of these are possible with the application of the principles of knowledge management.

In this unit you will explore the basics of knowledge management and look at how you can apply it to your area of responsibility. You will investigate the likely impact on your team of implementing knowledge management procedures. You will also identify the best methods of supporting them to ensure that these procedures are followed.

Assessing the current status of knowledge management in your area of responsibility is important and may reveal potential for further development. You will explore what this means for you as a team leader in the final part of the unit.

What you will learn:

- Be able to understand existing knowledge management in own area of responsibility
- Be able to develop knowledge
- Be able to share knowledge
- Be able to monitor and evaluate knowledge management in own area of responsibility

Links to the Technical Certificate

If you are completing your NVQ as part of an Apprenticeship Framework, you will find the following topics are also covered in your Technical Certificate:

- Know what knowledge sources exist to support the work of teams
- Understand how to use knowledge to support team working
- Be able to review the value of knowledge used by teams

Be able to understand existing knowledge management in your own area of responsibility

Knowledge management means the ways in which knowledge and information are obtained, developed and ultimately used to achieve the goals of the organisation. As most people work in teams, organisations need to ensure that the required knowledge and information are available and readily accessible to these teams in order to allow them to effectively carry out their work.

Knowledge management processes and procedures need to ensure that the required knowledge is made available to those who need it in a clear, well-presented format and that it is easily understandable, accurate and up to date. In this section you will investigate the ways in which knowledge and information are obtained, shared and utilised in your team or department. You will also go on to investigate intellectual property and look at the ways in which this can be protected.

How knowledge is gained and applied

Think about all of the different types of information, knowledge and expertise that you rely upon each day to carry out your work and to keep your team on track. When you arrive at your desk, probably the first thing you do is to check your email. Why is this? Checking your email is the quickest way to find out if someone has sent you important information that you will need to do your job, such as this week's shift rota, this month's sales targets and the new product price list.

No doubt you could probably add many more examples of your own to this list. The key point to note is that individuals and teams are all dependent, to a certain extent, on different types of knowledge and information in order to carry out their jobs. This can range from the simplest of details, such as the photocopier maintenance company's telephone number, to complex documents, such as annual corporate accounting reports.

Reasons why you need knowledge

You need access to accurate, good-quality knowledge to help you to:

- assess situations correctly and make sound judgements
- make effective decisions
- provide information to others
- plan and forecast
- monitor and keep up to date with trends in your industry
- watch out for early warning signals of potential problems, such as a drop in sales or an increase in production costs
- identify new business opportunities
- stay one step ahead of the competition.

The ultimate aim of obtaining knowledge is to become fully informed about all key relevant events – and especially changes – occurring within and outside the business. This will allow you to make better decisions and run your team more effectively. Importantly, it will also allow you to make well-informed and professionally relevant contributions in meetings with your line manager.

Sources of knowledge you need for your work

Knowledge can be acquired from a number of sources including:

- colleagues
- company databases
- departmental records and reports
- relevant trade press and websites
- specialist market research agencies
- the government's statistics website at www.statistics.gov.uk
- your network of industry contacts
- industry events, exhibitions and trade shows.

Types of knowledge

Internal and external knowledge

Knowledge can be internal or external. Internal knowledge is either generated or held within the organisation and can include important details about employees, customers, the organisation's products and services, financial data, design blueprints, inventions and even ideas.

External knowledge relates to the environment in which the organisation operates and includes legislation affecting the business, the economic climate, customer **demographics** and trends, competitor intelligence and **benchmarking**.

Formal and informal knowledge

Formal knowledge may consist of information given in a presentation by the managing director to all staff, or information contained in your staff handbook. Informal knowledge can consist of gossip and chat heard in the staff canteen. Both are potentially valuable in different ways.

Explicit and tacit knowledge

Explicit knowledge, sometimes called hard knowledge, is knowledge that is fact based, stated, published, or spoken and can be easily documented for later use. It can include information given to you at work in meetings, during presentations or via emailed documents.

Tacit knowledge, on the other hand, sometimes called soft knowledge, is the type of knowledge that often exists only in someone's head. It is usually not easily recorded; it is not normally a set of straightforward facts but instead is the result of the wealth of knowledge gained over

Activity 15 minutes

List the main sources of knowledge used by your team or department. Say whether they are internal or external knowledge sources and identify which are the most important ones for your particular team.

PLTS

When you are analysing and evaluating information, judging its relevance and value, you are practising your skills as an independent enquirer (IE).

Key Terms

Benchmarking – comparing business results and outputs with those of other businesses in the industry.

Demographics – characteristics of customer groups such as age, gender and income.

Key Term

Culture – a set of shared attitudes, values and practices that exist in an organisation.

many years' experience doing a certain job and of 'how things are really done'. Tacit knowledge can be learnt by methods such as on-the-job training, observation, mentoring and even informal conversations where you may pick up snippets of helpful information on how certain things are generally done – also called the **culture** of the workplace. Apprenticeships are a very good example of where acquiring tacit knowledge from other, more experienced staff is often a key part of the learning that takes place.

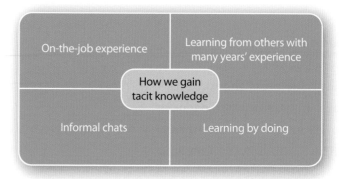

Figure E12.1 Different ways in which employees acquire tacit knowledge.

It is argued that this tacit form of knowledge is the most highly valuable type of knowledge that exists inside businesses and that finding ways to make this knowledge explicit is the key to exploiting commercial opportunities and gaining huge improvements in business.

Levels of knowledge

Knowledge exists at different levels within and around an organisation. It exists at individual, group, organisational and inter-organisational level. Inter-organisational knowledge is knowledge gained from other businesses such as suppliers and distributors. These different levels show the spectrum of knowledge available to the business and the key to maximising the value of it is to find ways to make links between the different levels. This can be done by increasing contact, collaboration and developing good working relationships.

Applying knowledge to your work

The process of applying knowledge to your work involves a series of steps as shown in the diagram below.

Figure E12.2 Steps involved in applying knowledge to work.

Analysing and interpreting

Analysing and interpreting knowledge means working through the raw data to ask yourself what it means. For example, if you were looking at raw sales figures for your department, you would need to look beyond the numerical spreadsheet data to identify any trends and examine the overall picture. Are monthly sales increasing or decreasing and by what percentage? How do the figures compare to last year's? Adding context in this way provides meaning and makes the information more useful to the end user. Identifying peaks, troughs and averages for such data over time is a very good method of benchmarking. This is a useful way to evaluate performance and to plan future improvements.

Refining

Refining knowledge means getting rid of unnecessary or redundant information and sifting out only what is relevant and pertinent to your needs. This is a very important skill that you will develop over time as you gain more experience. You can develop techniques for separating the relevant from the less relevant information.

Email at work is an excellent example of an area where you must develop techniques for refining and prioritising the information which arrives in your inbox. In many businesses, the sheer volume of information shared via email is more than anyone can hope to get through. An effective method of separating out the most important emails, so that you can easily view and deal with them first, is to set up filters and rules to all incoming mail. Also, make sure that your spam or junk filter is set to the maximum security setting to prevent unsolicited and irrelevant emails clogging up your inbox. You can periodically check the contents of your junk or spam folder to double check that nothing business related has inadvertently been caught in there.

Utilising

The ultimate aim of obtaining and refining all of the information available to you at work is to be able to use it to create business intelligence which can provide valuable improvements to your business, putting you ahead of your competitors.

Unit E12

Manage knowledge in own area of responsibility

Business intelligence on your customers' buying behaviour can be used to develop the most attractive special offers and promotions with the highest appeal to your customers. Similarly, intelligence developed on your competitor's new product range can be used to make decisions on your own organisation's product range and on ways of marketing this to maintain or expand the market share of your business.

Sharing knowledge

Sharing knowledge within the team is important for keeping everyone up to date and informed of latest developments relevant to their work. If team members are not given appropriate access to knowledge, they will feel alienated and excluded, be less able to carry out their work and the team spirit will be affected.

> **Remember**
>
> Make sure your staff are able to access all of the information they need. Remember, too, that these needs may well change over time, so be sure to check on this regularly.

Specialised job roles like archaeologists will always need to share knowledge.

In the early and mid-twentieth century, it was common practice among management to restrict the distribution of information and to limit access on a strictly need-to-know basis. More recently, however, there has been a shift away from this management approach to a focus on leadership, empowerment and involvement of staff.

Therefore, it is good practice to allow your team free access to all information except where there is a genuine reason for confidentiality. If no harm will be caused by the information being made freely accessible then there is no real reason for keeping it restricted.

Systems and processes for knowledge sharing

Knowledge can be shared among the team in a number ways including:

* company **intranets** or **extranets**
* computer networks
* web-based collaboration software, such as Microsoft SharePoint®, which provide a central location for file and information storage which can be accessed remotely from anywhere in the world

> **Key Terms**
>
> **Extranet** – an extension to a company's intranet to include password-controlled access to other individuals or businesses from outside of the company, such as suppliers or business partners.
>
> **Intranet** – a private communications network within a business.

- induction, training and coaching
- handbooks and procedure manuals
- product brochures and specifications
- regular team meetings.

Protecting intellectual property

Intellectual property (IP) consists of **assets** that a business owns, such as trademarks, logos and branding designs, patents, computer software, inventions and even drug formulations. It also includes creative materials, such as text, music, lyrics and artwork. As you can see, there are many different types of IP and each of them has a potentially great value to the organisation. IP is an asset to a business, just like land, buildings and stock. However, IP is different in that it is referred to as an **intangible asset**, mainly because it is difficult to put a financial value on it. IP can, in fact, be bought, **licensed** and sold by businesses and this is a good way of defining a value for it.

Methods of protecting IP

As with any other business asset, such as the cash held at the bank and the premises from which the business operates, IP must be kept safe. It belongs to the business and needs to be protected from unauthorised use, imitation, or outright theft.

Copyright material

Copyright material can include books, art, music, films and broadcasts, as well as websites and computer programs. All of these types of material are automatically protected by copyright law. There is no need to register copyright. This book that you are reading is protected by copyright. The text and images on all of the websites that you view are also copyright. You can identify copyright material by the © symbol, which usually appears along with the year and the name of the individual or organisation who owns it, for example, © 2012 Smith Ltd.

Trademarks

Trademarks include things such as branding, logos, designs, words and symbols that are associated with the identity of a business or its products. These can be protected by being registered. Once a business registers a trademark, it is then entitled to use it on its goods and has the right to take action against any third parties who attempt to use that trademark. No two businesses are allowed to have the same trademark. Each must be unique and must not be confusingly similar to any other. You can easily identify something which is a registered trademark, whether it is words, images or both, as it will appear with an ® symbol next to it. Unregistered trademarks appear with the symbol ™ next to them.

Activity 15 minutes

List three different methods by which knowledge is shared either within your team or between your team and others in the organisation. For each example, explain why such sharing of knowledge is important to the business.

PLTS

When you are analysing and evaluating information, judging its relevance and value, you are practising your skills as an independent enquirer (IE).

Key Terms

Asset – an item of value owned by a company.

Intangible asset – an asset that is not physical, such as a trademark or logo.

Licensed – the granting of authority to a third party to use intellectual property in some way, for example, to manufacture a product whose invention is protected by a patent held by the licence owner.

Designs

The design of a product refers to its unique appearance – its contours, shapes, colours, texture and material, rather than how it works. Designs can also be protected by being registered. Ownership of a registered design means that you are protected from others copying it or claiming it as their own. You can also sell your registered design, or license someone else to use it.

Inventions

Inventions, such as the cyclone technology that powers the Dyson range of vacuum cleaners, are protected by **patent** law. Patents prevent others from copying the inventions and profiting from the original creations of the patent holder.

Trade secrets

Confidential IP can be kept as a trade secret. An example of confidential IP might be a drawing or sketch of a new and unique product planned for future development. Keeping something as a trade secret means that anyone with whom you share information about it must sign a non-disclosure agreement. If they breach this agreement by telling others about your IP, you can take action against them under confidentiality law.

> **Key Term**
>
> **Patent** – a right granted to inventors to prevent others from copying, using or selling their invention.

> **Remember**
>
> IP is an asset to the business, just like buildings and stock. As such, appropriate measures must be in place to protect all the different forms of IP belonging to the business from imitation and theft.

> **Functional Skills**
>
> If you take part in a professional discussion as part of the assessment for this learning outcome, you will be practising your Level 1 Functional English Speaking and Listening skills.

Portfolio Task 1   60 minutes

Links to LO1: Assessment criteria 1.1, 1.2, 1.3

1. Write a short summary which describes how knowledge is gained and applied in your own area of responsibility. Identify how you get access to the sources of knowledge that you and your team need. Say whether they are internal or external and what access privileges are in place. Make sure you give examples of the types of knowledge that are gained and applied and include evidence of work products if available.

2. Give examples to explain how knowledge is shared in your own area of responsibility. State with whom this knowledge is shared and say why it is necessary. Outline any difficulties that may arise with knowledge sharing and say how you think these could be dealt with.

3. Define what you understand by the term 'intellectual property'. Give examples of some of the different types of intellectual property that exist in your team or department. Outline how these different types of intellectual property are protected in your own area of responsibility.

Your assessment could take the form of a written narrative or a professional discussion with your assessor. It could also include the production of workplace evidence, work-based observations or the use of witness testimonies, as appropriate.

Be able to develop knowledge

Taking existing information and developing it into new knowledge is the basis of innovation – a key component of business success and competitive advantage. For businesses, innovation means they can produce better products, create more satisfied customers and build a strong position in the market.

In this section, you will investigate methods of knowledge development and look at how you can support your team in using the appropriate knowledge development processes that are required for them to do their jobs.

Processes and procedures which can develop knowledge

This section will take you through the theory and then the practice of developing knowledge to create commercial business advantage. One of the key aims of the section is to show you that knowledge management can be applied to every business, not just large corporations.

Knowledge management theory

Knowledge management is concerned with organisational processes for the capture, development and utilisation of information to create new knowledge. This new knowledge can then be exploited to improve the performance of the business and, ultimately, to create competitive advantage.

There are three key areas of focus in knowledge management:

- the processes that take place within the business
- the people who work in the business
- the technology that makes all of these processes possible.

It is largely due to advances in technology and the growth of the internet that such widespread and immediate access to information and knowledge have been brought about. This technology, however, must fit with and fulfil the needs of the people who use it.

The building blocks of knowledge management are data, information and knowledge, which exist in a hierarchy as follows:

- Data – raw data, such as computer-generated figures in a spreadsheet is acquired.
- Information – raw data is given context and meaning to turn it into information, such as increases in capital expenditure over the year, or average customer spend per month.
- Knowledge – this information, by being combined with understanding, is turned into knowledge on which action can be taken. For example, if a trend is identified showing declining net profit margins, action can be taken immediately to identify the source of this decline and take appropriate action.

> **Remember**
>
> As a team leader, you need to find ways to nurture collaboration, trust and teamwork in order for knowledge management to operate effectively.

> **Activity** 15 minutes
>
> Think of three different types of knowledge that you are provided with in your job. For each, give an example of how this knowledge is, or could be, developed and used to provide improvements to the business.

> **PLTS**
>
> When you are supporting conclusions, using reasoned arguments and evidence, you are practising your skills as an independent enquirer (IE).

A collaborative environment

Knowledge management requires the environment of the organisation to foster sharing, collaboration, trust and teamwork. It also has a strong focus on innovation and continuous improvement. Without these factors in place in an organisation, the processes of knowledge management will not operate effectively. After all, you are unlikely to be willing to share information with others whom you do not trust! So, a good working environment is not just a nice-to-have; it is a fundamental requirement. It will therefore be a key task of management to cultivate such an environment. This is potentially difficult to achieve, especially in cases where the prevailing culture did not previously support such collaboration and trust.

Putting knowledge management into practice

Now that we've looked into the theory behind knowledge management, how can we apply this thinking to our own workplace? What sort of existing knowledge can we take and develop into something more useful, which will provide an improvement to the way the business operates?

Here's a very simple practical example of how a business could develop knowledge. By taking existing sales and customer data for the last twelve months, an analysis of repeat purchase patterns, average spend per purchase and category of purchases per customer could be produced and converted into a customer relationship management (CRM) database. CRM databases are superb tools, which can be used to identify exactly which of your customers are buying which products and how often. This type of information can be developed to create personalised marketing, tailored to the purchasing habits of each individual customer. Amazon uses this type of knowledge management approach and offers customers similar, or complementary, products to the ones they have recently purchased. Asda and Tesco's home grocery delivery services both use a similar approach by offering personalised offers and promotions tailored to customers' purchasing history – including the option of free home delivery on orders to customers who have not used their home delivery service for a while. This is an effective method of using purchase history knowledge to target repeat custom in the future.

Applying knowledge management in a range of diverse businesses

In order to demonstrate the universally applicable ideas behind the concept of knowledge management, the following section takes a look at how it could work and what sorts of information it might apply to for some different types of business.

A family run restaurant

The chef in a family run restaurant has the tacit knowledge of the secret recipe for special sauce that goes into their house speciality dish. This was given to him by his grandfather, the founder of the business. He must ensure that he passes on this knowledge to the next generation. The waiting staff know from taking food orders directly from customers, which dishes are the most and least popular. This information can be used to make improvements to the menu. The waitress knows that recently, more and more bookings taken by phone have asked whether there is a vegetarian option on the menu. This information can be used to provide a better vegetarian selection and even to add this as a key feature in their advertising.

A self-employed dress designer

The dress designer visits all of her clients in person, often for long periods. This is an excellent opportunity to gather customer feedback, such as on preferences for designs, fabrics and accessories. She can immediately use all of this information to develop improved dress designs that are matched to the requirements of her customers.

A dress designer will use customer feedback to improve her range.

A global chain of fast food restaurants

The fast food chain can use information gathered on sales volume by day of the week and even by time of day. This will tell them which are the busiest days of the week and which specific times of the day are most busy. Information gathered by this process can be used to plan the staff shift rota. They can also use sales data for the last twelve months to identify changing trends in products purchased. This will help them to plan menu changes for the forthcoming year to take account of changing customer preferences and eating habits.

As can be seen from each of these examples of very different businesses, the basic principles of knowledge management can be applied to the specific type of information to which the business has access. This knowledge can then be developed and used to make improvements to the way in which the business runs.

> **Remember**
>
> The principles of knowledge management are universal. This means that they can be applied to any business, small or large, to achieve improvements in efficiency.

Supporting individuals to ensure knowledge-development processes are followed

For knowledge development to work in practice, your team needs to be motivated and capable of carrying out the development tasks required. Team members also need to be able to understand the new knowledge that is developed, why it is important and how it benefits the business.

Training for knowledge development

Where new tasks, software and processes are introduced, this will have an impact on the job content of your team. If new skills are now required, then you will be responsible for arranging appropriate training of your team members to bring them up to speed with the new requirements.

IT training

One issue that is common in these circumstances is that staff who were previously non-users of IT now find that they are required to learn IT skills and use computers and software applications as part of their job. This is an area where you may experience resistance and low morale from your team. You will have to find the most appropriate methods of reducing this resistance during the introduction of such new tasks and skills. Nurturing the involvement of your team will be central to achieving this.

Documentation

New processes will also need to be included in the relevant job descriptions, procedure manuals and training guides. This will ensure that all employees have access to the correct operating information – this will be especially important in the early days after new knowledge management processes are introduced to your team.

Recognising and rewarding your team

A key part of supporting your team in taking on board new processes and learning new skills will be providing recognition and rewards where staff are performing well and correctly following the new knowledge development processes.

What this means in practice for you is that you need to keep alert to ongoing performance by walking around your team's work space and by chatting to them. Work alongside them and find out how they are getting on. Having a visible presence among your team will give you a good opportunity to spot good practice and give positive recognition of it.

Social events

Another good way of rewarding and recognising team effort is to encourage the social aspects of it. You could do this by arranging a team evening out, perhaps for a meal. You might even consider holding a prize-giving session to reward those who overcame the biggest barriers or who showed excellence in their work.

Activity   20 minutes

Give an example of knowledge development that could be implemented in your team. Say what training requirements would arise as a result of this new process and which training methods you would use.

Portfolio Task 2 60 minutes

Links to LO2: Assessment criteria 2.1, 2.2

1. Identify some examples of the established processes and procedures in your team or department that can develop knowledge. For each example, say in what way knowledge can be developed and why this is important, as well as who is responsible for making this happen. Include work-based evidence in your assessment to back up the examples you give.

2. Give three examples of ways in which you could, or do, support individuals in your team, to ensure knowledge development processes are followed. Again, it will help to provide evidence of your competence if you are able to include work-based products with your answer. This could include training materials, guidelines or procedure documents, for example.

Your assessment could take the form of a written narrative or a professional discussion with your assessor. It could also include the production of workplace evidence, work-based observations or the use of witness testimonies, as appropriate.

> **PLTS**
>
> When you are exploring issues, events or problems from different perspectives, you are practising your skills as an independent enquirer (IE).

> **Functional Skills**
>
> If you produce a written report as part of the assessment for this learning outcome you will be practising your Level 1 Functional English Writing skills.

Be able to share knowledge

In the work environment knowledge sharing is vital for successful team working. As team leader, you will be responsible for effectively communicating the correct processes and procedures for sharing knowledge within your team and for ensuring that these processes and procedures are followed. You will also need to learn methods of supporting your team to ensure that they know what is required of them and are able to perform their roles effectively.

Communicating established processes and procedures which share knowledge

Knowledge sharing is an effective way to get the most out of the information held by an organisation. But in order for this to happen, your team need to know what processes are in place, how to access them, how to navigate them once they have gained access to them and what types of information they should be uploading to, or filing in, shared areas.

Education and training

Getting these messages out to your team so they fully understand knowledge-sharing processes may require intensive education and training for your team. This is not something that can be achieved overnight and may take a lot of effort on your part. Do not be put off by this, as worthwhile changes – and especially potentially large-scale changes as this – need time to become established.

Take as an example the existing company extranet as a knowledge-sharing tool. How do you think you might communicate the workings of this established facility to your team? A good starting point would be to get the team together for a briefing meeting and give them a step-by-step demonstration of the extranet, what it is for, how it works, who uses it and what information they are expected to upload to it.

In addition, it may also be a suitable training technique to train up one or two of your team members who have good IT skills and to use them as mentors to provide ongoing training to the team when it is needed.

Establishing a sharing culture

Gaining commitment to knowledge sharing from your team may require overcoming cultural barriers, for example, where such sharing represents a huge difference to the way things were traditionally done. As we saw earlier, this means that such a change may not be an immediate success. This is because culture is something that is established gradually over time and, hence is not something that can be quickly changed. That is not to say that it cannot be achieved at all, but that it will require determination, focus and resilience from you as team leader in order to keep this culture change on track.

Communication methods

You need to select the communication methods most suited to your task and team. However, the following are some examples of methods which would work well, alone or in combination, to communicate to your staff the knowledge sharing processes and procedures:

- presentations
- demonstrations
- group training
- one-to-one training
- user guides
- procedure manuals.

A key benefit of materials such as user guides or procedure manuals is that they can be made permanently available to staff, for example, by being stored electronically in a centrally accessible area.

The learning organisation

The theory of knowledge management goes hand in hand with another concept – that of the learning organisation. A learning organisation is one that 'facilitates the learning of its members and continually transforms itself'. A learning organisation has five key elements:

- Systems thinking – using systems to measure the performance of the organisation and its departments.
- Personal mastery – commitment from individuals to learning.

- Mental models – challenging assumptions held about what people think they do compared with what they actually do.
- Shared vision – a universal focus for everyone, such as to be the best in the industry.
- Team learning – so that staff have better skills and expertise which ultimately improves the performance of the business.

As you can see, these features of a learning organisation provide an excellent environment in which knowledge management processes and procedures will operate effectively.

Methods of supporting individuals to ensure knowledge-sharing processes are followed

Training

Training is a key source of support that will allow your team to develop the required skills and expertise in following knowledge-sharing processes. Ongoing support can also be provided in the form of mentoring and coaching on the job.

An emphasis on team learning and sharing of skills and experience among team members will go a long way to creating the openness in communication needed for a truly successful knowledge-sharing organisation.

Monitoring

You need to keep a sharp eye on your team's performance against knowledge-sharing processes. Identify good performance and always recognise it. Also, identify poor performance and recurring errors, and take immediate action to remedy it. Use your team coaches and mentors to provide the extra support needed to bring about necessary improvements. Be sure, too, that you follow up on progress to make sure that performance has indeed improved.

It may be a good approach to set milestones or targets for the performance of your team members against following knowledge-sharing processes after they are implemented. These milestones could be:

- after one week, 50 per cent of the team are following the correct knowledge-sharing processes
- after four weeks, 75 per cent can now correctly follow the correct procedures
- after eight weeks, 90 per cent are now fully competent
- after twelve weeks, 100 per cent of the team are following the correct knowledge-sharing processes.

The above times and percentages are just examples and the ones which you choose to set may vary depending on your team and the nature and extent of processes which are introduced.

Activity 30 minutes

Answer the questions below to analyse how well your organisation measures up to the five key elements of a learning organisation.

1. Systems thinking – are there systems in place to measure the performance of the organisation and its departments?
2. Personal mastery – is there evidence of commitment of individuals to learning?
3. Mental models – do people ask questions about existing processes?
4. Shared vision – how well are people aware of the mission of the organisation?
5. Team learning – is there a focus on team learning?

PLTS

When you are asking questions to extend your thinking, you are practising your skills as a creative thinker (CT).

Remember

Always tell your staff exactly when and how you will monitor them. Be open and clear about this aspect of your management responsibilities, as this will increase trust between you and your team.

Unit E12

Manage knowledge in own area of responsibility

Creating team responsibility

Creating team responsibility for the process is the most effective method of ensuring that knowledge stored in the shared area is:

- properly filed
- regularly updated
- fit for purpose
- complete
- well presented
- error free.

If individual team members have explicit responsibility for taking care in the proper storage of their information, and if this is reinforced with a suitable monitoring process, then it will quickly become the norm to have well-presented and high-quality information available to your team on a regular basis. This will also make subsequent access, retrieval and transfer of the information more straightforward for all concerned.

Delegating the monitoring process

The monitoring process could quite easily be carried out by a suitably capable member of your team. It may be a good approach to identify a suitably qualified person and to brief them on the process. Delegating in this way takes the task away from you on a day-to-day basis, but you could request weekly reports as a means of keeping up to date with progress. Nominating a team member to oversee the process is also a good way of reinforcing the point that it is the team's responsibility to ensure professional standards of information presentation.

Portfolio Task 3 60 minutes

Links to LO3: Assessment criteria 3.1, 3.2

1. Demonstrate some of the ways in which you communicate established processes and procedures that share knowledge across your own area of responsibility. This could include guidance documents you might have produced, or training you have provided. For each method of communication, state its advantages and disadvantages.

2. Give reasons to explain why it is important to provide support to your team to ensure knowledge-sharing processes are followed. Give examples of suitable methods of providing such support and include evidence of work-based products to back up your answer, if possible.

Your assessment could take the form of a written narrative or a professional discussion with your assessor. It could also include the production of workplace evidence, work-based observations or the use of witness testimonies, as appropriate.

Functional Skills

If you produce a word-processed report as part of the assessment for this learning outcome, you will be practising your Level 1 Functional ICT skills in using ICT systems.

Be able to monitor and evaluate knowledge management in your own area of responsibility

No matter how well your organisation or department may be managing its knowledge-development processes, there is always a need for these processes to be suitably monitored and evaluated. This is for the simple reason that knowledge management takes time, costs money and requires a concerted effort from many staff over a long time. As with every aspect of business which uses resources, monitoring and evaluation are needed to make sure that the results or outputs justify the investment. They will also highlight any areas that are in need of change.

Assessing the knowledge-development process

How well does knowledge management work in your team? Is your team making every effort to exploit all of the existing information available to it and is it using this knowledge to create benefits to the business? Are there any gaps in knowledge management? What should you do about these? Remember that all of the information held by the team is an **intellectual asset**. However, in order for it to be truly valuable, it needs to be captured and used to develop intelligence to create opportunities. If it lies untouched in a customer database, for example, then no additional value can be created from it. In fact, this would be a waste of potentially valuable information.

Knowledge management is based on:

- technology
- people
- processes.

These three areas can be used as the focus to assess the quality of the knowledge development process in your area of work.

Technology

To make an assessment of the technology used in your team for knowledge management you need to ask yourself questions such as:

- What technologies do we currently have in place?
- Are technologies up to date, or are there newer and better technologies now available?
- Are these technologies providing us with the necessary knowledge and information in an easily usable format?
- Are the systems easy for your team to access and navigate?
- Are there any areas where the team's technology and systems cannot provide information that is needed?

> **Key Term**
>
> **Intellectual asset** – different forms of information held by a business, such as knowledge, research and development, software and patents.

> **Remember**
>
> The true power behind knowledge management lies in it being technology driven, so the more of your systems and processes that are electronic, the easier it will be to capture, develop, refine and utilise this information.

People

To assess knowledge management in terms of your team, you should focus on the following questions.

- Do your team members have the necessary skills – especially IT expertise – to effectively handle the knowledge-management tasks required of them, or are training or recruitment likely to be needed?
- Are there significant differences in the amount of knowledge management required between the individual team members and can tasks be allocated more evenly?
- How can you encourage your team to actively embrace the idea of knowledge management and see its relevance to their role?

Processes

Processes are concerned with how things happen in your team. How are orders processed? How are complaints processed? How are the arrangements for deliveries processed? Are these processes conducted manually or electronically? In order to make an assessment of knowledge management in terms of the key processes in your team, you need to analyse to what extent you are actively capturing the information provided by these processes.

If the majority of processes are technology driven, this will be a relatively easy task and you will be able to generate reports showing process history data. If most of your tasks are conducted manually, analysing information capture will potentially require a large amount of time and effort sifting through paperwork. It may be better to transfer this paper-based information into electronic format such as a database, to make it easier to analyse and manipulate.

Collating the results of your analysis

Once you have carried out your assessment of knowledge-management processes, you should have a fairly comprehensive picture of how well it is working covering:

- the areas in which information is being managed well and is being used for the development of new knowledge
- areas where there are gaps, such as where information capture methods need to be implemented
- skills shortages and training needs
- new technology requirements.

The results of your analysis can be presented in report format and will provide the basis for implementing changes, which you will look at in the following section.

Activity 20 minutes

Make a list of some of the knowledge-management activities that are carried out in your team using the three headings of technology, people and processes. If no knowledge management occurs in a particular area, say what you think could be done.

PLTS

When you are asking questions to extend your thinking, you are practising your skills as a creative thinker (CT).

Implementing changes to improve knowledge management

Implementing changes in the area of knowledge management may involve some quite large-scale developments, such as the installation of new technology and changes to job descriptions. This, in turn, may have quite a dramatic impact on your team members and on how they feel about their jobs. You may not yet have direct experience of dealing with such a significant change at work, but this is nothing to worry about. As you gain more experience in your role you will find out, by a process of trial and error, the techniques that work best for you and your team. The general guidance provided in this section is designed to be useful in most situations.

Involvement

Involving your team as much as possible in the process is probably the most effective method of successfully implementing changes to improve knowledge management. You could try to involve your team by allocating specific responsibilities to individual team members for completing certain knowledge-management tasks. You could also use team meetings to ask for their input and opinions on planned changes and on the best methods of implementing them. This is an effective method of creating ownership of the change by the team, which increases commitment.

Team meetings

You could also use your team meetings as an opportunity for team members to present to the rest of the team on progress against objectives. Knowing that they will be required to give a presentation to the team afterwards is a good way of focusing them on completing their tasks. Meetings are also an excellent forum for discussion, sharing of experiences, highlighting areas where help is needed and offering suggestions for solutions. This type of information sharing is, in fact, central to the idea of knowledge management.

Change by evolution

When changes are introduced based on alterations and developments to existing processes, rather than on wholesale transformation, they are:

- more easily implemented
- more likely to be accepted
- more likely to succeed in the long term.

So, if you have the authority to do so, try to find ways of introducing change incrementally to your team. If, however, the change-implementation process has been instigated by higher levels of management, then all you can do is to keep your team as involved as possible under the circumstances, monitor for signs of anxiety and low morale and take action to keep your team together.

Activity — 15 minutes

Think of three ways in which you could potentially involve your team in the implementation of changes to improve knowledge management. It might help to consider this in terms of before, during and after the change is implemented.

PLTS

When you are proposing practical ways forward, you are practising your skills as an effective participator (EP).

Monitoring change and development in the knowledge-development process

Once changes have been implemented, whether these are extensions to existing processes or the introduction of completely new ones, it is very important to monitor progress in the areas affected. Monitoring will tell you whether the changes planned have actually worked out as anticipated and will alert you to areas requiring further action or a change of plan.

Goals and targets

Change is not implemented for its own sake. It is carried out to achieve pre-defined team or organisational goals and targets. It also requires vast inputs of time and money. For these reasons, monitoring the outcome of change is a critical strategic activity, as it will tell you whether, and to what extent, these changes have met their intended goals. Ultimately, this is a test of whether the outcomes and benefits have justified the costs.

Systems

A key area in need of monitoring is that of systems and technology. Where new installations of hardware or software have been put in place, usually at huge cost, monitoring will require assessment of whether and how well they are providing the anticipated results and outputs. Issues which may well arise in the period immediately after implementation include:

- poor user performance – this could be due to the system itself being difficult to use, or it could be due to a lack of adequate training
- poor or overly complicated system outputs – possibly due to glitches in the way in which the system has been set up. Problems of this nature can usually be remedied by the intervention of IT support
- outputs incompatible with other systems – again, this issue is probably easily fixed by calling on the services of IT support.

Whatever systems issues you spot as part of your monitoring process, you need to speak to your team in detail about them, find out the underlying issues and arrange for solutions to be put in place.

Team

Monitoring of your team will involve discovering how well they think they are coping with the new processes. Are they generally happy with them, or are there any specific issues that need to be looked at? Ask your team whether they feel the training they received was adequate, or whether there are further areas in which they feel they would benefit from support.

How people react to change

There are certain categories of reactions to change which people can exhibit. It will help you as a team leader to be able to identify who in your team fall under each category. This will help you in finding the most appropriate strategy for dealing with them. It will also prevent you from losing confidence if you are experiencing resistance to change from your team. The categories are:

- trailblazers – fully embrace change and do not need much help
- pilots – know how to get somewhere but need a little direction from you as to where it is they are supposed to be going
- intellectuals – will say the right things but are slow and unwilling to truly change
- late bloomers – resistant for a time, but then accept the change
- traditionalists – will never be won over. A change of team or even organisation is the only real solution for this group of people.

Fact finding

One approach may be to issue a questionnaire to your team to gather information on how the changes have affected them. Allowing them the option of remaining anonymous is also a good idea. You could collate the results and present back the findings from your survey in a team meeting. This is beneficial in two respects:

1. It provides an ideal opportunity to open up free discussion and airing of issues.
2. It is an excellent opportunity to give further whole group training if this is necessary.

Activity 30 minutes

Draft a questionnaire consisting of approximately ten questions which could be used to assess your team's reaction to changes which have been implemented.

Describe how you would deal with any negative findings arising from your questionnaire results.

PLTS

When you are evaluating experiences and learning to inform future progress, you are practising your skills as a reflective learner (RL).

Functional Skills

If you produce a written report as part of the assessment for this learning outcome, you will be practising your Level 1 Functional English Writing skills.

Portfolio Task 4 60 minutes

Links to LO4: Assessment criteria 4.1, 4.2, 4.3

1. Carry out an assessment outlining the strengths and weaknesses of the knowledge-development process in your own area of responsibility. Give your opinion on how it could be improved and what resources would be needed to make these improvements.

2. Provide examples of any changes you have implemented to improve knowledge management. Such changes could include improvements in formatting of documents, timeliness of report production, improved presentation, or ease of access to information for those who need it, for example.

3. Write a short summary explaining how you monitor change and development in the knowledge-development process. What are the key things that you watch out for? What are some of the key issues that you uncover during the monitoring process? Say what are the best methods for dealing with them.

Your assessment could take the form of a written narrative or a professional discussion with your assessor. It could also include the production of workplace evidence, work-based observations or the use of witness testimonies, as appropriate.

Team talk

Alwin's story

My name is Alwin Mallik and I am 28 years old. I have been a team leader in a small, family-run catering business for two months. I have also just begun my NVQ in Team Leading.

As part of a drive to streamline business performance and reduce costs, we have recently invested in a computerised system that covers our stock control, purchases, sales orders, invoicing, customer records and supplier information. The only problem is that despite such a huge investment in this system, I am finding it almost impossible to sort through the massive amounts of data generated. I am not sure on which areas I should be concentrating and I am drowning in what I can only describe as information overload.

I have tried to discuss this with the business owners, but they are so busy themselves, looking after the food production side of things, that they never respond to me with an answer to any of my questions.

Top tips

Information systems are capable of generating huge amounts of data. It is important that, from the outset, you are clear and focused as to the specific information which you wish to receive and the frequency with which you need it. Prioritising information needs will help to reduce issues such as information overload, which is a common problem, as well as avoiding the production of unnecessary or redundant information.

Ask the expert	
Q	I work for a small business that has recently purchased a computerised business information software application. However, I am now in the position where I cannot cope with the sheer amount of information being produced by this system.
A	You need to decide on what specific information you need the system to produce for you, and on what basis, whether daily, weekly or monthly. Do not request more reports than you need, as this will become unmanageable. You would also benefit from finding out from the business owners what their information priorities are and then focusing on these. If they are busy, schedule a convenient time with them for a discussion to allow you enough time to talk through the issues.

What your assessor is looking for

In order to prepare for and succeed in completing this unit, your assessor will require you to be able to demonstrate competence in:

- understanding existing knowledge management in your own area of responsibility
- developing knowledge
- sharing knowledge
- monitoring and evaluating knowledge management in your own area of responsibility.

You will demonstrate your skills, knowledge and competence through the learning outcomes in this unit. Evidence generated in this unit will also cross-reference to the other units in this qualification.

Please bear in mind that there are significant cross-referencing opportunities throughout this qualification and you may have already generated some relevant work to meet certain criteria in this unit. Your assessor will provide you with the exact requirements to meet the standards of this unit. However, as a guide, it is likely that for this unit you will need to be assessed through the following methods:

- one observation of relevant workplace activities to cover the whole unit
- one witness testimony may also be produced
- a written narrative, reflective account or professional discussion

- any relevant work products to be produced as evidence.

The work products for this unit could include:

- examples of knowledge sources
- examples of applications of knowledge
- processes and procedures, training materials, or guidance documents used for developing knowledge
- examples of knowledge management and evaluation processes.

Your assessor will guide you through the assessment process as detailed in the candidate logbook. The detailed assessment criteria are shown in the logbook and, by working through these questions, combined with providing the relevant evidence, you will meet the learning outcomes required to complete this unit.

Task and page reference	Assessment criteria
1 (page 212)	1.1, 1.2, 1.3
2 (page 217)	2.1, 2.2
3 (page 220)	3.1, 3.2
4 (page 225)	4.1, 4.2, 4.3

Unit E15 Procure supplies

Acquiring the right suppliers at the right time means that the work of your organisation can continue without disruption and that your customers' expectations can be met.

This unit will help you to understand the importance of sourcing materials of quality at the best possible price while making sure that the selected supplier is reliable.

You will learn about the purchasing mix, purchasing planning and the importance of building supplier relationships. This will enable you to explore the usefulness of a supplier specification sheet and to understand the importance of agreeing the terms and conditions of the contracts with your suppliers. You will also look at the importance of monitoring your suppliers' performance.

What you will learn:

- Be able to identify requirements for supplies
- Be able to evaluate suppliers that meet identified requirements
- Be able to select suppliers and obtain supplies
- Be able to monitor supplier performance

Links to the Technical Certificate

If you are completing your NVQ as part of an Apprenticeship Framework, you will find the following topics are also covered in your Technical Certificate:

- Key principles of team leading
- Principles of decision making
- Management of knowledge

Be able to identify requirements for supplies

It is important for your organisation to **procure** items of high quality at the best possible price and at the right time! Knowing what your customers need and want is crucial if your business is to survive, but so is identifying the right suppliers to use. Often their expertise can help you to source the right items and building a sound working relationship with your suppliers can help your organisation to remain competitive. Don't forget you can also learn from others in your organisation (your internal customers) and by talking to them you can establish what is important to them and the experiences they have had when dealing with suppliers in terms of quality, price and delivery.

Whatever type of organisation you work in, materials, equipment, consumables, stationery or stock for re-sale will need to be purchased to enable targets to be met and for your customers' or service users' needs to be satisfied.

Once you and your managers have selected a supplier it is important to set about building positive relations with them. Knowing who to contact and building a rapport with that person can be very beneficial – after all the more often you work with a supplier and give them repeat business, the more likely you are to be able to negotiate price discounts!

Your organisation, like any other, will be concerned about **cash flow** and **budgets**. You may have to purchase services within the constraints of a departmental budget and you may purchase goods which are:

- raw materials
- components
- work in progress (WIP) or partly finished goods
- finished goods.

Some organisations outsource their production. In manufacturing for example, this means that they use the services of another organisation to produce their goods for them. An advantage of this is not having to invest in expensive machinery and equipment but a disadvantage is not having direct control over the quality of the products being produced.

Often, organisations will make a decision to either *make* or *buy* the products they provide to their customers.

An organisation is likely to make its own products, when:

- it can't find a suitable supplier of finished products
- reliable delivery times can't be met by a supplier
- there are no guarantees from a supplier of consistent supplies
- quality can't be guaranteed by a supplier
- the organisation wants to protect its own design or recipe.

Key Terms

Budget – an amount of money allowed to be spent on specific goods or services.

Cash flow – the total amount money coming in (income) and going out (expenditure) of a business.

Procure – acquire

Remember

When outsourcing to meet your own customers' expectations, you need to know that your supplier can meet your urgent requests for additional stock when required!

An organisation is likely to buy in products when:

- it's cheaper to buy in products of the appropriate quality than to make its own products
- it's cheaper to buy in products than invest in own machinery and equipment
- highly skilled staff are needed which the supplier already has.

Purchasing

A responsible purchasing officer will need to take into account their organisation's resources when purchasing goods or services. Your own team's resources will include time, money, equipment, materials, information and people.

You and your managers or purchasing officer will need to examine the *planning* of your purchasing activities to make sure the right people are involved. These should include your stock control, finance and warehousing personnel, to make sure items are ordered and received on time and that equipment and materials are purchased within budget.

Your purchasing strategy should ensure:

- you are supplied with high-quality goods or services
- you are getting your supplies at the best possible price
- that not too much stock has to be held.

To achieve this, whoever is purchasing should:

- liaise with other departments (for example research and development to meet design requirements)
- negotiate with suppliers (for example to obtain discounts/agree delivery times)
- look at opportunities for purchasing alternative items
- communicate with stock control clerks and monitor stock levels.

Selecting colleagues to agree requirements for supplies

In your organisation, you need to be able to select the right people to agree requirements for purchasing supplies. You should think about agreeing requirements for supplies with your:

- team members – they know exactly what is needed to carry out their roles efficiently and effectively
- line manager – to discuss requirements and make sure purchase requests are within budget
- finance department – you may need to liaise with finance for things like getting quotes

Activity 30 minutes

Identify which you think is the most important resource when purchasing. Write down your choice with reasons why and show your work to your assessor.

Remember

Agree at the outset with your supplier how damaged or inferior quality items can be replaced quickly and with minimum cost!

- customers – you need to understand their needs and wants which may influence your purchasing decisions
- colleagues (**internal customers**) – to find out what their criteria is when dealing with specific suppliers
- suppliers – you need to get quality items at the right time and at the best possible price.

Communicating with your team to identify the need for supplies

Depending on the nature of the business you are in, the process of obtaining supplies will involve having to communicate effectively with several of your colleagues. The size of your organisation will dictate how much activity is necessary to acquire your supplies. The purchasing function may be operated by one person or in a larger organisation it may be operated by a team of people.

Procurement experts suggest that effective purchasing relies on the principle of the five rights of purchasing. This suggests that organisations should aim to obtain supplies:

- at the right price
- that are delivered at the right time
- of the right quality
- of the right quantity
- from the right (that is, the best) source.

Portfolio Task 1 45 minutes

Links to LO1: Assessment criterion 1.1

Talk to the person/people who are responsible for purchasing supplies in your organisation. Ask them who they communicate with to agree requirements for obtaining supplies. Discuss your findings with your assessor. Your assessor will record this discussion to generate evidence for your portfolio.

Communication and functioning efficiently

For your team to perform efficiently, you will need to make sure it has sufficient stock of everything it requires, which may include:

- tools
- machinery and equipment
- stationery
- raw materials and components
- fuel
- protective clothing.

Talking to your team members on a regular basis is important so that you know what supplies they need, for what purpose, and by when, but you must also take steps to liaise with whoever is in change of stock control or your stores department. For example, to satisfy the requirement of your team your colleague in stores should be able to tell you how long it will take for a stock item to be purchased. This is known as the **lead time**.

Specifications for supply requirements

When agreeing requirements for supplies you must be aware of your budget for spending. Your line manager will have been in discussion with your finance department to establish budgets that will control spending on the stock items you and your team need.

In turn, you must discuss your spending requirements with your line manager. Often careful planning is necessary so there is enough stock to enable your team to function sufficiently, without finding yourself in a position of spending over budget.

Some organisations will use centralised purchasing and others decentralised purchasing:

- Centralised purchasing – purchasing is carried out at head office or by one department in the organisation. This gives the organisation opportunity to buy in bulk on behalf of every department in the business or on behalf of every branch or factory in the organisation. Buyers can then negotiate better prices as they buy many items at once, taking advantage of **economies of scale**. Using this method means everyone in the organisation uses stock of the same quality and standard.
- Decentralised purchasing – when each department or branch is responsible for its own purchasing. An advantage is that the requirements can be individually catered for to meet the needs of the organisations teams and customers. The smaller scale purchasing, however, means the organisation may miss out economies-of-scale opportunities.

Supplier relationship

The relationship between a purchaser and supplier should ideally be based upon mutual respect, trust, commitment and co-operation.

For this to happen, agreement must be reached over:

- costs – including delivery charges
- returns procedure
- delivery schedules
- consequences when contract conditions are not met
- minimum quantity order levels
- acceptable quality levels (AQL).

When spending on supplies, make sure you know the budget and do not exceed it.

Procure supplies **Unit E15**

Activity 30 minutes

Talk to your procurement officer/purchasing specialist in your organisation and find out what is contained in the specification for dealing with your suppliers. Show your findings to your assessor

Remember

It is good practice to ask your suppliers about alternative items they can supply that will fulfil the same criteria but may be available in different volumes or perhaps price. In the public or voluntary sector you should keep records that you have sought alternative prices for audit purposes.

Key Term

Supplier specification – a document drawn up by the purchaser that gives details of dimensions, weights, type of finish, colour, quality, volume and so on of the materials to be supplied.

Remember

Someone in your organisation will need time to draw up a specification, which then has to be approved by managers. In some cases, legal advice may have to be sought. This can take time and be costly.

In reaching agreement with your supplier, you will have negotiated to receive items to your specification. Make sure that you have checked with your chosen supplier that they will be able to meet your requirements consistently. Your customers' expectations need to be met and this can only be achieved by providing a product or service of the same specification over a long period of time. If your supplier cannot consistently meet your requirements, the quality and perception of your product or service may be undermined, resulting in disappointed customers!

Activity 30 minutes

Kellogg's® Cornflakes is a very popular breakfast cereal, but imagine what would happen if Kellogg's didn't form positive relationships with the farmers who grow and supply the corn they need. This would result in inconsistency of supply and if Kellogg's had to source new suppliers the taste of cornflakes might change.

Write down your views of the effect this would have on Kellogg's customers and the consequences for Kellogg's. Share your responses with your assessor.

Organisations usually draw up **supplier specifications** when dealing with their suppliers, especially if they are providing a product or service that is:

- of high quality to meet their customers' expectations
- needed in large quantities
- expensive to purchase
- needed to meet legal obligations.

Your procurement procedures and supplier specifications should enable you to:

- obtain high-quality items
- secure the best possible price
- obtain supplies when they are needed
- offer best value to your customers.

To enable a supplier specification to be drawn up, you need to decide what the supply criteria will be for your product or service. You need to think about:

- your budget (how much can you afford to spend?)
- who your customers are and what their expectations are
- for what purpose you are buying the items (why are they really needed?)
- where and how the items should be delivered
- how often you will need delivery.

These criteria will help you or your managers to draw up a supplier specification for each major item you need to purchase.

Below is an example of a supplier specification sheet:

Supply Specification Sheet for (*insert name of supplier*)	
Your organisation's name: **Address:** **Your email address:** **Tel No:** **Fax No:**	
Contact name:	**Tel ext.**
1. Glossary *In this section you would insert the meanings of symbols, abbreviations, acronyms or technical language that your supplier may not be aware of.*	
2. Introduction *This section should include an overview of market research or technical research that enabled you to identify the needs of your customers and therefore the purpose of the item you are seeking to purchase.*	
3. Scope *Insert here any specific requirements for the item such as **JIT**. Also, explain any potential for the demand from your customers to increase or decrease if external factors or your industry requirements change.*	
4. Delivery requirements *Procedures for gaining access on to your site should be included, as should details of your organisations' policy for acceptance or rejection of deliveries. Also, include warehousing hours and consequences of missing deadlines. Personal safety when loading and unloading, including **PPE** that must be worn, should be added.*	
5. Required goods or services *In this section, you should insert a description of the goods or service that you wish to procure. You need to include:* • *technical information (design requirements, colour, dimensions and assembly instructions)* • *end-user information (what your customers/end users expect)* • *performance measurement (if appropriate, your criteria for minimum and maximum performance from your supplier and how this will be measured)* • *industry standards (information that informs the supplier of your expectations to meet your current industry standards and an explanation that those may change)* • *testing (explain to the supplier that once received, the goods or services will be evaluated and tested to make sure they meet your expectations, your customers expectations and conform to your industry and any mandatory standards)*	
6. Meeting end-user needs *Under this heading, make it clear how you intend to keep your customers or end users satisfied with the goods or services they will receive from you. Explain that you will measure the performance of the supplier by checking:* • *quality of the goods or services* • *quantity received and timings of deliveries* • *costs and associated charges* • *improvements or modifications to meet industry standards.* *Explain to the supplier that you will carry out safety and other audits and that there will be penalties for missed targets and deadlines.*	

Remember

External parties (stakeholders such as shareholders, **HMRC** and auditors) may wish to scrutinise your supply criteria and supplier specifications to establish that steps are being taken to minimise spending costs while making sure quality items are purchased.

Key Terms

HMRC – Her Majesty's Revenue and Customs, which is the tax office.

JIT – Just in Time: suppliers agree to deliver items to you just when you need them, rather than you having to hold a minimum stock level in your warehouse taking up space and tying up money.

PPE – personal protective equipment – safety equipment, e.g. disposable gloves, aprons, safety glasses.

7. Policies, procedures and technology

Inform your supplier about your organisation's policies and procedures and that they are available for scrutiny. A supplier that you wish to forge positive relations with may be encouraged by your equality and diversity policy or evacuation procedure and that these (and others) will be of benefit to their staff when delivering goods or visiting your site. Explain that you wish to work with a supplier who will adopt best practice in terms of industry requirements and appropriate technologies when under a contract to supply with you.

8. Quality assurance

Let your supplier know what your accepted level of quality is. Give details of what you expect your supplier to do to make sure that what they provide is of high quality and reaches you as such. (This can reduce your staff costs, as less time will be needed to inspect when items are received.) Explain how you may randomly test items received and that it may be necessary for you to visit their site(s) to carry out your own audit of their policies, procedures and quality-assurance processes.

9. Documentation and record keeping

Explain what documentation will be used or requested and how information will be communicated between both parties. Explain how you expect processes for invoicing, statements of account and delivery notes to work and how technical drawing and so on will reach the supplier. Offer details of whether documentation will be paper-based, electronic or a combination of both and, if necessary, what compatible software will be needed. Explain how you intend to monitor access to records (for example, password protection) and how paper-based documentation will be stored.

10. Legal information

Insert what you consider are fair contractual terms and conditions. Explain any necessities to meet legal and industry specific requirements. Inform your supplier of any acts of Parliament or regulations that must be adhered to by them if they are to supply you, and those that will be adhered to by you if you are to serve your customers and meet their needs within the boundaries of the law.

11. Financial information

Explain that your budget may increase/decrease in any given financial year. You may suggest recommended unit costs or total costs that you have budgeted for and that you expect all charges (for example, delivery) to be made clear to you. Explain your expectations for terms and conditions of payment (for example, discounts for early payment). You may have intentions to seek economies of scale by buying in bulk and expect a discount for doing so. Liaise with your finance department so you can include details of how your organisation will process payments, accommodate VAT and so on.

12. Confidentiality

Finally, make it clear what your expectations are to protect personal confidential information in line with the Data Protection Act. Also explain that you seek a mutual understanding in relation to confidentiality of business information.

Figure E15.1 An example supplier specification sheet.

Portfolio Task 2 45 minutes

Links to LO1: Assessment criterion 1.2

Provide examples to your assessor of supplier specifications you currently have. Discuss the importance of these.

Be able to evaluate suppliers that meet identified requirements

Your organisation's procurement strategy should enable it to meet its customers' expectations by offering a high quality product or service at a lower cost than its competitors, but buying in goods or services can often be problematic, particularly in terms of quality. This means finding good and reliable suppliers.

Legal, ethical and organisational requirements also have to be considered when choosing a supplier(s) to work with. Your available resources will also play a part in this.

Identifying suppliers to meet requirements

Keeping your customers happy is a major organisational requirement, and to help you to achieve this there are three processes to consider:

- **Vendor** appraisal – you and your managers assess a supplier's ability to offer a reliable service or product of quality. You should do this before you even think about trading with them.
- Supplier evaluation – once you select a supplier, you evaluate their ability to supply you with a quality item on a consistent basis.
- Supplier rating – you monitor your supplier's capability to consistently meet all of your organisation's requirements and expectations.

You need to understand the importance of measuring your chosen supplier's performance in relation to your requirements. For this purpose, you could use a rating system similar to the one below:

Name of Supplier:		Date:	Evaluated by:
Supplier criteria	**Maximum score available**	**Awarded score**	
How flexible are they? (e.g. ability to increase/decrease supply as required	10	7	
How well do they compete on price?	10	9	
How serious are they about their quality control procedures?	10	8	
How serious are they about environmental concerns?	10	6	
An assessment of their ability to communicate effectively	10	7	
An assessment of their approach to dealing with returns	10	8	
How reliable are they in terms of meeting delivery schedules?	10	9	
	Total score	54/70	

Table E15.1 An example supplier rating sheet.

Key Term

Vendor – a person or persons selling supplies of goods or services.

Remember

You and your managers should make it your business to find out to what extent a supplier takes control of quality before supplying you with goods or services.

Activity 30 minutes

Talk to someone involved with procurement or finance in your organisation and find out what the total cost of annual purchases for your team were for the last financial year. Then, discuss your findings with your assessor.

You and your managers will need to carefully select the criteria you wish to use for your supplier rating exercise. You will need to use exactly the same criteria to rate each one of your suppliers. This will enable you to find out which supplier has the highest score and assess who should be the supplier you should choose to work with.

Be careful however, as a total score for one particular supplier may be higher than the others you are evaluating, but if one criteria score, say for example quality, is very low then you may need to reconsider.

Generally, you should adopt this approach before you start trading with a supplier but it is a useful tool to use to monitor and evaluate the suppliers you use on a day-to-day basis.

Evaluating your suppliers

Be aware that evaluating your suppliers' performances takes time, which is a valuable resource, so you should balance this against the risk of not doing it. But remember, failure to adequately monitor and evaluate your suppliers may result in your deadlines and promises to your customers not being met. Some of the ways you can evaluate your suppliers include reviewing whether they:

- consistently fulfil your chosen criteria
- meet delivery deadlines
- deal with rejects and returns promptly
- operate a stable pricing policy.

If you monitor and evaluate the performance of your supplier on a regular basis you should be able to identify shortfalls in the service they normally provide and therefore any improvements needed. By taking an active interest in your suppliers' activities you can enhance the working relationship you have with them. If they see that you are serious about working with them, they are more likely to be serious about working with you. This can help to negotiate the best terms to meet your organisations requirements.

When it comes to realistic delivery (or lead) times, you and your managers are the experts who can decide how quickly you need to receive items once an order has been placed.

It can be useful to evaluate several existing or potential new suppliers to find out how well they meet your delivery requirements and this can be done by producing a simple table like the one below.

> ### Remember
>
> You should think of **leasing** or **hiring** as the *purchasing of services* and should apply similar criteria to source the right supplier of the service!

> ### Key Terms
>
> **Leasing** – entering into a contract with an organisation to rent property, equipment or vehicles over an agreed period of time, for an agreed fee. The leasing organisation is often responsible for maintenance.
>
> **Hiring** – obtaining the use of an item (e.g. equipment) for a short period of time in return for a payment made.

Name of supplier:	Supplier location:	Delivery/lead time:	Delivery charge:	Mode of delivery:
Newshire Metals (Ltd)	Chester	3 weeks	£175	Articulated lorry
MTJ Metals	Oxford	5 days	£95	Courier van
Welsh Metals (Ltd)	Wrexham	2 weeks	£120	Rigid 8-wheeler lorry

Table E15.2 How suppliers could be evaluated.

The information that you put into the table can help to make informed decisions about the suppliers you use or intend to use. For example, it may be impossible for an articulated lorry to access your site and a three-week lead time may not meet your requirements. Of course this example relates to transport, but you can use the same process to consider other important factors, such as quality.

Portfolio Task 3 30 minutes

Links to LO2: Assessment criterion 2.2
Draw a table similar to the one on the previous page to evaluate the delivery performance of your current suppliers.

Record keeping

Effective record keeping will also help you to evaluate your suppliers' performance. Records should be kept about your suppliers' ability to:

- deal with rejects or returns
- control quality before items leave their site
- keep promises over lead times
- maintain stable pricing structures
- respond to fluctuations in order levels to meet your customers' needs.

A file should be kept for each supplier and these should be easily accessible. All of the above points should be addressed and recorded in the file. The information you collect will enable you to establish a purchasing pattern for each supplier you deal with.

Visiting prospective suppliers

If you intend to build long-term working relations with a particular supplier you should consider visiting their premises. This would give you the opportunity to inspect their site to see how motivated their staff are and what their working conditions are like. You could also inspect their procedures, which would give you an overview of their level of professionalism. While on site you could also:

- examine their approach to quality assurance
- meet the people you will be placing orders with
- examine their order-processing system to see how efficient it is
- assess how clean, tidy, secure and safe their site is
- discuss how they deal with rejects, returns and complaints
- examine the condition of the delivery vehicles they use
- find out how welcoming, helpful and responsible staff members are.

PLTS

By completing this task you will be evaluating the performance of your suppliers, giving you the opportunity to present a persuasive case for action proposing practical ways forward (EP2, 3).

Functional Skills

By completing the above portfolio task on a computer, you will be practising your Functional Skills in ICT at Level 1. You will be given the opportunity to present and communicate information using electronic means.

Remember

Purchase order forms, requisition forms and returns documentation will help you to gather information about your suppliers and help you to establish a purchasing pattern for each of them.

Procure supplies **Unit E15**

Key Terms

ISO 9000 – standards set by the International Organization for Standardization which deal with quality management and sets worldwide quality standards for organisations to work towards. This is a framework for quality assurance.

IIP – Investors in People standard – a government standard which organisations can apply for to show their commitment to their employees. Organisations will be assessed on the way they share their objectives with their staff.

Checklist

When evaluating the performance of your supplier you will need to consider:

- whether any standards have been awarded (e.g. ISO 9000)
- their processes for quality control
- how many years they have been trading for
- how effective their communication systems are.

When you and your managers evaluate the suppliers you use, the more detailed information you can find the better equipped you will be to make decisions about using them.

Evaluation of suppliers

You could establish criteria to use as part of your evaluation activity. For each supplier, you could find out:

- who their major customers in the market place are
- if you decide to trade with them, how dependent they will be on your orders
- how well established they are – how many years they have been in business
- if they been awarded any quality symbols (for example, **ISO 9000** OR **IIP**)
- what their processes for quality control are
- what their annual turnover is (an indication of how busy and successful they are)
- how rejects/complaints/returns are dealt with
- what their approach is to seasonal/fluctuating demands from you so that you can meet your customers' needs
- what administrative processes are in place (paper based/compatible software etc.)
- if they have product liability and other insurances
- what their approaches are to reducing waste and environmental issues
- how effective their communication systems are.

Bargaining with suppliers

You need to understand that some suppliers have more power than others when dealing with buyers. In 1979 theorist Michael Porter carried out some research into the bargaining power that both suppliers and buyers have. To illustrate this he devised a diagram entitled Porter's Five Forces:

Porter suggests that buyers' bargaining power is high when:

- there are many suppliers to choose from
- it would be possible for the buyer to make their own items if suppliers won't meet their requirements
- suppliers are willing to undercut each other's prices per unit.

Porter suggests that suppliers' bargaining power is high when:

- they supply specialist items or skills
- they have many customers and don't really need your orders
- they have a well-established recognisable, brand name.

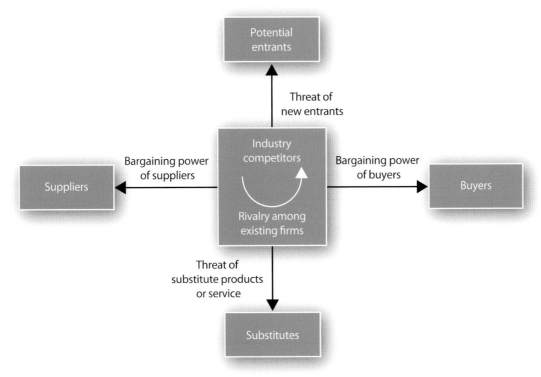

Figure E15.2 Porter's Five Forces.

Portfolio Task 4	45 minutes

Links to LO2: Assessment criterion 2.1
Provide examples to your assessor of suppliers that you currently use that meet resource, organisational and legal requirements. Discuss your findings with your assessor.

Remember

It may be a requirement of your organisation to work with a supplier who is socially responsible and has a responsible attitude towards sustainability. These issues may form part of the criteria you use when evaluating your suppliers.

Be able to select suppliers and obtain supplies

The procurement process involves knowing exactly what you want to purchase and then selecting the right supplier who will meet the requirements of your specification.

Having evaluated the suppliers you intend to use you will be armed with useful facts that will help you and your managers to make informed decisions about who to select.

Your purchasing strategy should be linked to your organisation's business objectives. In other words, how much will the service you get from your selected supplier help your organisation to achieve its objectives?

Activity 20 minutes

The Institute for Supply Management gives definitions for:

- sustainability.
- social responsibility.

Find out what these are, write them down and discuss them with your assessor.

> **Remember**
>
> If you rely heavily on one supplier and it closes down or there is strike action this can seriously affect your organisation's chances of achieving its business objectives. Be aware however, that it is not always cost-effective to have too many suppliers to deal with!

> **Activity** ⏱ 30 minutes
>
> Some organisations will select suppliers purely based on price. If one supplier charges less than another then they will be chosen. Write down the potential problems you foresee for organisations that do this. Discuss your responses with your assessor.

> **Remember**
>
> Your supplier specification sheet should link to your purchasing mix.

Selecting suppliers that best meet requirements

Procurement specialists often refer to strategic and non-strategic suppliers when deciding who they should deal with:

- strategic suppliers – provide items which your organisation couldn't manage without if they are to meet their objectives (for example, suppliers of components or finished goods)
- non-strategic suppliers – provide important items, such as stationery or catering suppliers, although not as essential as strategic supplies and could be sourced elsewhere if need be.

The purchasing mix

Purchasing mix analysis is a tool that allows organisations to carefully examine how well a supplier meets its requirements. It is used to make sure organisations purchase items that will fulfil the requirements of the organisation.

- Quantity – taking into account possible future disruption to deliveries (for example, strike action or production delays) the size of each order is worked out to make sure that enough stock – but not too much – will be available to satisfy customers expectations. Often an automatic re-order level is agreed.
- Quality – discussions should be held with colleagues working in research and development, production and marketing departments to agree the acceptable level of quality for the items being purchased so that they satisfy customers' needs.
- Price – as part of your purchasing strategy you should monitor prices over time to make sure you get the best value for money without compromising an quality. Changes in supply and demand factors and sometimes seasonal trends may affect prices and this should be carefully monitored.
- Delivery – to help with production planning and stock control, it is important to know what the lead time between placing an order for goods or services and receiving them will be. You also need to know this so that you can advise your customers about how long they have to wait before you can sell your goods or services to them.

> **Portfolio Task 5** ⏱ 45 minutes
>
> **Links to LO3: Assessment criterion 3.1**
> Use the purchasing mix tool to analyse how well one of your selected suppliers meets your requirements. Discuss your findings with your assessor.

When dealing with your selected supplier your purchasing strategy should enable you to:

- add value to the purchasing process by seeking the best price, quality and reliable lead time
- develop a deeper understanding of the industry and market place you work in
- improve the two-way communication process with your supplier
- understand what is important to enable your team and organisation to operate efficiently and effectively
- involve your team members and colleagues at other levels when deciding what to purchase
- examine which goods or services are purchased most often and for what purpose
- estimate the quantity or volume of goods and services you intend to purchase over your financial year.

All of these factors will help you and your managers to negotiate better deals with your selected supplier.

It is important for you to trust your selected supplier. Their reputation feeds into your organisation's reputation and in turn your customers' perception of what you do.

Once a decision has been made to work with a chosen supplier you should assess their professionalism by:

- talking to other organisations in your industry who use the same supplier to see if they recommend them
- asking the supplier for references or **testimonials** from other organisations who use them
- using opportunities such as **networking** events or trade association meetings to talk to other people in your industry and find out whether they recommend your chosen supplier
- reading trade journals and magazines to see if there are any reviews about your chosen supplier
- obtaining a copy of their company annual report (if they trade as a company) and reading its content.

Taking these steps will help you to find out how trustworthy and reliable your suppliers are likely to be.

Supply chain management

Sometimes, many organisations are involved in the process of producing one item. For example before you buy an item of clothing from your favourite shop, it will have been through many different stages of the supply chain. Managing this process from beginning to end is known as **supply chain management**. In most cases, each organisation is dependent on the others if they are to succeed.

Key Terms

Networking – attending events and meetings where other people connected to your industry will be present to share information and best practice.

Supply chain management – managing the entire chain of supply from raw materials assembly to final delivery to the customer.

Testimonials – written statements outlining someone else's perception of how well the supplier performs.

Remember

It is always a good idea to inform your selected suppliers of your environmental policy (if you have one) or to ask them how they dispose of waste materials or show concern for the environment. Your stakeholders will want to know that you deal with reputable suppliers!

A typical chain of supply is shown below.

Step 1: An organisation designs item of clothing.

Step 2: Material is produced by another organisation.

Step 3: The material is passed on to another organisation to be dyed (different colours).

Step 4: The coloured material is sent to another organisation to be cut out and sewn.

Step 5: The finished products are dispatched to another organisation to be packaged.

Step 6: The packaged goods are sold to wholesalers.

Step 7: The final goods reach the retailer to be sold to end customers.

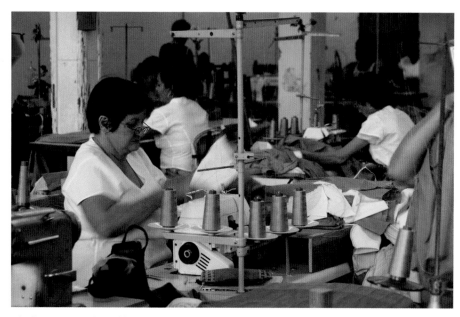

Clothing is produced by many organisations, some overseas and others in the UK.

Remember

If any supplier in the chain is behind schedule or if production is halted, then every other organisation in the chain will also be behind schedule. If contracts with major customers are lost as a result of this, then jobs could be put at risk.

Each organisation will have carefully selected which supplier of goods and services it wishes to work with. If there are difficulties with any supplier at any stage of the process, the knock-on effect for every other organisation in the chain could be disastrous! Ultimately customers may be forced to buy their clothing from a competitor.

You need to understand that occasionally a supply chain might exist on a much smaller scale. Take the example of a garden centre that:

- plants and grows its own strawberries
- harvests its own strawberries
- washes its own strawberries
- packages its own strawberries
- sells its own strawberries to its customers.

Stock control

When selecting your supplier you should consider the support it will offer to help you with your stock control requirements. Some suppliers will be able to offer the following forms of support.

Just in time (JIT)

This technique originates from Japan. It enables you to order supplies only when you actually need them (say within two days) rather than having to wait for a specific lead time. The benefits of JIT are:

- less stock will be held by you (freeing up space)
- less money will be tied up in stock sitting in your warehouse
- you can respond quickly to seasonal demands or the needs of your customers.

It is suggested by procurement specialists that approximately 25 per cent of the value of stock held goes towards warehouse costs and paying for someone to look after it. JIT can help to reduce these costs. However you must be sure that the supplier you select will be able to deliver immediately when requested to do so.

Electronic data interchange (EDI)

This technique allows you to set up IT networks with your selected suppliers. You must share compatible software for this to work, however. Orders can be placed quickly and your supplier can respond quickly to advise you of the availability of what you wish to purchase. Marks and Spencer was the first UK retailer to use EDI and the network connected all of the organisations in its supply chain for its clothing items. Sometimes an organisation uses an **extranet** for a similar purpose.

Radio frequency identification (RFID)

This technique helps to track items you are purchasing as they work their way through the supply chain. Your RFID reader will transmit and receive radio signals and the information the reader collects will be processed on special computer software.

Nowadays, some county and district councils select their suppliers of services online. For example, Construction Line is a national database of building contractors that can be used to find suitably qualified suppliers of building services.

Contractual terms and conditions

You enter into contracts everyday without thinking about it. If you buy a magazine, for example, you will have entered into a contract. At work however, agreeing contractual terms with your selected suppliers needs careful consideration. If you have a specialist member of staff who deals with purchasing, then they will be responsible for agreeing contracts and perhaps you and your managers may share some of the responsibility for doing this.

Key Term

Extranet – an extension of an intranet linking organisations to their suppliers and technical help desks to speed up responses to enquiries.

Activity 60 minutes

Spend some time researching JIT, EDI and RFID and write down the advantages and disadvantages of your organisation using each technique. Show your responses to your assessor.

Remember

Your purchasing strategy may involve you buying from overseas suppliers. Careful planning is needed to obtain these goods, which will probably reach you from ships loaded with large containers. This mode of delivery is often referred to as deep sea transportation, often taking months to reach you!

In very large organisations however the legal team will oversee the exchange of supplier contracts.

Agreeing contractual terms and conditions means examining:

- costs
- timescales
- terms and conditions.

If you are involved in agreeing contractual terms with your selected suppliers be aware of your limits of authority. You need to discuss this with your managers so that you are clear about how much decision-making power you have.

An agreement to do something does not become a contract unless the parties involved actually *intend* to create legal relations. This means that:

- agreements with family and friends (for example, you agree to pay a relative to wash your car) will not usually be considered legally binding (there was no legal intention)
- agreements between business organisations or an organisation and an individual will be considered legally binding, as the parties involved set out to create legal relations (for example, you employ a valeting company to clean your car).

To prove that a contract has been entered into, there must be evidence of:

- an offer being made
- an acceptance of that offer
- consideration (something of value passing between both parties)
- legal intention
- capacity (are the parties capable of entering into the contract, for example, of sound mind).

If you are entering into a contract with a selected supplier it follows that:

- you will place an order (an offer to buy)
- the supplier will accept your order (an acceptance to supply)
- there will be consideration (you will give money in exchange for the goods or services you purchase)
- there will be legal intention (you and the supplier both agree to enter into a legal relationship)
- you and your supplier will have the capacity to enter into the legal agreement (both representatives will be of sound mind and over 18 if it is a financial agreement, such as **HP**).

When you enter into a contract with a supplier, documentation should be drawn up that confirms:

- the length of the contact period (with agreed renewal dates if appropriate)

Key Term

HP – hire purchase. This is when you purchase an item on credit terms. You don't actually own the item until the last payment is made.

- how long the quoted price can be held
- payment terms (30, 60, 90 days or more and options for discounts for early payment)
- delivery patterns
- confirmation of insurance (for example, the supplier agrees to have **product liability insurance**)
- the length of notice that must be given if either party wants to back out of the contract (these are sometimes referred to as rollover contracts).

Sometimes 'standard form contracts' will be prepared by very large organisations. These contracts are drawn up to offer every customer the same terms and conditions without room for negotiation. Electricity and water suppliers use standard form contracts.

A contract doesn't always have to be in writing. When you buy a newspaper, for example, you are entering into a contract but usually there will be no documentation to support the exchange process.

Some of the contractual terms and conditions you must agree with your selected suppliers are:

- a description of the goods or services you require – the items you receive should meet the requirements of your supplier specification sheet and purchase order form
- delivery lead times and arrangements – suppliers must inform you in writing if they are unable to meet delivery deadline. Your supplier must deliver on the date on your purchase order form or agree a new delivery date if this is not possible
- duties of the buyer – confirms that you promise to accept and pay for deliveries that meet your requirements when received on time
- breach of contract – outlines what actions you will take if your selected suppliers fail to fulfil their legal obligations
- confidentiality – you and your supplier will not share financial information, trade secrets or other business affairs with other parties
- cancellation of orders – you may cancel any order before it is delivered in writing with sufficient notice
- changes to the order placed – your supplier must inform you in writing if they need to change make changes to your order. You have 21 days to inspect and approve modified goods
- risk to the delivery of the goods – under normal circumstances, you will become the owners of the goods when they are dispatched from the supplier's premises and not before
- the agreed price of the goods or services ordered and payment – you will agree to pay the purchase price providing the goods or services are delivered to you as specified.

Key Term

Product liability insurance – protection against claims from customers when injury or damage has been caused by a product.

Activity 30 minutes

Think back over the last two days and write down how many contracts (e.g. buying petrol for your car) you have entered into. You may be surprised at how many! Discuss your findings with your assessor.

Procure supplies Unit E15

The list on page 247 shows suggestions only and the terms and conditions you use in your contracts will depend upon the nature of your business and the goods or services you are purchasing.

PLTS

This activity will give you the opportunity to use a practical method to break down your task into manageable steps. You will also communicate your learning from this activity to different audiences, including your assessor (RL 6; EP 3).

Functional Skills

By completing this task, you will be practising your Functional Skills in English at Level 1. You will be communicating information using an appropriate language. Also, by preparing your headings electronically, you will be practising your Functional Skills in ICT at Level 1.

Remember

Some suppliers will insert the acronym 'E&OE' on their invoices. This stands for Errors and Omissions Excepted and is a legal disclaimer against administrative errors made by the supplier.

Portfolio Task 6 45 minutes

Links to LO3: Assessment criterion 3.2

Talk to your manager, or whoever is in charge of purchasing, and obtain a recent contract that has been drawn up with a selected supplier. Write down the headings that were used to agree the terms and conditions of your contract and discuss these with your assessor. Your assessor will record this discussion to generate evidence for your portfolio.

Public sector contracts

Public sector organisations, such as county councils, are governed by UK and European law when purchasing. Very large contracts for purchasing goods or services have to be advertised in the *Official Journal of the European Union* (OJEU), but even small contracts have to be written in line with the Local Government Act 2003.

Other procurement policies that public sector organisations are expected to adhere to include:

- the Race Relations (Amendment) Act 2000, now incorporated into the Equality Act 2010, states that selected suppliers of goods and services should be representative of the local population
- the UK Government's Sustainable Development Policy suggests that sustainability and environmental concerns should be included in supplier specification documents.

An example of a public sector organisation is the Highways Agency which monitors the safety and use of roads and motorways. It must adhere to government policy, which dictates that it must carefully select its suppliers to meet with purchasing requirements. Suppliers must:

- make sure they don't get involved with any fraudulent activities
- make sure they meet the agency's customers' expectations (for example, safe roads and reliable journeys)
- deliver high levels of quality as agreed in the terms of the contract
- show a consistent approach towards supplying an efficient service
- deliver a high-performance service that fulfils their contract
- adhere to all applicable legislation in line with the agency's obligations and policies.

Be able to monitor supplier performance

You should monitor your suppliers' performance on a regular basis to establish how:

- well their goods or services help you to meet your customers' needs
- well your supplier offers support, such as technical backup
- regularly your supplier communicates with you
- well agreed terms and conditions are adhered to.

You should also monitor how they:

- respond to changes in your requirements
- respond to fluctuations in the quantity of supply you need at short notice
- keep to delivery schedules
- support you with compatible software for stock control purposes.

The procurement process involves getting the right goods and services into your organisation at the right time.

Monitoring supplier performance against contractual terms

The contract between your organisation and your supplier will dictate the terms and conditions that both parties must adhere to. It is important that you monitor your suppliers to make sure that they are not in breach of the agreed terms and conditions. There are many methods and techniques that you can use to assist you with this process.

Examples of monitoring methods include Michael Porter's value chain model and Key Performance Indicators (KPIs).

The value chain model

In 1985, theorist Michael Porter developed the value chain model (as shown in Figure E15.3 on the following page), which examines procurement activities, logistics and other functions in an organisation. In the model, primary activities are:

- inbound logistics – how effective are your procedures for receiving deliveries such as safe handling, unloading and storing of stock?
- operations – how efficient are your procedures for testing goods, machining, assembly and packaging?
- outbound logistics – your processes for warehousing, outbound goods and transportation should be evaluated
- marketing and sales – how well does your organisation raise customer awareness so that sales can be made?
- service – what do you do to add value to your core product? (for example, a customer help-desk service).

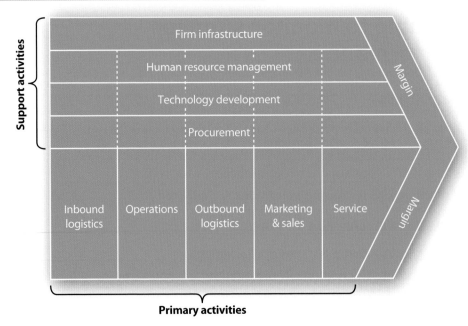

Figure E15.3 Value chain model.

Monitoring support activities

Support activities in the value chain model are:

- infrastructure – how does your workplace culture, quality control systems, information processing and planning affect your primary activities?
- human resources management – recruitment and training must be effective to make sure you have skilled staff members to carry out primary activities
- technology development – having staff with the right knowledge to use systems effectively is vital to support primary activities
- procurement – purchasing the right goods and services at the right time is vital so that primary activities can function effectively.

You must understand the importance of monitoring your suppliers' performance and delivery against your agreed contractual terms and conditions. To do this, you should:

- produce a plan for managing and monitoring the contract
- set KPIs to help you to measure your suppliers' performance
- find a mutual understanding that will enforce supplier compliance to the terms and conditions of the contract.

Key performance indicators (KPIs)

When you draw up a plan, you should date it and give it a heading such as 'Supplier performance monitoring plan'. Its content should include the:

- name and contact details of the supplier you are in a contract with

Activity  45 minutes

Use Michael Porter's value chain model to evaluate how effectively inbound logistics operate in your organisations. Present your findings to your assessor.

Remember

Procurement experts suggest that two per cent of the value of a large contract goes towards the costs to manage it (e.g. staff time).

- name of the nominated person(s) in your organisation who will monitor the contract.
- dates and frequency of contract reviews
- methods of communication
- KPIs associated with the contract (the KPIs should be based on your contract's terms and conditions)

KPIs are likely to measure your suppliers' performance in relation to:

- agreed delivery times
- keeping promises to deal with returns and rejects
- availability of goods or services
- flexibility to meet the changing demands of your organisation
- acknowledgement of the orders you place
- agreeing payment terms and prices
- requests for technical information
- requests to supply appropriate paper work and records or electronic updates
- quality control systems.

Your plan should include a paragraph stating that each KPI and term and condition of the contract will be assessed against your supplier's actual performance. A supplier performance rating sheet can be used for this purpose.

Portfolio Task 7 · 45 minutes

Links to LO4: Assessment criterion 4.1

Explain to your assessor how your organisation currently monitors your suppliers' performance and delivery against the agreed contractual terms. Find out if your organisation has a plan in place to do this. If you find a plan, write down a summary of its content and show this to your assessor.

Other monitoring methods

Other ways of monitoring your suppliers' performance against the requirements of your contract include:

- customer feedback surveys
- **benchmarking** yourself against other organisations in your industry
- arranging monthly face-to-face meetings with your suppliers.

Key Term

Benchmarking – a process that compares your activities to those of another similar organisation.

Dealing with breaches of contract

Suppliers of services have a duty to make sure that they provide their service to you within a reasonable time, for a reasonable fee, and that reasonable skill and care is used. If they fall short of this duty, it can lead to a breach of contract.

If one of your selected suppliers consistently fails to meet the terms and conditions of your contract they will be considered to be in breach of contract. Examples include:

- refusing to perform within the agreed terms and conditions
- failing to deliver goods or services as agreed
- supplying defective or sub-standard goods or services on a consistent basis.

The following is a list of different types of breach of contract.

- Repudiatory breach – this is when a serious breach of contact occurs and the injured party can claim damages.
- Anticipatory breach – this is when one party anticipates that a term or condition of a contract cannot be performed. For example, your supplier knows that they will not be able to fulfil their legal obligations and informs you of this in advance.
- Frustration – a contract may in certain circumstances, be discharged by frustration. For example, your supplier sends your order by ship, which hits rocks at sea and needs repairs. This would be considered an event of frustration and the contract would be discharged.

There are some circumstances where failure to perform legal obligations will not be considered the fault of the supplier. These include such things as strikes, wars, fires, floods, extreme weather conditions and earthquakes and all fall under the legal term, force majeure.

It can also sometimes be the case that a supplier is unable to deliver on time because of conflict with a member of staff in your organisation. Perhaps someone is being difficult by closing the warehouse ten minutes early and turning deliveries away! Monitoring how your own staff members behave is important too.

Cases for breach of contract of small value will be heard in county courts and cases for high values will be heard in the High Court. In exceptional cases, contracts of very high value will be heard in a specialist court called the Commercial Court.

Once a contract has been broken the injured party can seek compensation through the courts. Claims can be made for:

- damages – monetary reward to cover losses
- specific performance – an equitable remedy and an alternative to a monetary reward. Instead the judge may agree to make a party complete the contract.

Remember

A breach of contract means that the contract that was in place between you and your supplier will come to an end and you will be able to claim compensation if your supplier is at fault.

- quantum meruit – as an alternative to a claim for damages, this remedy restores the injured party to the position they were in before entering into the contract. For example, if you prevent a supplier of a service from entering your site to finish off works, they could seek compensation for the amount of work already done.

- injunction – another example of an equitable remedy. In this case the judge will make an order preventing a party from continuing to do something.

An equitable remedy is awarded when normal remedies such as money are not enough. A judge may use equity, meaning fairness, to force a party to complete their side of the contract.

Exclusion clauses

When negotiating the terms of a contract, a supplier may ask to have an exclusion clause inserted into it, excluding their liability for damage to goods during transportation for example. These types of clauses are sometimes thought of as an attempt to avoid responsibility.

The Unfair Contracts Terms Act 1977 places legal control over the use of exclusion clauses and this act of Parliament makes it illegal for a supplier to attempt to avoid their legal responsibilities as written into:

- the Sale of Goods Act 1979
- the Supply of Goods and Services Act 1982
- the Sale and Supply of Goods Act 1994.

You need to be aware that the UCTA 1977 offers protection to your customers if you include exclusion clauses in your contracts that are considered to be unfair.

Activity 60 minutes

Talk to your managers to find out if you can access a copy of a supplier contract that has an exclusion clause in it. Examine the clause, write it down and discuss it with your assessor.

Portfolio Task 8 30 minutes

Links to LO4: Assessment criterion 4.2

Explain to your assessor your organisational procedure to deal with breaches of contract. Your assessor will record this discussion to generate evidence for your portfolio.

Team talk

Sophie's story

I'm Sophie and I work as a team leader for High Fly Kites Ltd. We are a small company manufacturing traditional quality kites for the tourist and leisure industry and depend on supplies of tissue paper, wood and string.

We have recently been having problems with our tissue paper supplier. We never receive deliveries on time and when we do receive them the quantity is often wrong, which holds up production. This has upset some of our customers who have had to wait for their stock of kites. In today's economic climate these retailers are telling us they may have to look elsewhere if we can't get our kites to them on time. My team members get fed up when production is halted while we wait for the supplier to deliver the shortfall. This affects my team's morale but my managers tell me they have used this supplier for years and don't want to upset their contact, whom they know personally, by complaining to her.

Top tips

Organisations shouldn't use the same supplier just because they have always used them or because they know the owners well. A supplier should only be used because they are the best.

By using a supplier specification sheet, evaluation processes and a careful approach to selecting a supplier some of the problems that Sophie and her team are experiencing can be eliminated. A contract should be drawn up with terms and conditions carefully agreed upon. The best method for effective and regular communication with your selected suppliers should be established so that inadequate performance relating to deliveries can be reported to suppliers quickly.

Ask the expert	
Q	What can I do to get my managers to realise that this supplier is causing major problems for my team, our customers and our production schedules?
A	You should write down all of the facts to back up your concerns and ask your line manager for a meeting. Diplomatically point out how unreliable this supplier has become and what the consequences of this are. You could produce a short report for your manager to read through after your meeting. You could suggest that a supplier specification sheet should be drawn up which would make it clear to your supplier that terms of delivery must be adhered to. You could also discuss with your manager that you would like the opportunity to carry out an evaluation of your suppliers, the results of which would indicate that your current supplier of tissue paper is not meeting your organisational requirements.

What your assessor is looking for

In order to demonstrate your competency within this unit, you will need to provide sufficient evidence to your assessor. You will need to provide a short written narrative or personal statement, explaining how you meet the assessment criteria. In addition, your assessor may need to ask questions to test your knowledge of the topics identified in this unit.

Below is a list of suggested documentation that will provide evidence to help you to prove your competency in this unit.

Work products for this unit could include:

- vendor appraisal documentation
- supply specification sheet
- supplier rating sheet
- delivery requirement documentation
- examples of contracts with suppliers
- key performance indicator
- minutes of meetings which discuss procurement activity

- emails which refer to procurement activity.

Your assessor will guide you through the assessment process as detailed in the candidate logbook. The detailed assessment criteria are shown in the logbook and by working through these questions, combined with providing the relevant evidence, you will meet the learning outcomes required to complete this unit.

Task and page reference	Assessment criteria
1 (page 232)	1.1
2 (page 236)	1.2
3 (page 239)	2.2
4 (page 241)	2.1
5 (page 242)	3.1
6 (page 248)	3.2
7 (page 251)	4.1
8 (page 253)	4.2

Index